THE ANCESTORS OF HENRY STONE

The Ancestors of Henry Stone
Abdill Family History, Volume I

By Richard J. Abdill III

First edition

2017
Minneapolis, Minnesota

Cover design by Anna Gindes.

Cover image, portrait: Henry Stone and Mary Lynn Wade, likely on their wedding day, 29 Nov 1894. Courtesy of Sally Abdill.

Cover image, background: View from Blue Ridge Parkway, near Shenandoah National Park, Virginia. Photo by the author.

Photo of St. Simon and St. Jude Church copyright Norwich Historic Churches Trust Ltd. Used by permission.

Photo of Spindle house excavation copyright James Madison University. Used by permission.

First edition, 2017

ISBN: 978-0692840474

Library of Congress Control Number: 2017902200

"Time is the longest distance between two places."

—Tennessee Williams,
The Glass Menagerie

Contents

Abdill Family History

This is the first volume of what will eventually be a series of books detailing the ancestry of the author and his siblings. The planned volumes:

- I: **The Ancestors of Henry Stone**: A study of all the known ancestors of Henry Stone (1866–1940), a great-great grandfather of the author.
- II: **The Ancestors of Sally Abdill**: A continuation of Volume I, it completes the ancestry of Sally (Stone) Abdill's father, plus traces the known ancestry of her mother, Esther (Rager) Stone (1899–1996).
- III: **The Ancestors of Richard Abdill**: An examination of the remaining lineage of the author: The direct ancestors of Richard Abdill Sr. (1928–2014), the husband of Sally Abdill, plus the known ancestry of Nancy (Siegel) Abdill (b. 1959), mother of the author.
- **The Abdill Family History**: A casebound, archival-quality compilation that will combine the information of all previous volumes, plus an extended narrative examining the Stone family's fight in the U.S. Civil War.

Introduction

I'm so glad you found this book. If you're reading this, I'd guess you're either lost or looking for information about a relative whom we have in common—if the latter, I'm thrilled this work may help someone in our family get a clearer picture of their background. In the case of the former, I don't think anyone would hold it against you if you stopped reading now, but you may want to stick around anyway: There are some good stories hidden in here, including soldiers from the Revolutionary War,[i] Civil War,[ii] and both world wars.[iii] A knight makes a brief appearance in Part I,[iv] as do several English mayors.[v] Part II holds even more adventure; you should check for yourself. I think it's a pretty compelling collection, but I'm probably a little biased.

There will be a little misty-eyed nostalgia later on, but for now, it's time to explain how all of this is organized:

---

[i] Benjamin Alsop *9-330*.

[ii] John Stone *6-40*.

[iii] Henry Stone Jr. in WWI; his uncle John Allen Stone in WWII.

[iv] John Pettus, son of Thomas Pettus *16-41472* and Christian Dethick *16-41473*.

[v] Thomas Pettus *16-41472* and his son, Thomas Pettus *15-20736*.

The numbering system

You'll see what appears to be a pretty complex numbering system used for identifying people. At the least, it will help you differentiate between people with identical names (looking at you, "Thomas" and "William"), but once you get the hang of it, it's a powerful framework that should be helpful in understanding who's related to whom.

Since this is predominantly a collection of my direct ancestors, it uses *Ahnentafel* numbering,[vi] a system designed to trace ancestry backwards from someone ("all the ancestors of Jim"), rather than other, more popular systems for tracing ancestry forward ("all the descendants of James").

Everyone is assigned a number, starting with me (1) and moving backward, to my father (2), mother (3), and so on—because everyone in the family tree has only two biological parents, the number *2* is an important one: To find the number of a person's father, simply **double that person's number**; to find their mother, **double the person's number and add one**. (This also means spouses are one number apart.)

A simple example: Sally (Stone) Abdill is number *5*. Her father, Henry Stone Jr., is $5 \times 2 = 10$. Henry's father is $10 \times 2 = 20$. To find someone's mother, the process is similar: Each woman in the tree has a number one greater than her husband's. For example, Henry's number is *10*, which means his wife, Esther Rager, is number *11*. So, if you wanted to find Sally Abdill's mother, you would take her number, *5*, and double it (to *10*, Henry's number), then add 1, to get Esther's number, *11*. Siblings do not get a number, nor do spouses that are not a direct ancestor.

This gets more helpful in older generations, when there are more people in each layer: For example, Thomas Wigglesworth

---

[vi] Also sometimes referred to as the Sosa-Stradonitz Method.

is number *166*; to find his mother, you'd need to look one generation back, for someone numbered *333*. (It's Philadelphia Fox, and her mother, Philadelphia Claiborne, is number *667*.)

You'll notice that many entries in the book are not consecutive: To maintain the numbering system, people who are missing from the tree still have their place "reserved." Richard Lamb, for example, is number *326*, but we don't know who his biological parents were—so, numbers *652* and *653* remain blank, because those numbers are where his parents would be located. By extension, the parents of numbers *652* and *653* are also unknown, and their parents, and so on, so all the numbers of Richard's ancestors (652/653, 1304/1305, etc.) are missing.

Generations

The Ahnentafel numbers in the book also have "generational indicators"—those are just to add a little clarity to a number like "326," which at a glance isn't much help. Richard Lamb's actual reference number in the book is *9-326*, which simply means he is number *326* in the tree, and that he is in the ninth generation. His parents would be in generation 10, his grandparents in generation 11, and so on. I am the only person in generation 1, so my number is *1-1*; my dad, because his number is *2* and he is one generation removed from me, is *2-2*. To continue the example from above, Sally Abdill is *3-5*. Henry Stone Jr. is *4-10*, because he is one generation older than his daughter. Esther Rager, Henry's wife, is number *4-11*; she is in the same generation (4) as her husband, but her Ahnentafel number (11) is one greater than his (10).

Dates

There are a lot of dates in here, some of which are considerably removed from the present. The problem we run into is the Julian calendar, which most of the world used until the late 1500s, when the modern Gregorian calendar was adopted. However, Great Britain (and its colonies) was a little behind, and didn't adopt the new calendar for another 170 years, which takes us into the 18th century and many people who are included in the tree.

The most substantial difference between the two is the "first" day of the new year: Though we now flip our calendars to a new year on January 1, the Julian calendar did so on March 25. This means an "Old Style" date of 10 Feb **1620** is, in our modern calendar, actually 10 Feb **1621**—our calendar had our new year on January 1 and the year changed to 1621, but the Julian calendar hadn't "flipped" yet. Between March 25 and the end of December, the years line up, and there isn't an issue.

So, for almost two centuries, we have a set of dates that would have been recorded in two different years, depending on where the recorder lived. Whenever there is a conflict between the old and new styles, I have gone with the Gregorian year, to make comparisons easier and avoid the "double dating"—writing years such as "1620/1621"—that comes along with so many books dealing with that period. (Before Gregorian dates were used anywhere, Julian dates were the *only* option—those dates have been unaltered.)

Even this, unfortunately, comes with some caveats: The actual dates don't line up too well, either. By the time the U.K. switched over in 1752, their calendar was 11 days behind the Gregorian calendar, up from a 10-day difference when the "new" calendar was adopted elsewhere in 1582. I have **not** converted any of these dates—while the text does use modern years, be aware that it uses whatever dates were recorded during that transition period, so the actual day may be off by almost two weeks. I was tempted to adjust the dates to be more exact, but if you want to figure out the actual conversion, there are websites that can help; leaving them as-is here is designed to help future researchers—if everybody's gravestones have the "wrong" date on them, it would take forever to figure out who lines up where.

Citations

I've done my best to be thorough in citing facts and where they came from, and hope to improve these in later editions. Any superscript numbers in the text are references to endnotes that appear at the back of the book. Any superscript Roman numerals are references to footnotes that should be at the bottom of the page on which they're referenced. These aren't citations, just side notes I thought should be pulled out to avoid confusing the main text.

Format and Organization

All direct ancestors have a small biography and appear side-by-side with their spouse and a list of any known children. The child in the direct line of descent is indicated in capital letters. So, for example, the list of children of William and Clarissa Stone uses names like this: "William, Mary, Susan, JOHN," because John Stone is the child of theirs that is a direct ancestor of mine, and the next person to be profiled. Most times a person is referenced, their Ahnentafel number directly follows their name, in italics, like this: "Esther Rager *4-11*."

Most "Ahnentafel charts" using this system just start with number 1 and go backwards in order. This approach is the easiest to navigate if you're using the book as a reference and are looking up individual people, but reading it from front to back doesn't make as much sense: As the tree grows "out" and the number of people in each generation grows, people get farther and farther away from their parents in the text. In the 10th generation of such a list, for example, there could be as many as 512 people listed before the next generation even starts; this number grows exponentially with each successive generation.

To avoid this, I've instead organized the chapters by last name, starting with the oldest person we know in that line. In the "Stone" chapter, for example, we start with the earliest Stone we know of: William Allen Stone *7-80*, born about 1802, and his wife Clarissa *7-81*. We then move on to their son John *6-40*, my direct descendant, then John's son Henry *5-20*, and so on. The families of the wives in each chapter are broken out into their own chapters, according to their last names as well. So, while Clarissa Pettus *7-81* married William Stone *7-80* and is included in the "Stone" chapter, her ancestors are in the next chapter, for the "Pettus" family. The overlapping person (Clarissa, in this case) is included in the chapter of her husband.

I readily admit that this is approach probably puts an unfair focus on the male ancestors, a pattern that you'll likely see repeated throughout the book. I could have written an entire book just about the exploits of John Stone *6-40* in the Civil War; his wife Maria *6-41* gets only a few lines—she may not have even gone by the name "Maria." My only excuse is that this obnoxiously patriarchal approach mirrors the societies of the time: In addition to the husband's name dictating the family's, almost all the women here were homemakers without any documentation except for (if we're lucky) birth, death, and census records; not one female ancestor of Henry Stone had the right to vote. When there was enough information to make informed inferences about what their lives were like, I did my best to include it; most of the time, however, we will have no idea.

Figure 1: L–R: Claire, Richard 1-1, Lauren and Katie Abdill in New Jersey, December 2016.[1]

I was worried that including my thoughts in the book's preface would be seen as self-indulgent, and it probably is— my justification is that all genealogy work is at some level a self-indulgence, the manifestation of a need to put a life into perspective. But it's not just my history in these pages, which is why I am hopeful about the utility of this work, however self-centered its motivation may be. The people in Part I alone have thousands of descendants, people who, like me, owe their very existence to this long list of beautiful, flawed people and their children. Their history is our history: the ministers and bullies, the orphans and murderers, the postal carriers and Confederate soldiers. Some live on in the remembrances of the living, but most are preserved only by the wisps of smoke they left behind—government files and church records that obscure lifetimes of glory and heartbreak but offer us a precious connection to the past.

Through these documents, our people reach out to us through the ages and say, "I was here." One day, I hope this book will do the same, and it is dedicated to the generations to which we'll be reaching out next—the Abdills and Bluntners and Spindles and Holloways and Foxes that we will never get to meet. We were people who loved each other. We had a heritage. We were here.

—Rich Abdill
August 2016
Minneapolis, Minnesota

Prologue

Henry Stone *5-20* is the youngest person profiled in Part I. To help things get oriented, included below are the descendants of Henry and his wife, Mary Lynn Wade *5-21*, who are in the direct line of the author. Sally (Stone) Abdill *3-5* and her husband, Richard Abdill *3-4*, will be profiled in a future volume, as will the family of their son, Richard Abdill *2-2*, so those entries are abbreviated here.

Henry Thomas Stone Jr. (*4-10*), Esther Amanda Rager (*4-11*)

Henry *4-10* was born in Christiansburg, Virginia[4] on September 25, 1895.[5],[6] He arrived in the city (population 660)[7] the same year as Booker T. Washington, who served as

Figure 2: Signatures of Henry Stone Jr., from his draft registration for World War I[2] (top) and World War II.[3]

9

superintendent of
the Christiansburg
Institute, one of Virginia's most prominent boarding schools
for black children, founded after the Civil War.[8],[9] At a
public event during a visit by Washington, institute Principal
Edgar A. Long, a son of former slaves, described Montgomery
County at the turn of the 20th century: "You are today in
a county where there has never been a lynching, where the
jail is empty and the schoolhouse is full. During my thirteen
years of residence in this community, I have never known a
serious altercation between a white man and a black man."[10]

In early March 1913, Henry (and a small group including
his uncle,[11] Guy F. Ellett) made a 260-mile trip to Washington, D.C. to see the first inauguration of President Woodrow
Wilson.[12] (His daughter Sally *3-5* said Henry was a "dyed-in-
the-wool Democrat" for his entire life, though it's safe to say
the Democratic Party of turn-of-the-century Virginians was
far different from the party we know today.)

He attended Washington and Lee University for the
1914–1915 school year, when he joined the school's band[13] (his
daughter said he could play the piano)[14] and was a member
of the "South-West Virginia Club."[15] That academic year
does not appear to have included any exceptional events, save
a 103–0 football victory over Morris–Harvey College[16] and a
campus-wide outbreak of pinkeye the following spring.[17] (It
was reported in the *Richmond Times-Dispatch* that Henry
would be returning for the following year,[18] but there is no
evidence he did, and his memoirs state he had "a year at
W&L.")[19] Given his family's interest in genealogy, it's possible
they were aware that Henry's fourth-great grandfather, Gen.
Andrew Lewis, had helped found the university in 1776.[vii]

[vii]When Lewis was involved, the university was called "Liberty Hall."
He will be profiled in Volume II.

By 1917, Henry had left Christiansburg and was living in Buffalo, New York, working as a clerk for the prominent construction company Stone & Webster,[20],[viii] which had just completed construction of the Buffalo General Electric Company's Niagara River Station in November 1916.[21]

In December 1917, just as the the American fighting force in Europe was ramping up, Henry quit his job to enlist in the U.S. Army "to go over and clean the war up for the Democrats." He reported that he was disqualified because of his poor vision, and he returned to work.[23] The following May, the American Expeditionary Forces in Europe had ballooned from 129,000 to 424,000 strong,[24] and Henry received his draft notice—the medical inspections were apparently more lax than before, and he was sent to France, where he served in Company I, 323d Infantry Brigade, 81st Infantry Division, and participated in the final days of the Battle of the Argonne Forest.

Figure 3: Esther Stone 4-11 and her daughter, Sally 3-5.[22]

For an annotated transcription of Henry's war memoir, see Appendix E.

He returned to Virginia in late June 1919,[25] and, in about 1925,[26] married Esther Rager.

Born in rural St. Clair Township on September 10, 1899,[27],[28] Esther Rager *4-11* grew up in Pennsylvania coal

---

[viii]The "Stone" in the company name is of no known relation.

country, the daughter of Elmer *5-22* and Catherine Rager *5-23*. (Elmer and Catherine will be profiled in *Abdill Family History*, Volume II.) Her family had moved several miles north by 1910, to the newly incorporated[29] town of Seward,[30] a tiny town along the Pennsylvania Railroad.[31]

In September 1916, Esther likely traveled to Cumberland, Maryland with James Gatehouse, a coal miner[32] and fellow Seward resident, and the two obtained a marriage license[33] (the date of the wedding is unknown). At some point in the following year, the couple moved to Fayette County, on the Pennsylvania–West Virginia border. It was here, about 75 miles from Seward, that Esther gave birth to a son, Thomas Rager Gatehouse, in Point Marion.[34]

Sometime between late 1918[35] and 1920, Esther and James moved to Philipsburg, Pa. with James's parents. Thomas is also living there, though he's listed in the 1920 census as the son of Esther's in-laws.[36] Thomas appears in the same household in the 1930 census too—but this time as the grandson, and without Esther or James.[37] They were divorced, but exactly when is unclear; it must have been some time before 1925. By the time the 1930 census-takers came to Philipsburg, Esther was already living in Los Angeles with her new husband, Henry,[38] and James was living with his wife, Sue. (James reported in that year's census that he was "first married" in 1927;[39] Esther similarly reported she was first married in 1925[40]—long after the birth of their son, and after their description to 1920 census-takers as husband and wife.)

Henry was working as a "purchasing agent" for a construction company, and the couple had a daughter with them—Sally Anne (later just "Sally"), their only child.[41] They soon returned to the east coast, where Esther would spend the rest of her life—Henry died in 1972,[42] and she remained in Burlington until her death in 1996, at the age of 96.[43]

(a) Henry Stone,4-10 Richard Abdill 2-2, Esther Stone 4-11, and Peter Abdill, likely at Richard's fourth birthday party in 1964.[44]

(b) Henry 4-10 and Esther 4-11 Stone, likely at the wedding of their daughter Sally 3-5.[45]

Sally Anne Stone (*3-5*),
Richard John Abdill (*3-4*)

Henry and Esther's daughter Sally (b. 1 Mar 1929) will be profiled with her husband Richard (1928–2014) in Volume II of the *Abdill Family History.*

Richard and Sally had four children:

- **Anne Louise**, b. 22 Nov 1951, d. 14 Mar 2012. Married Edward L. Holloway 16 Feb 1974.
- **Kathy Jeanne**, b. 10 Feb 1955. Married Michael S. Somogy 1975, then Philip J. Mesmer 19 Aug 1995.
- **RICHARD JOHN** *2-2*, b. 20 Apr 1960. Married Nancy E. Siegel.
- **Peter Henry**, b. 3 Oct 1962. Married Lisa S. Anderson 16 Aug 1987.

Richard John Abdill (*2-2*),
Nancy E. Siegel (*2-3*)

Richard and Nancy (b. 4 Nov 1959) will be profiled in Volume III. They had three children:

- **RICHARD JOHN** *1-1*, b. 1 Nov 1989; married Lauren M. Redding.
- **Katie Rebecca**, b. 26 Feb 1992.
- **Claire Victoria**, b. 22 Mar 1996.

Part I

Ancestors of Henry Stone

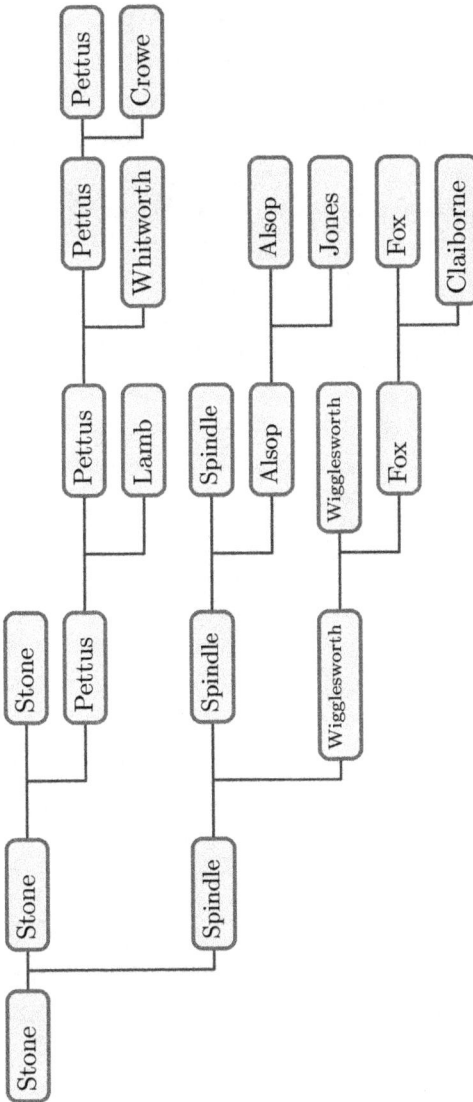

Figure 5: A diagram of families covered in Part I and how they are related by marriage. (There may be multiple generations for each name; this diagram just charts which families married which.)

18

Chapter 1

Stone

When Henry Stone Jr. *4-10* moved away from Christiansburg, Virginia in the mid-1910s, he left an area in which his ancestors had lived for almost 300 years. The first American ancestor we know of was one of the original settlers of the Jamestown colony—George Percy *15-21322* was aboard the *Susan Constant*, one of the three ships bringing colonists to Virginia in 1607,[i] but he returned to England several years later. When John West *14-10660*[ii] arrived in 1618, there was a permanent ancestor in the colonies for the first time. The Pettus family arrived in Virginia at various points over the next 15 years,[46] slowly migrating north. Clarissa Pettus married William Stone and moved in about 1850 to Montgomery County, where Christiansburg is the county seat. The city's Sunset Cemetery is the resting place of many relatives.

Christiansburg itself is today a city of about 22,000 peo-

---

[i] Also aboard was John Smith, the English soldier and explorer rescued from execution, according to legend, by Pocahontas.

[ii] Profiled in Part II in "Generation 14," along with George Percy *15-21322*.

ple,[47] though in 1900 there were less than 660 residents on census rolls.[48]

Henry Junior was a child during the legendary presence of the "Black Sisters" in Christiansburg: A school in the town, Montgomery Female Academy, was put under the care of a woman named Virginia Wardlaw around 1905. She was followed by her sisters Mary and Caroline (and their respective families) shortly after. The sisters, who had taken to wearing thick layers of black veils, all had bizarre interactions with the community and their own children: Caroline's son Hugh died after what is suspected to have been a push down a flight of stairs; Mary's son, John, burned to death in Christiansburg in 1906—his bed was later found to have been doused in kerosene. Both had large life insurance policies taken out in their names.

The family's reputation in the town soured around 1908, when the school was closed[49] and the sisters finally left for New York. A year later, Caroline's daughter, Ocey, who also had multiple life insurance policies in her name, was starved and drowned by the sisters. Virginia starved herself to death while awaiting trial for murder,[50] and is buried in Christianburg's Sunset Cemetery.[51]

The tales of the sisters have survived in local lore for more than 100 years, including in a municipal planning document from 2014[52] and an account on the website of Christianburg's Montgomery Museum that claims, "people were afraid to go on the streets at night. The sisters were known to visit the cemetery often ... Legend says girls would awaken at night to find the black robed sisters standing on each side of the bed... withdrawing without explanation of their presence."[53] Henry's daughter Sally says she can't recall her father ever talking about the Black Sisters, but there is still a connection: His great-aunt was Bessie (Wardlaw) Spindle, the fourth sister, who brought them to the town to begin with.

William Allen Stone (*7-80*), Clarissa Ann Pettus (*7-81*)

The earliest "Stone" in the direct line is William Allen[55] Stone, born in Virginia probably between July 1801 and July 1802,[56] died 13 Nov 1861 in Montgomery County.[57]

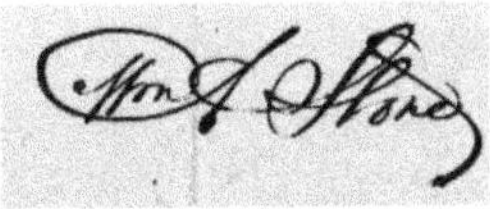

Figure 1.1: The signature of William Stone 7-80, from an 1859 I.O.U. written to his son William.[54]

William worked as a farmer[59] and married Clarissa (sometimes Clara) Ann Pettus 14 Aug 1822.[60] Clarissa was born abt 1807 in Lunenburg County, Va., and died 24 Dec 1878.[61] Her parents were Samuel and Sophia (Lamb) Pettus —for more information about that (long) branch of the family, see the "Pettus" chapter.

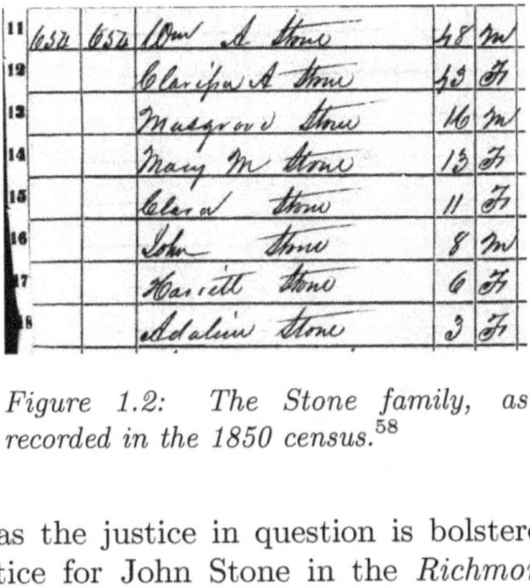

11	652	652	Wm A Stone	48	M
12			Clarissa A Stone	43	F
13			Musgrove Stone	16	M
14			Mary M Stone	13	F
15			Clara Stone	11	F
16			John Stone	8	M
17			Harriett Stone	6	F
18			Adaline Stone	3	F

Figure 1.2: The Stone family, as recorded in the 1850 census.[58]

Though it appears "William Stone" was a popular Virginian name about this time, a "William A. Stone" was a county justice who appears to be ours. He served a term in 1826, then consecutive terms from 1831 through 1852, excluding 1839 and 1840.[62] That our William was the justice in question is bolstered by a 1907 death notice for John Stone in the *Richmond*

Times-Dispatch in which he's described as "a son of Captain
William A. Stone"[63]—there's no record of William ever
serving in the military, and military titles were sometimes
used in an unofficial, honorary capacity for other government
service. For example, James Wade *6-42*, the father-in-law of
William's grandson Henry *5-20*, was a prominent court official
who was described in one newspaper article after his death
as "Colonel James Wade,"[64] despite having been a lieutenant
in the Civil War.[65] It also appears that this William Stone
held a leadership role in the Restoration Church movement in
Lunenburg County, at least in the late 1830s, when he appears
in the church's magazine, *The Millennial Harbinger.*[66]

William and Clara had 10 children (three of whom, Musgrove, John Richard, and Sophia Adaline, share their names
with Clara's siblings):[67]

- **William Elliott**, b. 1 Nov 1829,[68] d. 24 Feb 1885.[69]
  Married Mary H. Miller 10 Oct 1849.[70] Fought for the
  Confederacy in the Civil War: In the Stonewall Brigade
  with his brother John in 1861,[71] then with the 14th Virginia Cavalry Regiment until 12 Nov 1864, when he was
  captured during a Confederate loss[72] at Cedarville. Was
  freed in a prisoner exchange 15 Mar 1865.[73] May have
  operated a hotel in Christiansburg before his death.[74]
- **Susan Elizabeth**, b. 5 Sep 1829,[75] d. 23 Jan 1877 in
  Pulaski, Va.[76,77] Married Miles A. Wilson 19 Oct 1846
  in Lunenburg County, Va.[78]
- **Musgrove Colgate**,[79] b. Jun 1834,[80] d. late June
  1901.[81]
- **Mary**,[iii] b. abt 1837,[82] d. 24 May 1895 in Waukesha,
  Wisconsin.[83] Married Dexter Bullard[84] 5 May 1858 in
  Montgomery County, Va.[85]

[iii]Her middle initial is variably given as "S," "M," "F," or "Mcf," so
is omitted entirely here.

- **JOHN RICHARD** *6-40*, b. abt 1842,[86] d. 1 Nov 1907.[87]
- **Harriet L.**,[iv] known as "Hattie."[88] b. abt 1845,[89] m. Philip[90] B. Sale 15 Dec 1875.[91] Date of death unconfirmed.
- **Sophia Adaline**,[92] "Addie,"[93] b. abt 1847 in Lunenburg County,[94] married John N. Williams.[95] Died 5 Jun 1869 in Greene, Va., age 22.[96] The document describing her cause of death is mostly illegible, but her 7-month-old son Elisha died of "summer complaint"[v] the following month.[97]
- **Franklin Newton**,[98] b. abt 1852 in Virginia.[99] Attended the Agricultural and Mechanical College of Kentucky[vi] in 1868.[100] Appears in the 1870 census,[101] but died before 1881.[102]
- **Clarissa Ann**, went by "Clara,"[103,104] b. abt 1838 in Virginia;[105] m. Robert Miller 5 May 1858,[106] apparently on the same day as her sister Mary. Died before 1881.[107]
- **Samuel A.**,[108] dates of birth and death unknown, but is referred to in William's will as his son.[109] Married a Mary (or Molly)[110] Wade bef 1875 and moved to Texas.[111] Was living in Hubbard City, Texas in 1900, according to a social column in the *Clinch Valley News*, where he is described as a doctor (and the brother of John R. Stone).[112]

[iv] Her middle name may have been "Lamb," the maiden name of her maternal grandmother.

[v] A colloquial reference to a diarrheal condition found most commonly in children.

[vi] This school would later form the nucleus of the University of Kentucky.

The Stone farms

In 1830, William and Clarissa held 21 slaves, including 10 children under the age of 10.[113] In 1840, there were 24 people enslaved on their farm.[114] In 1850, we know more about the farm itself: There were 23 slaves[115] working on the 775-acre plantation,[vii] which was also home to a considerable flock of livestock.[116]

The numbers look much the same in 1860, after the family moved to Montgomery County, though the farm was startlingly more valuable: 800 total acres now,[117] but, while the Stone farm in Lunenburg County was valued at $4,075 in late 1850,[118] their new farm in 1860 was estimated at $20,000—in 2016 currency, more than half a million dollars.[119] While there are several other valuable farms in the area, the Stone farm was certainly on the high end—of the 80 closest properties, it is the fifth-most valuable in 1860, and only one property had farm equipment listed as more valuable than theirs ($400). Also in the inventory was livestock worth $2,000, more than all but two properties in the area:

- 12 horses
- 4 mules
- 8 milking cows (plus 25 "other cattle")
- 8 oxen
- 40 sheep
- 50 pigs

The real money, however, was in the Stones' crops. While some farms out-produced their plantation in various categories, the Stones appear near the top of almost every category, far more often than the other farms:

- 600 bushels of wheat, third-most in the area
- 200 bushels of rye, the most by far

[vii]Though 275 acres of the farm is categorized as "unimproved," likely indicating they weren't used for cultivation.

- 2,000 bushels of "Indian corn," third-most
- 400 bushels of oats, second-most
- 10,000 pounds of tobacco, second-most
- 20 bushels of peas and beans, tied for the most
- 100 bushels of Irish potatoes, the highest yield in the area
- 365 pounds of butter, third-most
- 20 tons of hay, fifth-most
- 12 pounds of hops, more than the only other hop producer in the area

In addition, there may have been as many as 55 slaves living on the Stone plantation in late 1860: 23 owned by William, two by his son Musgrove, and another 20 owned by Whitehead M. Coleman,[120] a wealthy "trader" who was living on the farm; his relationship to the family is still unclear, but he appears in court cases after the war in which the Stone siblings appear to owe him a significant sum of money: "Some people say they are glad the Negroes were freed and that [...] labor is cheaper," William E. Stone wrote in a letter to him, in 1880. "I am not one of that kind, give me back my Negroes as in 1860 and you will see me paying my debts in a hurry."[121]

Which William?

There is evidence the Stone and Pettus families were friendly for decades even before William was born; there are William Stones involved in land transactions with the Pettus family as early as 1777.[122] There were several consecutive generations of Williams—it's possible one of them was the father of our William, but it's not clear which. Families in that area (including other members of the Stone family), when naming their children, frequently re-used names of their siblings, their parents' siblings, or their nieces and nephews, which obviously makes genealogical knots all the more difficult to untie.

William may have also had a sister (or niece) named Sophia
A. Stone, who married Chester Bullard 1 Nov 1842; William
acted as surety.[123] William and Clarissa had a daughter named
"Sophia A. Stone," and their other daughter Mary married
Dexter Bullard. The relation between them all is unknown.

Clarissa's father Samuel had an uncle named Isaac Stone,
who married Samuel's maternal aunt, Rebecca Whitworth.[124]
in 1793.[125] Isaac and Rebecca had a son named Asher who
could be the same "Asher Stone" who acted as surety for
William and Clarissa's marriage bond,[126] but the common ancestor between Isaac, Asher and William is unknown. William
W. Pettus, a genealogist living in Ashburn, Virginia, said in
an email that William and Clarissa's marriage record lists
William's father as another William Stone, but this is unconfirmed. Pettus's research forms the foundation of the "Pettus"
chapter, so it is tempting to take his word for it.

A candidate for William's mother was Tabitha Neal, who
married a William Stone in 1791[127] and had a son named
William. That son, however, appears to have moved to North
Carolina.

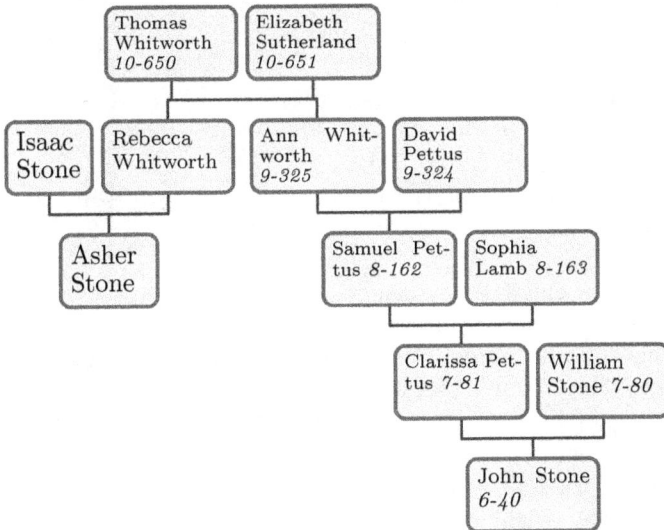

Figure 1.3: Isaac Stone married Rebecca Whitworth. The relationship between him and William Stone 7-80 is unknown, as is whether their son, Asher, is the same one who acted as surety for the wedding of William and Clarissa.

John Richard Stone (*6-40*),
Maria Virginia Spindle (*6-41*)

John Richard, the fifth child of
William *7-80* and Clarissa *7-81*, was
born abt 1842,[129] when the family
was still living in Lunenburg County,
Va.[130]

Virginia was born 20 Jul 1839[131]
to parents Benjamin and Maria
(Wigglesworth) Spindle. Though
her first name in multiple documents is given as "Maria," her tombstone[132] and subsequent documents
filed by her children[133] make it appear that she more commonly went
by her middle name, "Virginia,"
and possibly "Jennie" for short.[134]

*Figure 1.4: An undated
photograph of Virginia
Stone 6-41.*[128]

Though John's pre-war occupation is listed as "student" on mil-
itary paperwork,[135] he may have at one point served as a
remarkably young postmaster of Montgomery County: A
small newspaper story in the *Richmond Dispatch* says that
a "John R. Stone" was appointed to the post in early 1859
at the same time "vice Wm. E Stone" resigned.[136] Though
John was likely not yet 17 years old, there are no other known
people named "John R. Stone" living in the county at the
time, and "Wm. E. Stone" was the name of his brother.
Postal records confirm William E. Stone was appointed to
the position at Dry Valley 19 Jun 1857;[137] John may have
been the deputy as early as that,[138] and was appointed to the
post on his own 17 Jan 1859.[139] This bit is based on entirely
circumstantial evidence—given his young age at the time, it

could very well have been a different John, though he doesn't appear anywhere else in records that would otherwise have been confused with "our" John. (Another possibility is that he was a more reasonable age for the position, and we have incorrectly identified the year of his birth.)

The War

On April 13, 1861, the first shots of the Civil War were fired at Fort Sumter. Two days later, President Abraham Lincoln issued a call for 2,340 Virginians to join the federal cause of suppressing the insurrection. Two days after that, Virginia instead voted to secede from the Union. Later that day—April 17, 1861—John enlisted in the Confederate Army.[140]

He was placed in Company G of the 4th Virginia Infantry Regiment,[141] which was organized into "Virginia's First Brigade,"[142] under former military-school professor Col. Thomas Jackson. However, the unit and its commander would soon receive new monikers: Their rally in the First Battle of Bull Run on July 21 helped turn the tide of the battle in favor of the Confederates, and the (disputed) declaration of Gen. Barnard Bee—"There is Jackson, standing like a stone wall!"—led Virginia's First to furthermore be known as the "Stonewall Brigade." The man who had started the war as the eccentric Col. Thomas Jackson would die less than two years later as Southern hero Gen. Stonewall Jackson, his "foot cavalry" known throughout the army for their grueling marches and unlikely victories.

Shortly after Bull Run, John was sent to "General Hospital"[viii] for an unspecified illness. He was back with the unit by winter,[143] and appears to have been with the brigade for Jack-

---

[viii] Possibly a reference to Charlottesville General Hospital, a makeshift Confederate military hospital just east of Staunton, Va.

son's famous "Valley Campaign" of spring 1862. However, he
likely missed the Second Battle of Bull Run (28–30 Aug 1862),
as he was hospitalized again in early August and spent time
in Confederate hospitals in Charlottesville and Lynchburg,
Va.[144] He may have still been away from the unit as late as
the end of October.[145]

In May 1863, he was likely at the Battle of Chancellorsville,
in which his regiment reportedly "lost 140 men out of a total
of 355."[146]

The brigade lived on, however, and arrived at the Battle of
Gettysburg the evening of July 1,[147] after fighting had already
started. They took up positions around Culp's Hill, where
they spent the majority of the battle trying (unsuccessfully)
to dislodge Union troops at the top.[148] Though evidently in
good health at the start, John was one of 78 in his regiment[149]
wounded on July 2 or 3, described in military records as,
"wounded Breast flesh."[150] He was admitted to the Confederate
hospital in Charlottesville two weeks later; it's not clear if the
wound was the reason.[151]

He returned to his unit later in 1863 and fought at the
Battle of the Wilderness in May 1864. At that battle, which
featured an estimated 61,000 Confederate troops, there were
11,400 casualties[152]—including John, who was shot in the
right forearm. He carried a Union musket ball lodged in
his arm bones for the rest of his life.[ix,153] (The American
Civil War Museum in Richmond, Va. has a battle flag of the

[ix] John claimed to have been shot with a Minié ball, the conical bullet
that first enabled the widespread use of rifled barrels, but it's not clear
how he could have known this. It would seem more likely that his arm
held a more traditional musket ball, as the Minié balls, made of softer
lead that mushroomed out on impact, were notorious for causing catas-
trophic damage that frequently required the amputation of arms rather
than simply being left alone.

4th Virginia Infantry[x] that was captured by the 3rd Michigan Infantry at the Battle of the Wilderness.)[154,xi]

There are no records indicating John spent any time away from his unit after his injury, though he would have been almost one-handed the following week at the Battle of Spotsylvania Court House. It was a horrific scene, featuring some of the most grisly fighting of the entire war.[155] Many members of the Stonewall Brigade were reduced to hand-to-hand combat after their gunpowder was doused with rain[156]—at one stage, the Confederates at that point in the line fought against troops from Pennsylvania and New Jersey by swinging their muskets like clubs.[157] Later, after the smoke cleared at the battle's infamous "Bloody Angle," the Stonewall Brigade was dead: All but 200 had been killed or wounded.[158]

John was evidently placed into the "consolidated"[159] Stonewall Brigade, which by this time was the size of only a small regiment. It was placed within the (actual) brigade of Brig. Gen. William Terry, who as a colonel had commanded John's regiment the previous year at Chancellorsville.[160] (Terry's brigade was placed within the infantry corps of Confederate Gen. John Breckinridge, who two and a half years earlier had been vice president of the United States.)

The newly formed troops—the "Army of the Valley," under Gen. Jubal Early—fought the Battle of Monocacy near Frederick, Maryland on 9 Jul 1864, then charged south, toward Washington, D.C. for what would be the Battle of Fort Stevens. A portion of that battle, fought on the outskirts of Washington, was personally observed by President Abraham Lincoln, in what became the only instance of a sitting presi-

---

[x]The flag is for the same regiment as John's, but a different company.

[xi]You can send a request to see the flag in person; there would have been a picture of it here, but they charge publications $150 per image.

dent coming under enemy fire. (In this case, enemy fire that may have been coming directly from an ancestor of ours.)

The battlefield, situated north of the fort because of the direction of the Confederate approach, was mostly untouched after the war, save for a small Union cemetery established on Georgia Avenue. This changed around 1925, when developers were allowed to build homes in what is now the Brightwood neighborhood of D.C. In 1928, a two-unit row home was built[161] exactly along the Confederate position from July 11[162] and given the address of 6415 8th Street NW. For six months in the beginning of 2014, Richard Abdill *1-1* lived in its basement.

Back in 1864, John continued fighting, until he was wounded again: He was shot in the shoulder[163] at the Third Battle of Winchester in September 1864.[xii] Again, there are no records of his leaving the unit for medical care, but these records may have either been lost or never existed.

After more than three and a half years with the 4th Virginia, John was transferred in November 1864 to the 25th Virginia Cavalry Regiment,[164] a unit that seems to be almost entirely undocumented in the last months of the war. An 1893 congressional report compiled from Confederate documents puts the 25th in a division under the command of Maj. Gen. Lunsford L. Lomax,[165] but that's most of the evidence uncovered by the author.

It appears that when John arrived at the 25th, he was mis-recorded in the company muster roll as "John W. Stone." This explanation (rather than John W. simply being a different person) could be supported by the remarks in the document: "Transferred from Co G 1 Va Inf to Co E 25 Va Cav"[166]—so,

---

[xii]The state legislation detailing John's wounds says only, "at Winchester," the location of three separate battles. John's 1896 pension application gives the date as "19th September 1864," which is the date of the third battle.

for this to be a different person, there would have needed to be two John Stones in the same company, transferred to the same company of a different unit, in the same month of 1864. The confusing part is that "John W. Stone" is listed as coming from Company G of the *1st* Virginia Infantry, and our "John R. Stone" transferred from the 4th. This appears to have confused even the government recordkeeper who compiled the information—on the cover of the report for "John W. Stone," the "See also" section gives the unit as "1 Va Inf," but underneath, someone has written "(4?)" Supporting this theory is that records from the 4th Virginia definitely refer to our John being transferred, and there is no record in the 1st Virginia of any solder named "John Stone" ever serving.

The complete text of those sloppy remarks is even more vexing: "Transferred from Co G 1 Va Inf to Co E 25 Va Cav Since Dec the 15 1[8]64 absent wounded from date of"— the report looks to have been cut off, either on the original document or on the compiled record from which this quote is pulled. It seems the person who recorded John with the wrong middle name and incorrect unit also forgot to finish the sentence in which he explained when John left for medical care. In any case, we have no evidence indicating whether he returned. He was marked as "absent" in his last known entry in Confederate muster rolls.

This is also the last record we have of his service, which is particularly problematic because of the unit he was with: The Army of the Valley was largely disbanded in November 1864 after a string of embarrassing tactical decisions by Gen. Early, who saw most of his troops sent to Petersburg to join up with the army of Gen. Robert E. Lee. Early was left with a "skeleton crew" to defend the Shenandoah Valley. The group is poorly defined in extant records, but it's possible at least one company from the 25th Virginia Cavalry–Company E, John's

unit—was part of it: A sickly soldier in John's company was
recorded in a 31 Dec 1864 muster roll as "assigned to light
duty by order of Gen Early," suggesting Early was still in
command of that unit.[167]

We don't know where
John was at the close of
the war—the 25th surrendered at Cumberland Gap,
Va., on 25 Apr 1865,[168]
but John, while he is listed
on rosters of the unit, does
not appear to have re-
ceived an official parole on
that day.[169] This could be
because he wasn't there,
but documentation at the
end of the war (and specifically from this surren-
der) is haphazard and relatively unreliable.[170]   (A
more in-depth narrative of

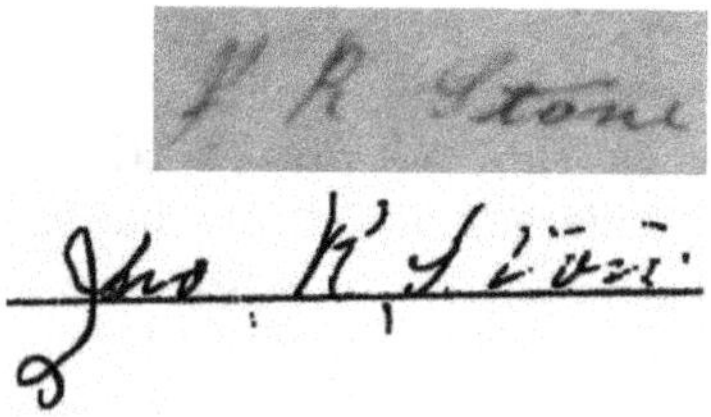

*Figure 1.5:   Two signatures of
John R. Stone—the first from an
1862 Confederate payroll receipt,
the latter from an 1896 pension
application, 32 years after he'd
been shot twice in the right arm.*

the Civil War experiences of John and his brother William is
planned for the compiled edition of the *Abdill Family History*.)

Post-bellum life

On 21 Dec 1865, John married Virginia Spindle, the sister
of Thomas Spindle, with whom he had served in both the
4th Infantry[171] and 25th Cavalry.[172] Their eldest son, Henry,
was born in November 1866, and by 1870 the young family
was living on what was likely the 400-acre portion of William
Stone's plantation that John inherited in 1861 after William's
death:[173] Their "neighbors" in the census include John's
brother Musgrove and his mother Clara.[174]   Though John

and Virginia were only 28 and 30 years old, respectively, their $1,500 "estate" was worth about $28,000 in 2015 cash, and they had three live-in servants: Lucinda Hungate, age 19, Spencer Cheese, 22, and George Jenkins, age 14. (Neither Spencer nor George could read or write, and it's likely several of the Stone family's postbellum servants were actually emancipated slaves.)[175]

John declared bankruptcy around 1877; his brother Musgrove may have done the same, and both gave up hundreds of acres of land in an attempt to pay their debts.[176] He first applied for financial assistance from the state of Virginia in about 1879, when he submitted a letter from a doctor saying his wartime injuries had made him "incapable of performing hard manual labor for any length of time."[177] There are several applications filed between then and 1898, the final of which describes John as "poor + needy."[178] It appears this was the one approved by the Virginia legislature.[xiii]

Virginia died 26 May 1884,[179] in Christiansburg[180] at age 44. She and John had four children:

- **HENRY THOMAS**, b. 7 Nov 1866, d. 6 Sep 1940.[181]
- **John Allen**, b. abt 1869, d. June 1877, age 8.[182]
- **Mary**,[183] known as "Mamie,"[184] b. 22 Oct 1871 in Christiansburg,[185] m. Charles Lyde[186] Alexander 21 Feb 1900,[187] d. 29 Jun 1958 in Norfolk, Va.[188] Worked as a high school music teacher.[189]
- **Virginia E.**, b. 19 Oct 1878 in Christiansburg,[190] d. 25 Aug 1970 in Chesapeake, Va.[191] May have moved to Hubbard City, Tx., in 1900 to live with her uncle, Samuel Stone.[192] Did not marry.[193] (Middle name probably "Ella" or "Ellen.")[194]

John moved about 11 miles west, to New River, sometime in the early 1890s[195] and was probably the same "John R.

[xiii]See Appendix D.

Stone" who got a job transporting patients to the newly
opened[196] Southwestern Lunatic Asylum.[197] He remarried on
6 Jan 1892,[198] when he was 49 and his wife, Ida V. Gillespie,
had just turned 30.[199]

Later that year, the *Roanoke Times* wrote about "John R.
Stone, the well known attendant who conveys patients to the
asylum at Marion," who was struck by lightning after being
caught in a storm.[200] He apparently made a quick recovery.

Ida worked as a teacher[201] and served as principal of the
school in New River in 1901–1902.[202] John and Ida had one
child, **Clara**, in 1895. John fell ill with Hodgkin's lymphoma
less than 10 years later,[203] and his daughter Mamie is mentioned in the *Richmond Times Dispatch* as visiting "her sick
father" in New River in early 1906.[204] He died 1 Mar 1907.[205]

Ida, who died in 1948,[206] is buried at Sunrise Burial Park
in Fairlawn, Pulaski County, as is Clara, who died in 1973.[207]
However, it's likely John is buried elsewhere.

The Old Stone Burying Ground

John's 1907 obituary says he was to be interred at the "old
Stone burying ground by the Confederate veterans," with no
elaboration.[208] There is another reference to "the old Stone
burial-grounds" six years earlier, in a burial announcement
after John's brother Musgrove died within days of his own son,
Dr. John Stone.[209] Musgrove's wife Mary died the following
year, and her death announcement says her burial "will be
made at the old Stone burying ground, at Dry Valley."[210]

Musgrove and Mary's son John is buried at West View
Cemetery in Radford, Va.,[211] according to crowdsourced data
about the cemetery. Though it would seem all four were buried
in the same place (and Radford is around the area that used
to be called "Dry Valley"), the database says Musgrove's son

News reached Salem yesterday of a remarkable accident which happened Wednesday afternoon on the road between Snowville and Radford, to John R. Stone, the well known attendant who conveys patients to the asylum at Marion. He was with a companion in a storm and of a sudden was struck by lightning which ripped his clothing from head to foot down one side, burning and stunning him. After a few hours rest he recovered sufficiently to continue his journey.

(a) A June 1892 article about John Stone being struck by lightning.[212]

John Stone.
[Special to The Times-Dispatch.]
EAST RADFORD, VA., March 1.—Mr. John Stone died this afternoon at his home, at New River, after a long illness. He was sixty-five years old and leaves a wife and four children—Mrs. Charles Alexander, of Tazewell; Mr. Henry Stone, of Christiansburg; Miss Virginia Stone, of Pulaski, and Miss Clara Stone, of New River. He was a son of Captain William A. Stone, and was a member of the Stonewall Brigade.
Burial will be made to-morrow at the old Stone burial ground by the Confederate veterans.

(b) A death announcement for John R. Stone.[213]

is the only "Stone" from that time interred there, and the author has not yet been able to go to research in person.

Henry Thomas Stone (5-20), Mary Lynn Wade (5-21)

Henry was born 7 Nov 1866[214] and grew up working on his father's farm in Christiansburg.[215] When he was 10, his 8-year-old brother, John Allen, died of unspecified causes;[216] Henry and his wife Mary named their third son after him.[217]

Mary Lynn Wade was born in Christiansburg 27 May 1869,[218],[xiv] living with eight older siblings, a 24-year-old cook named Catharine Brown, and Catharine's two children, Nannie and Lewis. Mary was a year younger than Catharine's oldest, Nannie.[219]

Mary's father James died suddenly[220] when she was five, but there were plenty of people in her home growing up: In addition to the siblings closest to her age, her older brother

---

[xiv]Mary's gravestone lists her year of birth as 1868, not 1869—the latter was given precedence because it was listed in her death certificate and lines up more accurately with her age as recorded in census records.

Charles remained living there into his 20s, when his wife Fannie moved in as well.[221] (The Wade family will be profiled in *Abdill Family History*, Volume II.)

Henry and Mary were married 29 Nov 1894.[223],[xv] It's unclear what Henry's occupation was, but they were evidently relatively well-to-do: In 1900, they had a live-in cook, an 18-year-old woman named Mary Howard.[224]

In the 1890s, Henry was part of a mercantile partnership called "Spindle, Harless & Stone" that appears to have sold farming supplies.[225] One of his partners, "R.B. Spindle," was likely his uncle,[xvi] Richard Buckner Spindle.

In 1910, Henry was employed as a traveling salesman for a "dry goods store,"[226] though it's not clear if it was the same business as he was in 20 years prior. He retired sometime in the 1930s.[227]

Figure 1.7: The sons of Henry 5-20 and Mary Stone 5-21: Henry 4-10 (wearing his U.S. Army uniform), Charlie, and John Allen, in spring 1918.[222]

[xv]A photograph believed to be from their wedding is on the cover of this book.

[xvi]Technically, his mother's half-brother.

His granddaughter Sally *3-5* remembers him: "I think he was in sales. They would talk about 'the store.' ... Even after he retired, he would get up and put on a black suit and a black bow tie and a white shirt, and he'd sit on the porch." she said. "There weren't a lot of stories about him. He was just a quiet gentleman."[228]

Henry and Mary had six children:

- **HENRY THOMAS JR.,**[229] b. 25 Sep 1895, d. 6 Dec 1972. (Henry is profiled in the prologue.)
- **Charles Ingles Wade,**[230] b. 27 Mar 1898,[231] d. 12 Nov 1928, lost at sea in the sinking of the S.S. *Vestris*.[232]
- **Margaret Alan,**[233] b. 10 Mar 1900,[234] d. 24 Jul 1900. Buried in Sunset Cemetery.[235]
- **Agnes McClanahan,**[236] b. 26 Jul 1901 in Christiansburg,[237] m. John Henry Stephens 3 Sep 1918,[238] d. 6 Aug 1924 in Christiansburg, of complications from childbirth.[239] Their daughter, Mary Marshall Stephens, was raised by Mary and Henry.
- **Frances Hartwell,**[240] b. 26 Feb 1905 in Christiansburg, d. 15 Apr 1972 in Blacksburg, Va., of congestive heart failure;[241] m. John Gibson Davis 6 May 1927.[242] Widowed, Frances married again, John Roedel of St. Louis, 1 Jul 1939.[243]
- **John Allen,**[244] b. 1 Feb 1907,[245] probably Christiansburg, d. 20 Aug 1977, Radford, Va. of pneumonia.[246] Veteran of World War II. Went by "John Allen."[247]

On 3 Sep 1940, Henry (then 73) sought medical treatment for a fall in which he'd broken several ribs. He died three days later, with the fall cited as the main cause.[248] He was buried 8 Sep 1940, in Sunset Cemetery.[249] Mary remained in Christiansburg until her death on 21 Feb 1955.[250] She was buried the next day[251] in Sunset Cemetery.[252]

Figure 1.8: Frances H. Stone, daughter of Henry 4-10 and Mary Stone 4-11.[253]

Figure 1.9: Mary Lynn Stone 4-11 in 1918.[254]

Chapter 2

Pettus

This chapter is a listing of the ancestors of Clara Ann Pettus *7-81*, who married William Stone *7-80*. Much of the information here is based on the life's work of William Pettus IV, a distant cousin living in Virginia as of 2016. His two-volume history of the Pettus family is the definitive source I can only hope to one day produce—for more information about the people in this chapter (or other descendants of the Pettus clan), his *Thomas Petyous of Norwich, England and His Pettus Descendants in England and Virginia*, from Otter Bay Books, is the place to go. Though I was able to piece together some of the Pettus line before finding his book, his sourcing (featuring excursions on both sides of the Atlantic) is far better, and where the two perspectives conflict, I have deferred to his.

PETTUS, OF RACKHEATH.

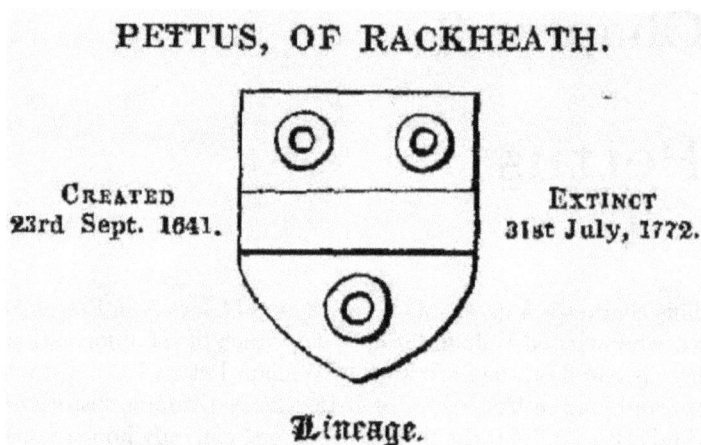

CREATED
23rd Sept. 1641.

EXTINCT
31st July, 1772.

Lineage.

Figure 2.1: The arms received by Thomas Pettus 16-41472 in the 1590s.[255] The dates referenced in the illustration refer to the Pettus baronetcy: Thomas's son John was knighted in 1607. John's son Augustine was knighted in 1611.[256] Augustine's son, also named Thomas, was awarded the Pettus Baronetcy, a hereditary title that was passed down for six generations before no more male heirs were living to inherit it.

Thomas Petyous (*18-165888*)

A tailor,[257] dates of birth and death unknown. He moved to Norwich, a city in Norfolk County, England, in 1492,[258] likely putting his date of birth at 1470 or earlier. He had one son, possibly with a woman named Agnes: **JOHN** *17-82944*.[259]

John Pethous (*17-82944*)

Born about 1500, died sometime after 25 Jul 1558, when he made his will.[260] Married first an unknown woman around 1518, and had three children:

- **THOMAS** *16-41472*, b. abt 1519, buried 12 Jan 1598.
- **Anne**, buried 1 Oct 1554.
- **Jone**, buried 28 Mar 1542.

Another history of the Pettus family[i] states that John's first wife was named Jone, which lines up nicely with the name of their second daughter but does not appear to be substantiated anywhere else.[261]

W. Pettus outlines numerous public offices John held during his life: two terms as constable (1523 and 1532), multiple terms as a city councilor and two terms as coroner, among others.[262]

At some point after 1522, John's wife died. He then married Cecily Capon, a widow. She and John moved to a house he purchased in 1536, next to St. Simon and St. Jude Church (where the majority of English Pettuses in this branch are buried). A section of "Pettus House," as it is called, is still standing on Norwich's Elm Hill.

On 28 Mar 1542, John buried both Cecily and his daughter Jone, in what was likely an outbreak of disease in the walled

---

[i]From Rudd and Stacy, see bibliography.

city. A year later, John got married again, on 1 Feb 1543, to
a widow whose married name appears to have been Beatrice
Duckett.[263] He died 15 or 20 years later.

Thomas Pettus (*16-41472*), Christian Dethick (*16-41473*)

Thomas, born about 1519, was a tailor like his father, and
likely apprenticed under him.[264] He too served as constable,
councilor, and in other offices, including a term in 1566 as
sheriff of Norwich. This qualified him to run for mayor, which
he did (unsuccessfully) in 1580. He won election in 1590, and
the sword rest he used while attending church services that
year was on display at a now-defunct Norwich museum in the
1970s.[265]

He married Christian Dethick
29 Oct 1548.[267] She may have died
25 Oct 1566.[268]

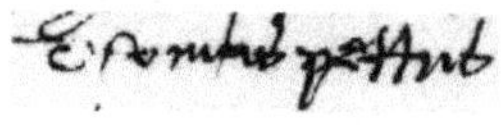

Thomas was the Pettus to purchase the family estate at Rackheath,[269] held for generations afterward.[270] He was also the family
member to receive, some time after
1590, a coat of arms.[271]

*Figure 2.2: The signa-
ture of Thomas Pettus
16-41472, from a 1594
document.*[266]

He died 7 Jan 1598, and he and
Christian have a prominent monument at St. Simon and St.
Jude Church in Norwich.

Christian and Thomas had eight children,[272] many of
whom rose to prominence in the Norwich area:

- **John**, b. abt 1550, d. 9 Apr 1614 in Norwich. Married
  Bridget Curtis 25 Jan 1581.[273] Served as sheriff of
  Norwich 1598–1599, elected to the British Parliament's

Figure 2.3: Pettus memorial at St. Simon and St. Jude Church. Thomas, in his red mayoral robes, can be seen kneeling to the left of the table. Christian is to the right, and their children are crowded around in the background.

House of Commons in 1601 and 1604,[274] which likely meant he was present at the King's Speech on 5 Nov 1605, the date the Gunpowder Plot was foiled. He would probably have seen in person both Queen Elizabeth I (in 1601) and King James VI (in 1604 and 1605). Knighted 29 Jun 1607 "at Whitehall,"[275] a reference to the Palace of Whitehall, the home of English monarchs until 1698. Also served as mayor of Norwich, and was later a shareholder in the Virginia Company.

- **Isabell**, baptized 28 Jun 1551 in Norwich.[276]
- **THOMAS** *15-20736*, baptized 17 Sep 1552, d. 1 Jun 1620 in Norwich.[277]
- **Elizabeth**, baptized 28 Jun 1554,[278] m. Augustin Whall 29 Aug 1573.[279]
- **William**, b. 1556,[280] d. 1608. Married Elizabeth Rolfe 13 May 1594.[281] Elizabeth's father, Henry Rolfe,[282] was

possibly an uncle (or, more likely, grand-uncle)[283] to
John Rolfe, husband of Pocahontas.

- **Alexander**, birth date unknown, died after 1597.[284]
- **Cicely**, b.   1560;   married   Humphery   Camden[285]
  13 Sep 1581.[286]
- **Anne**, baptized 16 Apr 1564, d. before 29 Jun 1634.[287]

Thomas Pettus (*15-20736*),
Cecily King (*15-20737*)

Thomas Pettus was baptized 17 Sep 1552 and died 1 Jun 1620.
He and Cecily King were married in 1574;[288] she was the
daughter of William King *16-41474*. Thomas, like, his father
and brother, was elected mayor, he in 1614.[289] Cecily died
about 1641.[290]

They had 17 children:

- **Ann**, baptized 10 Jul 1582, buried 7 Sep 1582.
- **William**, baptized 12 Aug 1582, buried 19 Dec 1648; m.
  Mary Gleane 21 Dec 1607.[291]
- **John**, baptized 12 Oct 1584, buried 1618–1620.
- **Edward**, baptized 17 Nov 1585,[292] d. 1620. Did not
  marry.
- **Henry**, baptized 25 Oct 1586, buried 14 Aug 1588.[293]
- **Susan**, baptized 19 Mar 1589. Married Geoffrey Might.
- **Elizabeth**, baptized 12 Jul 1590, d. bef 1620; m.
  Nicholas Sadler.
- **George**, baptized 1 Dec 1591.[294] Died at sea in sum-
  mer 1629, bound for the East Indies. Married Frances
  Palgrave 1624.
- **Frances**, baptized 24 Mar 1593,[295] d. aft 1620, when
  she inherited a rental property from her father.
- **Mary**, baptized 19 Apr 1594.[296]

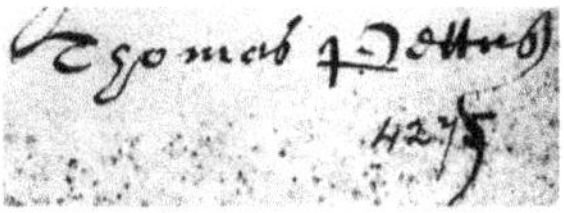

47

Figure 2.4: The signature of Thomas Pettus 15-20736 from 1614.[303]

- **Thomas**, baptized 8 Aug 1596, buried 31 Dec 1597.[297]
- **THOMAS** *14-10368*, baptized 19 Feb 1599,[298] died bef 1668 in Virginia.
- **Theodore**, baptized 18 Jul 1600, d. after 1626. Likely the first Pettus to North America;[299] appears in Jamestown records in 1623.[300]
- **Christian**, baptized 26 Jul 1601,[301] d. after 1620, when she inherited a rental property from her father.
- **Ann**, baptized 17 Jan 1605, d. bef 5 Feb 1662, when her will was proved. Buried at All Saints Church, Rackheath, Norfolk, England. Never married.
- **Henry**, died at sea in 1673, aboard the *Dover Castle*.
- **Robart**, baptized 28 Feb 1608.[302]

Thomas Pettus (*14-10368*), Elizabeth Freeman(*14-10369*)

Thomas and Elizabeth Pettus are the first Pettuses in North America in the direct line being traced. (Thomas's brother Theodore may have arrived earlier.)[304] Thomas immigrated in about 1630.[305]

Thomas's uncle, Sir John Pettus (son of Thomas Pettus *16-41472*) was an investor in the Virginia Company, but what pushed Thomas to America was likely a trial for manslaughter, in which he was accused of stabbing a William Sheppard in the stomach on 24 Mar 1629; Sheppard died the next day, and Thomas was arrested at some point after August 10 of that year and imprisoned in the jail within the Norwich city hall. He was acquitted by a jury, but records show he sold most of his inherited property in England in early 1630 and likely sailed to America later that year.[306]

There are several layers of unsubstantiated lore adding up to the notion that Thomas Pettus was married to a Native American woman named Ka-Okee, of the nearby Patawomeck tribe. This alone would not be particularly controversial, but for the second half of the tale: that Ka-Okee was the daughter of Pocahontas. A modern recording of the lore of the related Mattaponi tribe says Pocahontas had a husband before her marriage to Englishman John Rolfe, and that this union with Kocoum[307] produced a child. The Mattaponi tradition holds the child was a son (called "Little Kocoum").[308]

However, this is partially contradicted by modern tribal lore from Pocahontas' tribe: According to William "Night Owl" Deyo, a Patawomeck tribal historian, the child was a daughter (Ka-Okee), who married a member of the Pettus family.[309] While DNA testing has at least partially corroborated the connection to Ka-Okee (or at least a Native American ancestor),[310] there is no contemporary evidence for any relation between Ka-Okee and Pocahontas. Any chance to test the remains of Pocahontas was lost in the collapse of the London church in which she was buried, and no known evidence has been found linking her modern descendants to those of Ka-Okee.

Deyo also suggests another connection, that "the famous Matoaka portrait of Pocahontas was found in England in a Pettus home"—apparently that of Elizabeth (Pettus) Rolfe, daughter of Thomas Pettus *16-41472* and Christian Dethick

16-41473, who may have inspired the name of Ka-Okee's daughter, Christian. However, available evidence points toward the painting being in possession of a different family, not Elizabeth's, and in 2011 a researcher claimed the portrait was almost certainly of a different Native American woman, painted 150 years after Pocahontas had died.[311]

However, W. Pettus talked at length with Deyo, which, combined with his extensive research in the area, led him to conclude Thomas most likely married Ka-Okee when he first immigrated to America, and had two children with her:

- **Christian**
- **STEPHEN** *13-5184*, b. abt 1642.

Around 1638, Thomas married Elizabeth Freeman,[ii] who had immigrated to America around 1632. Elizabeth was a widow when she and Thomas were married; her first husband was Richard Durrent. There *is* evidence of the marriage of Thomas and Elizabeth; if Ka-Okee (or her marriage to Thomas) is a fiction, then Elizabeth is the most likely mother of the children.

Thomas was nominated to the Virginia Council of State on 9 Aug 1641 by King Charles I—a sharp turn of events for an accused murderer that W. Pettus speculates was related to the king buying support in England for his impending conflict with Oliver Cromwell. Two of Thomas's cousins, still in England, were given lofty titles around the same time. Thomas stayed on the council for 19 years, during which time he acquired thousands of acres of land, mostly under the "headright" system, in which land patents were awarded in exchange for bringing colonists to North America.

Thomas died some time in the 1660s; his place of burial is unknown, but is likely hidden somewhere on the grounds of

---

[ii]The overlap between Stephen's birth and Elizabeth's marriage to Thomas is another complicating factor.

his former home. Elizabeth's date of death is also unknown, but she did remarry after Thomas's death, to John Grove.[312] They likely had one child together (Thomas, b. abt 1652, died around February 1688 in Holland), but there is no evidence ruling her out as the mother of Stephen and possibly Christian.

Thomas and Elizabeth's home, "Littletown," was excavated by archaeologists in the early 1970s.[313]

Stephen Pettus (*13-5184*)

The connection of Stephen to the known Abdill family tree is the most tenuous of them all: W. Pettus was not able to find any data about his birth, death or marriage, nor direct evidence of his children. It is also at this point that multiple other family histories of the Pettus family diverge, mostly, one would assume, confused by the prolific use of the "John" and "Thomas" family names, particularly within the same generation. W. Pettus's research has shown, with far more certainty than I could offer, that Stephen had two children:

- **JOHN** *12-2592*, born possibly around 1662, in Blisland Parish, New Kent County, Virginia. Died after 1704.
- **Susanna**, born around 1667. Married Evan Ragland (b. 1656), according to Ragland family tradition.

John Pettus (*12-2592*)

Like with John's father Stephen Pettus *13-5184*, we trust at this point the research of W. Pettus, which resulted in the conclusion that John had a son, also named JOHN *11-1296*.

We know John (son of Stephen) was alive in 1703 or 1704, when he signed a letter from his parish to the royal governor of Virginia.

John Pettus (*11-1296*),
Anne Overton (*11-1297*)

John was likely born in 1672. He and Anne Overton (b. 1673) were married in 1703,[314] before migrating from New Kent County to Hanover County, near present-day Old Church, Va.,[315] where John was one of the largest landholders in the parishes of St. Paul and St. Peter.[316] He is found in numerous land transactions in that area. He and Anne had four children:

- **Anne Overton**,[317] b. 1702, d. 24 Oct 1736; m. Joseph Eggleston abt 1720.
- **THOMAS** *10-648*, b. 25 Dec 1712, d. 18 Mar 1780 in Lunenburg County, Va.
- **John**, died 1770.
- **Lucy**, born abt 1718, m. William Humphries.

Thomas Pettus (*10-648*),
Amey Walker (*10-649*)

Thomas was born 25 Dec 1712, Amy 25 Jan 1718. They were married 10 Nov 1735[318,319] (Amey's parents were David *11-1298* and Mary *11-1299*.)[320]

It looks like Thomas and Amey moved to Amelia County (nearer to Richmond) in January 1746, clearing land to live on with the help of three servants, Glasgow, Jemmy, and Juda.[322] (It's not clear if these people were slaves; as a tobacco planter from a wealthy family, they almost certainly owned many.) The family moved to Lunenburg County,

Figure 2.5: The signature of Thomas Pettus 10-648 from about 1750.[321]

where Thomas appears to have been an avid land speculator, sometime around 1751.[323]

It was from Lunenburg County that Thomas was elected to the Virginia House of Burgesses in 1769[324]—he served consecutive terms through 1775, and then again in 1777 and 1778.[325] He was definitely one of the 89 "late burgesses" who met in Williamsburg's Raleigh Tavern in May 1774, after the royal governor dissolved the House for being too politically antagonistic. Other attendees included George Washington, Thomas Jefferson, Patrick Henry, and many other prominent Virginians, all of whom are now listed on a bronze plaque at the rebuilt tavern.

Thomas and Amey had nine children:

- **John**, b. 24 Sep 1736, d. Apr 1799 in Charlotte County, Va.
- **Overton**, b. 13 Oct 1739, d. 20 May 1749.
- **Thomas**, b. 10 Mar 1742, d. abt 1797.
- **Mary**, b. 6 Nov 1746, m. Thomas Branch Brown. Moved to Kentucky.
- **Ann**, b. 31 Jan 1749, d. 9 Mar 1831 in Lunenburg County, Va.; m. James Shelburne 22 Sep 1765.
- **Samuel Overton**, b. 1 Mar 1751, d. 10 Dec 1759 in Lunenburg County. Two of his sons, Freeman[326] and William,[327] were members of the "Old 300," the settlers in Stephen F. Austin's first Texan colony and the first white settlers of Texas officially recognized by the Spanish government.[328]
- **William**, b. 30 Apr 1753, d. 10 Dec 1759 in Lunenburg County.
- **DAVID WALKER** *9-324*, b. 3 July 1755, d. 8 Nov 1805.
- **Rebecah**, b. 21 Jun 1759 in Lunenburg County.

David Walker Pettus (*9-324*), Ann Whitworth (*9-325*)

David was born 3 Jul 1755, in Virginia.[329]   He married Ann Whitworth 25 Nov 1776.[330],[iii] (She was born 30 Oct 1750,[331],[332] to Thomas and Elizabeth Whitworth; see the "Whitworth" chapter for more.)

Just weeks before their wedding, David was commissioned an ensign[iv] in the militia of Lunenburg County.[333] He almost certainly fought in the Revolutionary War, but his role is unclear.

Ann died 13 Mar 1802.[334],[335] She and David had 13 children, though only six survived to adulthood:

- **Elizabeth**, b. 24 Sep 1777.
- **Thomas**, b. 27 Feb 1779; d. 1854 in Madison County, Ala.
- **David W.** (likely "Whitworth"), b. 20 Dec 1780; d. Jan 1852 in Madison County.
- **Infant**, b. 13 Aug 1782, d. 14 Aug 1782.[336]
- **Infant**, b. 6 Jul 1783, died same day.[337]
- **SAMUEL** *8-162*, b. 22 Aug 1784, d. 10 Sep 1857.
- **Infant**, b. 19 Apr 1786, died same day.[338]
- **John**, b. 29 Mar 1787, d. 19 Aug 1790.
- **Infant**, b. 1 Jan 1789, died same day.[339]
- **Mary**, b. 15 Mar 1790, d. 12 Jul 1790.[340]
- **Infant**, b. 10 Jun 1792, died same day.[341]
- **Infant**, b. 31 May 1793, died same day.[342]

[iii]Pettus p. 373 puts this date as 28 Nov instead; both sources refer to family bible records, but the 25 Nov date appears to have come from a record possibly started by David Pettus himself.

[iv]At the time, "ensign" was the lowest rank of military officers, but still outranked the enlisted soldiers.

- **Nancy**, b. 21 Apr 1795, d. sometime after November 1805, when she was mentioned in her father's will.

David remarried, to Elenor Willson, on 25 Sep 1802.[343]

Samuel Pettus (*8-162*),
Sophia Musgrove Lamb (*8-163*)

Samuel was born 22 Aug 1784, likely in Lunenburg County, Virginia. Sophia was born 20 Sep 1784[344] to Richard *9-324* and Clarissa Lamb *9-325*,[345],[346] and the two were married 29 May 1806,[347] when they were both 22 years old.

In 1830, Samuel and Sophia owned 27 slaves;[348] 10 years later, that number was down to 15.[349] In the 1850 census, slave inventories were split out into a separate form; the record for Samuel is missing.[v]

Samuel died 10 Sep 1857,[350] Sophia on 19 Mar 1861.[351] They had five children:

- **CLARISSA ANN** *7-81*,[352] b. 23 Jul 1807,[353] d. 24 Dec 1878;[354] m. William Stone *7-80*.
- **Musgrove Lamb**,[355] b. 11 Oct 1808, d. 3 Sep 1881. Lived for a period in Tennessee,[356] but moved back to Virginia several years later.[357]
- **Elizabeth Harriott**,[358] b. 20 Nov 1811.
- **John Richard**,[359] b. 12 Sep 1818 in Lunenburg County, d. 26 Sep 1870 in Fort Bend, Texas. Likely fought in the Civil War in the Confederate 16th Texas Infantry

---

[v]An important caveat: There is very little identifying information in census records prior to 1850; we know there was a man named "Samuel Pettus" living in Lunenburg County in those years, with that number of slaves. There are no other records in that county for a different Samuel Pettus, and the one in the records in question was living near Walker Pettus, his cousin.

Brigade. Buried in Morton Cemetery, Richmond, Fort Bend County, Tx.[360]

- **Sophia Adaline**, b. 17 Apr 1820, d. 1898.[361]

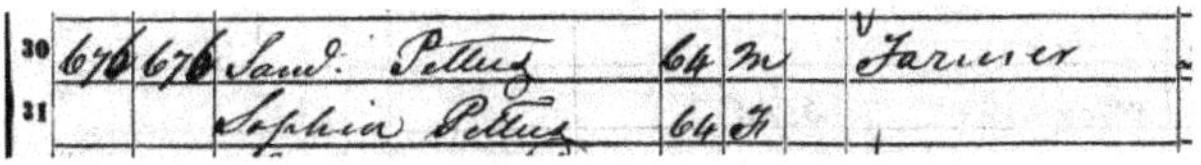

30	676	676	Saml. Pettus	64	M	Farmer
31			Sophia Pettus	64	F	

Figure 2.6: Samuel and Sophia Pettus, recorded in the 1850 census.[362]

Chapter 3

Crowe

Christopher Crowe (18-165894), Christian (18-165895)

We know essentially nothing of Christopher and Christian Crowe; according to *The Pedigree Register, Vol. III*, Christopher died 7 Dec 1527, and that his father was "Richard Crowe of Longham, Norfolk." The same book also says there is a "brass" in St. John the Baptist's church in Mileham commemorating the couple.[363] We know of one child: ROSE *17-82947*.[364]

Simon Dethick (17-82946), Rose Beatrice Crowe (17-82947)

We know Rose Crowe was probably born around the turn of the 16th century,[365] but not much more. Simon Dethick lived in Wormegay, North Elmham, Norfolk, in England,[366] and died between about 1 Nov 1541 and 1 Feb 1542.[i,367] The couple had about eight children:[368]

- **Christopher**
- **Richard**
- **Thomas**
- **John**
- **Henry**
- **CHRISTIAN** *16-41473*, whose monument at St. Simon and St. Jude Church in Norwich includes a family crest, indicating Simon's ancestry likely included some form of nobility.[369]
- **Rose**, married William Batch.[370]
- **Elizabeth**, married Richard Swift.[371]

Simon was buried 1 Mar 1543[372] at St. James's Church in North Elmham, England. Rose died some time between the completion of her will on 25 Oct 1566 and 21 Nov 1566, the day it was proven.[373]

---

[i]When Rose made her will on 1 Feb 1542, it was "within three months after his decease."

Chapter 4

Whitworth

John Whitworth (12-2600), Mary Claiborne (12-2601)

Whitworth Family History, Vol. 1 states John Whitworth was born in 1673 and his son Thomas in 1690. However, the only historical documentation we have currently (indexed marriage records) indicates John was born in 1665[374] and Thomas in 1685,[375] which also provides a more likely chronology on both accounts.

According to those same documents, Mary Claiborne was also born in 1665, and married John in 1684.[376] **THOMAS** *11-1300* was their only known child.

Thomas Whitworth (11-1300), Mary Winston (11-1301)

According to a marriage record for the couple, Thomas Whitworth was born in 1685, and Mary Winston five years later. They were married in 1725.[377] Their date of marriage lines up with other evidence (their first child was born the following year), however, if the other dates are correct, that means Mary would have had her first child at about 35, and her last at age 46. No other corroborating evidence has been found for their births, but it's possible the couple was younger than this record indicates.

The couple had six known children:

- **THOMAS** *10-650*, b. 1726.[378]
- **Catherine Mary**, b. 1728.[379]
- **Mary**, b. 1730.[380]
- **William**, b. 1732.[381]
- **Samuel**, b. 1734.[382]
- **John**, b. 1736.[383]

Thomas Whitworth (10-650), Elizabeth Sutherland (10-651)

Thomas Whitworth was born probably 26 Jun[384] 1726.[385],[386] in Amelia County, Virginia.

He and Elizabeth had 12 children:

- **Samuel**,[387] b. 14 Dec 1745[388] in Amelia County, Va., d. 1 May 1819, Hall County, Ga.[389]
- **Thomas**,[390] b. 29 Jun 1748.[391]
- **ANN** *9-325*,[392],[393] b. 30 Oct 1750.[394],[395] See chapter "Pettus" for more.

- **Elizabeth**,[396] b. 29 Oct 1752[397] in Lunenburg County, Va.[398] Married a Mr. Robertson.[399]
- **Mary Fendall**,[400] b. 30 Jul 1755[401],[402] in Lunenburg County.[403] Married Edward V. Couch (b. 31 Jul 1761)[404] in North Carolina.[405]
- **Fendall**, b. 17 Dec 1757[406],[i] in Amelia County, d. 20 Aug 1826.[407] Married Elizabeth Willis 30 Oct 1783.[408] Also appears as variants of "Fendalph"[409] and possibly "Randolph."[410]
- **John**,[411] b. 17 Oct 1759[412] in Amelia County, d. 21 Dec 1801 in Sumner County, Tenn.; m. Sarah Cunningham, then Elizabeth Claybrook on 18 Dec 1778.[413]
- **Loviney**,[414] b. 9 Mar 1762,[415],[416] married a Mr. Harvey.[417]
- **William**,[418] b. 8 May 1764[419] in Lunenburg County, d. 22 Mar 1853, Cleveland County, NC.[420] Married Mary. Buried in New Prospect Baptist Church in North Carolina, for some reason under the name "William Whitter," the name he used later in life.[421]
- **Sarah**, b. 1 Sep 1766[422] in Lunenburg County.[423] Likely the daughter "Sally" mentioned in Thomas's will who married a Mr. Jone.
- **Sutherland**,[424] b. 24 Dec 1769[425] in Lunenburg County; d. 14 May 1837 in Gumlog Creek, Franklin County, Ga.[426] Married Mary Hood (b. 3 Jan 1772, Ireland)[427] on 3 Jan 1792 in Gaston, NC.[428][ii] Died 14 May 1837 in Gumlog Creek.[429]

---

[i]The Pettus bible puts this date at 17 Oct.

[ii]Though we don't have anything definitive showing the "Southerland Whitworth" who married Mary is the same as our Sutherland, the assertion is helped by his unique name and the knowledge that many of the Whitworths we know about at some point moved to North Carolina.

- **Rebecca**,[430] b. 17 Jan 1774[431] in Lunenburg County;[432] d. 28 Aug 1861 in Tennessee.[433][434] Married Isaac Stone (d. 16 Jan 1843)[435] in 1793.[436] Middle name possibly "Elizabeth."[437]

Chapter 5

Lamb

Richard Lamb (9-326),
Clarissa Boswell (9-327)

We know of Richard Lamb *9-326* only what can be pulled to-gether from scattered scraps of records from Virginia—there is evidence of another "Richard Lamb" living in Orange County, Virginia from the same time, and there are few supporting documents from colonial America that we have access to.

The most detailed biographical data we have is from a 1956 genealogical book by Frances Beale Hodges. According to this, Richard Lamb immigrated to Virginia from England, arriving "with ample means & established himself in business in the Port of Norfolk & Portsmouth."[438] This is corroborated by the mention of a "Richard Lamb" in a 1749 immigration list arriving in Virginia,[439] though that date of immigration has also been ascribed to the Orange County Richard Lamb.

Lamb appears in several 1769 newspaper advertisements in a context supporting a role as a merchant: On Jan. 5[440]

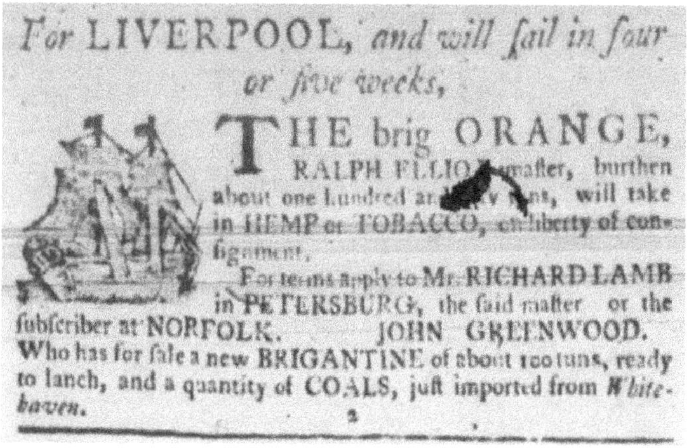

Figure 5.1: A shipping advertisement mentioning merchant Richard Lamb, from the Virginia Gazette.[443]

and 12,[441] advertising shipping space available on the *Brigantine Orange*, sailing for Liverpool, and repeatedly in 1772 for renting out "a commodious well built STORE in the Town of Petersburg." The ad describes it as "adjoining the Tobacco Warehouses,"[442] but that isn't as helpful as it sounds for locating its current location: By 1770, the town's central location had made it a focal location for the tobacco trade; warehouses were everywhere.

Even if Lamb's store was rented away (or sold), it appears he stayed in Petersburg for at least a little while: In January 1773, he took out an ad in the *Gazette* looking for help locating a 17-year-old runaway slave. The ad mentions a contact named John Greenwood, who also appears in the other advertisements and was probably a business partner.[444]

Our best connection between Richard Lamb and his daughter, Sophia (Lamb) Pettus *8-163*, is unfortunately also secondary documentation: In volumes 64 and 65 of the Daughters of the American Revolution lineage book,[i] Richard Lamb and Clarissa Boswell are described as the parents of Sophia and a son, William Boswell Lamb. The DAR has documentation requirements for proving familial connections, but we don't have access to the documents used in this particular case.

Both of these entries mention Richard's role as "quartermaster, Continental Army" and are used as one of the qualifying ancestors for applications to the DAR. This differs somewhat from the Hodges account, which says of him, "when the Revolutionary War broke out he retired from business and removed his family to the interior of the State. He contributed largely of his private fortune to the patriotic cause, & at his death the debt was unpaid, & from the loss of the vouchers in Washington, his descendants were never reimbursed."[445]

Interestingly, both of these accounts may be true: There are numerous letters that mention a "Mr. Lamb" from winter 1780 between Thomas Jefferson, then governor of Virginia, and Continental Army Gen. Horatio Gates, who had left his army behind in North Carolina after a disastrous defeat at the Battle of Camden, ostensibly to gather resources and soldiers back in Virginia. In a letter to Jefferson on 9 Oct 1780, Gates explained that the "Southern Army" is "much Distress'd for Carriages to Transport Provisions and Stores for this Army."[446] Jefferson responded 15 Oct, telling Gates that Virginian soldiers were "now on their march to join you," and that he had written "a power to Mr. Lambe Q.M." to commandeer 50 Virginian wagons from southern counties. The accompanying letter, giving a quartermaster permission to requisition the wagons, has "To Mr. Lamb" written in the upper margin; scholars

---

[i]Pages 291 and 271, respectively.

from the National Archives believe the addressee to have been
Richard Lamb.[447]

One other clue can be connected here: on 20 Oct 1780,
Gates again wrote to Jefferson, expressing discomfort that
Lamb was acting as both quartermaster and commissary when
"these Offices are incompatible, as they ought to be checks
on each other." He asks Jefferson to send a trusted man "to
reside at Mr. Lamb's as Commissary,"[448] which could suggest,
though not conclusively, that Lamb was operating out of his
home. This situation could be corroborated by an 1835 letter
from a Revolutionary War soldier named Stephen Biggs, by
then 80 years old, who was explaining (through an apparently
foggy memory) the details of his service in order to get pension
payments that had recently been approved by Congress.

Biggs enlisted early in the war, and he had just returned
from a three-month tour of duty in summer 1781 when "there
was a call for men to serve in guarding the Magazine[ii] which
was kept in Brunswick County at one Richard Lamb's." It had
been stated in a "proclamation," Biggs said, that anyone volunteering for three months at the magazine would be excused
"from the next tour of duty in marching against the enemy";
Briggs went immediately. He joined a group of about 30 men
guarding the magazine under Richard Lamb, "who was called
by the company Captain Lamb." (After the British surrender
at Yorktown, "Captain Lamb" apparently discharged the company by simply sending them home, and Biggs had never tried
to get any documentation of the discharge, which left him
without the necessary paperwork to apply for his pension.)[449]

The life of Clarissa Lamb *9-327* is an even foggier mystery:
Beale says she was "born & reared in Mecklinburg [*sic*] Co.,
Va.," and a collection of marriage records puts her date of
birth in 1740.[450] From Clarissa's documents we can infer that

---

[ii]A store or warehouse for weapons and military provisions.

Richard died in about 1786: Though the author has been unable to find the relevant state tax records from 1787, several sources reference Clarissa's appearance in the documents evidence that her husband, who would normally have appeared in her place, had died. (This date is also asserted in both DAR citations, and in Beale.)

She remarried 30 Nov 1790, to William Whitehead, in Petersburg Virginia.[451]

According to Beale, Richard and Clarissa had seven children:[452]

- **William Boswell**,[453,454] b. 8 Sep 1774, d. 14 Nov 1852;[455] m. Margaret Stuart Kerr (b. 1 May 1777, d. 12 Apr 1844).[456]
- **Mary Elliott**,[457] b. abt 1773; may have married John Moody Robertson 1 Mar 1792.[458]
- **Clarissa H.**,[459] b. abt 1778,[460] m. John Booth[iii] 19 Jun 1826;[461] both died after 1850.[462]
- **SOPHIA MUSGROVE** *8-163*, b. 20 Sep 1784, d. 19 Mar 1861, m. Samuel Pettus. See "Pettus" chapter for more.
- **Harriet**,[463] m. John Day 23 Jul 1804.[464]
- **Elizabeth**.[465]
- **Margaret Patience**, the youngest, according to Beale, who also says she married Richard Whitehead.[466] There is a record of a Margaret P. Lamb marrying a Richard Whitehead on 13 Jan 1800,[467] but for both of those facts to be true, Margaret would have been maybe 16. (Another potential inconsistency to consider: Beale says a man married the daughter of Margaret and Richard in 1809,[468] which would require the daughter to have

---

[iii]Almost certainly no relation to the other famous southerner named John Booth; the assassin of Lincoln was a first-generation American, while this John was descended from several generations of Virginians.

been, discounting very unusual circumstances, about nine years old.)

Another revolutionary Richard Lamb

In addition to the Richard Lamb in Orange County, Va., several documents mention a Captain Richard Lamb who commanded a company of artificers in Baldwin's Regiment, in the Continental Army. He enlisted as a lieutenant in 1777, according to military documents, and was promoted to captain in 1778 before resigning the following year.[469] There is no location given for Capt. Lamb's service, but a "Captain Lamb" appears as a signatory to several 1779 letters to the Continental Congress that are addressed to "the Quartermaster General of the Army of the thirteen United States of America."[470] This Capt. Lamb indicates he is from Connecticut.[471]

There is a significant likelihood that this is the same Capt. Lamb serving in Baldwin's Regiment: Artificers were teams of skilled mechanics or craftsmen who helped make sure troops were properly equipped, and they reported up through the same chain of command as the quartermaster corps. So, we have reason to believe there were at least two Richard Lambs who served in the Revolution, one a direct ancestor from Virginia, the other a craftsman and officer from New England.

Chapter 6

Spindle

William Spindle (8-164), Elizabeth C. Alsop (8-165)

Other than the names of William and Elizabeth's children, we know little about them: It appears Elizabeth was born in about 1780 and died in April 1860.[472],[i] They likely held 22 slaves in 1830,[473] but the only other early census record from the family is from 1810, when there was more than one William Spindle living in Spotsylvania County, so it is difficult to say for certain whether that is the same family.[ii]

Most of what we know about the couple comes from Spotsylvania chancery court records, particularly a lawsuit regard-

---

[i] An 80-year-old "Elizabeth Spindle" is recorded in an 1860 mortality schedule immediately before Harriet Leavell, Elizabeth's daughter. Both died of pneumonia in April 1860; it's possible this is a different person, but unlikely.

[ii] A lawsuit over the "other" William Spindle's estate suggests he died in the early 1810s and was married to someone named Lavinia.

ing William's estate after his death in 1836.[474] From that, we can glean the names of their children (other information is pulled from independent sources):

- **Jefferson**, b. abt 1802,[475] died probably 1861,[476] and before 1880.[477] Married Maria Tackett.[478]
- **William W.**, b. abt 1805, d. Apr 1868, in Fredericksburg, Va.[479]
- **Harriet Alsop**,[480] b. 7 Apr 1806, d. 17 Apr 1860[481] of pneumonia.[482]   Married Edmund S. Leavell 7 Sep 1837.[483]   Both buried in the family cemetery at Snow Hill Plantation.[484]
- **BENJAMIN** *7-82*, b. abt 1808.[485]
- **Ellen E.**,[486] b. abt 1815, d. 4 Mar 1866. See information in entry below for Benjamin Spindle *7-82*.
- **Emily**, b. aft abt 1815, d. aft 1836, m. William G. Cross. Buried at Snow Hill Plantation.[487]
- **John A.**, b. aft abt 1815,[iii] d. aft 1836.
- **Frances A.**, b. abt 1816 in Virginia,[488] m. James M. Quesenberry 9 Jun 1840.[489]

We have one other lead on the Spindle line: According to a biographical sketch of William and Elizabeth's great-grandson, Richard Buckner Spindle Jr.,[iv] he was "a descendant of Robert Spindle, a native of England, who came to America in the period of Colonial settlement and located in Virginia."[490] No documentation of a Robert Spindle has been found, but he was allegedly William's father.

[iii]Frances, Emily and John were described as "infants" in the lawsuit in about 1836, indicating they were younger than 21.

[iv]Grandson of Benjamin Spindle *7-82* and his second wife, Sarah Buckner.

Benjamin Spindle (7-82), Maria C. Wiglesworth (7-83)

Benjamin Spindle was born in Virginia in about 1808.[491] He married Maria C. Wigglesworth at some point before 1834, when the couple's first son was born.[492] They lived in Spotsylvania County for most of their lives, and had four children:

- **William Henry**, b. 14 Feb 1834, d. 3 Sep 1883.[493] Served in the Confederate Army, first in the 30th Virginia Infantry Regiment,[494] then in the 9th Virginia Cavalry.[495]
- **Thomas W.**, b. abt 1835,[496] d. 12 Feb 1905.[497] Married Lavinia C. Shelburn 25 Jan 1870.[498] Served in the Confederate Army, first as a private in the Stonewall Brigade[499] and then as a cavalry officer.[500]
- **Mary E.**, b. abt 1838,[501] d. 8 Sep 1903.[502] Married J. Wade Shelburne.[503]
- **MARIA VIRGINIA** *6-41*, b. 20 July 20 1839, d. 26 May 1884.[504] Married John R. Stone *6-40*; see the "Stone" chapter for more.

It's not clear what happened to Maria (Wiglesworth) Spindle, but it appears she died after July 1839, when their last child Maria was born, but before 1850, when Benjamin and sons William and Thomas appear in the federal census without her. Their daughter Mary, 13 years old in 1850, appears in that census with Benjamin's sister Frances and her husband James Quesenberry nearby in Spotsylvania.[505] The location of Maria V. Spindle, then 11 years old, is unknown. Between 1840 and 1850, Benjamin's other sister, Ellen, moved in with him and the boys.[506]

Ellen's fate is a sad and interesting one: In the 1860 census 10 years after she was recorded living with her brother, Ellen appears with the Quesenberry family[507]—the household of her sister, Frances.

Then, on 30 Nov 1865, an unmarried 50-year-old named Ellen E. Spindle from Spotsylvania was admitted to Western State Hospital in Staunton, 100 miles west. At the time, the facility was known as Central Lunatic Asylum; she appears in the intake records on the same page as murderer[509] Annie E. Kirby, with a note that Ellen's (unnamed) condition had lasted "several years," with the "supposed cause" listed, as with many other patients, as simply, "the war." She died of malnutrition four months later, on 4 Mar 1866.[v]

T. W. SPINDLE,
ROANOKE, VA.

Figure 6.1: A portrait of Thomas W. Spindle, age 67, from a 1902 edition of Confederate Veteran magazine.[508]

Benjamin remarried, to Sarah Hill[510],[vi] Buckner,[511] on 16 Nov 1853,[512] when Benjamin was about 53[513] and Sarah about 29. (Sarah was born in Virginia abt 1824; her mother's name was likely Esther.[514]) They had two more children together:

- **Richard Buckner**, b. 17 Aug 1853 in Spotsylvania, d. 26 Sep 1928, in Christiansburg. Married Bessie Gertrude Wardlaw in about 1885. (Richard's date of birth is curious: A biographical sketch of Richard's son in *Virginia:*

---

[v]These records were obtained by the author from researcher Dick Johns, who accessed the originals at the Library of Virginia.

[vi]Benjamin's state death record only includes Sarah's middle initial; *Rebirth of the Old Dominion* states that it stands for "Hill," as do the death certificates of their daughter children Ella and Richard, but all of these are secondary sources.

Rebirth of the Old Dominion says he was born in 1854,[515] which would make sense given the wedding date of his parents. However, his gravestone says he was born in 1853,[516] he is listed as 7 years old in the 1860 federal census (recorded 6 Aug 1860),[517] and his death certificate gives his date of birth as 17 Aug 1853;[518] evidence points toward his being born prior to his parents' marriage, but nothing conclusive.)

- **Ella T.**, b. 23 Oct 1855 in Spotsylvania, d. 2 Jul 1948 at the Confederate Home for Women, Richmond, Va. Never married.[519]

Benjamin contracted "consumption"[521] (likely tuberculosis) and died 24 Jan 1860,[522] leaving the farm and 18 slaves[vii] in Sarah's care.[523] Sarah, in addition to raising her

Figure 6.2: The signature of Maria (Wiglesworth) Spindle, from an 1839 lawsuit.[520]

two children, also was stepmother to Benjamin and Maria's four children, all of whom moved back to the Spindle farm at some point.[524] One possible exception is Thomas, who was listed in the 1860 census as living with the young family of Robert and Clara Miller in Christiansburg, about 200 miles southwest.[525,viii]

Thomas's move would prove significant: When the Civil War broke out the following year, many enlistees from the Christiansburg area were placed into the unit that would come to be known as the "Stonewall Brigade," including Thomas.

[vii]It appears 17 slaves worked on the Spindle farm; one worked nearby, on the farm of Neil McCoull.

[viii]It's not clear how Thomas came to know the Millers, but Clara (Stone) Miller was the sister of John Stone *6-40*.

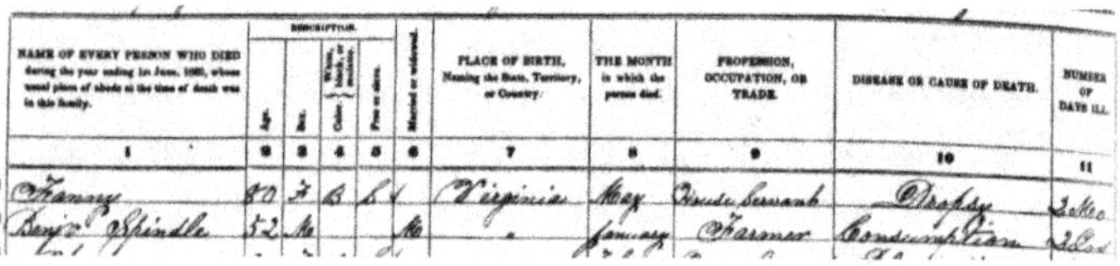

Figure 6.3: Benjamin Spindle's 7-82 entry in 1860 federal mortality records. He is on the second line.[530]

He was placed in the 4th Virginia Infantry Regiment,[526] in the same company as a 19-year-old farmer named John Stone. Five years later, John would marry Thomas's sister Maria; both are profiled in the "Stone" chapter as the parents of Henry Stone *5-20*.

The Civil War touched the rest of the family as well: The Spindle farm was a major landmark in the Battle of Spotsylvania Court House in May 1864, and was host to some of the bloodiest fighting of the war.[527] The first day, May 8, was of particular note: With Union forces mobilizing in the family's fields, scholars believe the engagement at "Laurel Hill" was actually fought at the Spindle farm.[528] Confederate forces shot incendiary shells into the Spindle farmhouse, which was positioned between the opposing armies; there are conflicting reports about whether soldiers believed anyone was inside.[529]

"And then," wrote a young Confederate private, "I saw a sight I never wanted to see again. A woman bareheaded, her long hair streaming behind, ran out of the big house and across the field to the left between the two fighting armies and reached shelter in the woods on the Po River."[531] Historians[532] and the National Park Service[533] believe that woman was Sarah (Buckner) Spindle, with at least some of her children. (Available evidence suggests the regiment of John Stone, Sarah's future son-in-law, was involved in fighting about two

Figure 6.5: The signature of Benjamin Spindle 7-82, from an 1841 court filing.[540]

miles away at the time. It's not known if Virginia Spindle, John's future wife, was at the house during the attack.)[534]

There was more fighting on the farm over the following four days,[535] but the Spindles would have long since fled.

The house burned to the ground and was apparently never rebuilt, but the site has several historical markers nearby with information about the family's role in the battle. In 2004, after years of failed[537] (or inconclusive)[538] attempts, archaeologists found what was determined to be the basement of the Spindle house.[539]

Figure 6.4: A brick section at the north end of the Spindle house basement, uncovered in 2004.[536]

Though there was at least one other "Sarah Spindle" living in Virginia during that time, evidence points to Benjamin's wife dying some time before 1868, when the "last wife" of Benjamin Spindle was mentioned in a lawsuit as "now dead."[ix] *Rebirth of the Old Dominion* also mentions that Richard Spindle "was only a boy when both

---

[ix]The lawsuit, filed in Spotsylvania Chancery Court, was brought by Benjamin and Maria's daughter, Maria Virginia Spindle 6-41, and her husband, John Stone 6-40. At issue was Benjamin's $2,000 estate, which his son Thomas had invested in Confederate war bonds and subsequently lost.

his parents died," but no official records have been located to
confirm this.

Finding Maria's family

"Maria Claiborne Wigglesworth" is mentioned as Benjamin's
wife in several unsourced secondary documents,[541,542] but
there are no official records that link Benjamin to Maria
in which her maiden name is specified. There is, however,
some evidence we can glean from a lawsuit from the late
1830s in which "Benjamin Spindle and Maria C his wife" sued
several members of the Wiglesworth family (it is spelled in-
consistently with one 'g' until this generation) regarding the
estate of Maria's aunt, Elizabeth. This was a vital source for
finding Maria's siblings and, ultimately, her father, Thomas
Wiglesworth *8-166*. In addition, records from the Daughters
of the American Revolution, though uncited in their publicly available "lineage books," say Maria's father was named
Thomas Wigglesworth.

Chapter 7

Alsop

Genealogist Jerry David Alsup has done the most definitive work on the Alsop family—his *Alsop's Tables* series is full of documents and context going back to the Norman invasion of 1066; if you are interested in reading more about the family in colonial Virginia (and before), part I of the series is a good starting point and the volume with the most data about our piece of the tree.

While some documentation for the Alsop family has been found by the author, most citations in this chapter point to *Alsop's Tables*, based mostly on extant legal documents from 18th century Virginia, to avoid duplicating his meticulously completed work.

George Alsop (13-5280), Anne (13-5281)

George and Anne emigrated from England as indentured servants around 1664 and lived in Accomack County, Va.,[543]

though not much else of their life is known. They had two
children:

- **GEORGE** *12-2640*[544]
- **William**, may have been born in America.[545]

George Alsop (12-2640), Anne (12-2641)

George appears to have been born in Derbyshire, England,
and immigrated to America at some point before October
1669.[546] It's likely he arrived after his parents.

George married a woman named Anne,[547] and with her
had two children:

- **WILLIAM** *11-1320*, d. 1761.
- **Anne**. Had a son, apparently out of wedlock, named
  Isiah.[548]

William Alsop (11-1320)

William's date of birth is unknown, but he was living on his
own plantation in King George County, Virginia in 1721.[549]
We don't know the name of his wife (or wives), but he had
about six children before his death in 1761:[550]

- **WILLIAM** *10-660*, b. abt 1720.
- **Benjamin**, d. 1777. Married Nellie.[551]
- **John**, d. abt 1751.[552]
- **George**, b. 1735,[553] d. 1797 in Caroline County, Va.
  Married Delphia.[554]
- **Elizabeth**, married William Jones abt 1750.[555]
- **Sarah**, d. 1793. Married Stapleton Crutchfield.[556]

William Alsop (10-660),
Sarah Jones (10-661)

William Alsop was born in Richmond County, Va., in about 1720.[557] The identity of his first wife is unknown, but she and William had a child, Margaret ("Peggy") in 1742.[558] The first wife must have died before 1758, as that is the year William had a son by his second wife, Sarah Jones.

Sarah was born in 1735[559] and died 8 Jan 1808—other than that (and the identities of her parents, in the "Jones" chapter), we know nothing of her life. William died in fall 1778.[560]

Alsup finds nine children of William and Sarah, though this author has not been able to confirm some of them:

- **BENJAMIN** *9-330*,[561] b. 17 Mar 1758, d. 1 Dec 1832.[562]
- **Elizabeth**, married Bartlett Collins.
- **Jane,**, known as "Jennie,"[563] b. October 1760, d. 5 Oct 1815 in Lexington, Ky.;[564] married James Wood.
- **Phoebe**, married Fielding Smithy.
- **Sarah**, b. 1772;[565] married Thomas Walden.
- **Martha**, married John Holladay.
- **William**, b. abt 1772. Married Amy Ann Scott abt 1796.[566] Died bef 1850 in Scott County, Kentucky.
- **John**, b. abt 1768, d. abt 1801. Married Lucy Spindle.[567]
- **Ignatious**, b. abt 1760. Likely died bef 1808, when he is omitted from his parents' inheritance.[568]

Benjamin Alsop (9-330),
Frances Boswell (9-331)

We have needed to pull lots of information from unconventional sources, especially for the time before about 1840 when official documentation becomes increasingly rare. For Benjamin Alsop, however, our information is unique, if possibly flawed: Most of what we know comes directly from him. Benjamin applied in 1832 for a program approved by Congress granting pensions to an expanded group of Revolutionary War soldiers;[569] the application has survived, and includes sworn accounts given by Benjamin and transcripts of testimony given in open court, plus corroborating statements from four soldiers who served with him.

Benjamin was born 17 Mar 1758 in Spotsylvania County, Va. It was here he enlisted as a minuteman in autumn 1775, about 5 months after the conflicts at Lexington and Concord. This unit was disbanded several months later, and he reenlisted, likely in early 1776, in the 6th Virginia Regiment of the Continental Army. Eventually, they were

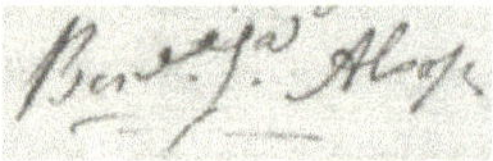

Figure 7.1: The signature of Benjamin Alsop from a 1790 court filing.[570]

ordered to march north to New York in August 1776. That month happened to be the beginning of the end of the Continentals' hold on New York City: The troops under Gen. George Washington lost the Battle of Long Island, and by the time Benjamin and the 6th Virginia made it to Newark, New Jersey, the army was already in retreat toward Pennsylvania. He and the rest of Washington's army camped for the winter at Valley Forge.

On Christmas morning 1776, Benjamin claims to have

been part of a 200-man reconnaissance outfit that crossed the Delaware River to gain information in preparation for the attack planned that night. When he eventually returned back to the Pennsylvania side of the river, he found the army preparing for what would become the famous "Crossing of the Delaware," in which 2,400 American troops (including Benjamin) attacked Hessian mercenaries in the Battle of Trenton and captured more than 800 soldiers fighting for the Crown; not a single colonist was killed in the battle.[i]

Benjamin stayed with the army on its subsequent march through New Jersey, fighting in Gen. Nathanael Greene's division at the Battle of Brandywine, where he was wounded. The court document describes his statement: "He was struck with three balls, only one however wounding him, that in the left shoulder, whilst in the act of reloading his musket. The blanket slung along to his back had 16 bullet holes through it." He was also at the besieged Fort Mifflin in fall 1777, possibly among the reinforcements that arrived under Virginian Lt. Col. John Green. He says he was at the eventual abandonment of the nearly destroyed fort, in which the 300 survivors rowed away from Mud Island under the cover of night.

Benjamin's enlistment was up in 1778, and he returned home to tend to the affairs of his father, who had died while Benjamin was away. However, he was drafted back into service two years later, and his unit marched south, eventually joining up with the southern army under Gen. Horatio Gates. He appears to have been on the losing side of the Battle of Camden in August 1780, in which 3,700 American troops suffered an estimated 1,900 casualties. Returning to Spotsylvania, Benjamin was then named a lieutenant, and received a commission signed by then-Governor Thomas Jefferson. (When asked

---

[i]At least two soldiers, however, did die of exposure on the march to Trenton in the middle of the night.

about the document in court, Benjamin said "I have lost or mislaid it.") He joined the army of the Marquis de Lafayette, which was marching toward the Siege of Yorktown; however, Benjamin was discharged two weeks before the siege ended there with the surrender of the British under Gen. Charles Cornwallis.

There is a small collection of documents supporting this: Information compiled by the U.S. War Department indicates Benjamin enlisted in the Continental Army on 29 Jan 1776 and was discharged 31 Jan 1778,[571] which lines up perfectly with his story. (He was in a different unit when he was drafted again in 1780, which would have been documented, if anywhere, in a separate record. This has not been found.) There are also two pay ledgers listing him being paid for active-duty service.[572,573]

However sparse the documentation, the government ultimately accepted his testimony and granted him the pension.[574] While some dates in his account are possibly off by several months, all other details—commanding officers, timelines of battles, etc.—appear to line up well with available documentation about the war. Other details may not be correct, but they are as correct as they will ever be: Benjamin's only record of his birth, for example, is an entry in a family bible. In any case, for all information in this section not otherwise cited, we are taking him at his word.

As for Frances Boswell, Benjamin's wife, we know very little: She married Benjamin shortly after the war, and died 6 Jan 1799,[575] but her age and parentage are unknown. She almost certainly lived with her family on the 313-acre plot that appear under Benjamin's name in tax records,[576] called "Snow Hill."

Frances and Benjamin had two children together:[577]

- **ELIZABETH C.** *8-165*, d. April 1860. See the "Spindle" chapter for more.
- **Ann G.**, died at some point after 1832. Her married name was "Parker."[578]

Benjamin remarried after Frances's death, to Mary Byrd Rogers, b. abt 1769.[579] They had one daughter, Sarah Ann ("Sallie"), born in 1812.[580] She married Stapleton Crutchfield III on 13 Jun 1833[581] and died August 1850.[582] (A Stapleton Crutchfield served as the chief of artillery under Gen. Stonewall Jackson; it appears he was a different person than Sallie's husband, who appears to have died in 1859.)[583]

Benjamin spent at least some time instructing infantry in the 2nd Battalion of Spotsylvania County.[584] He died 1 Dec 1832[585] and was buried at Snow Hill Cemetery. His headstone was replaced in the early 1900s by the Daughters of the American Revolution and was still visible in the 2010s.[586]

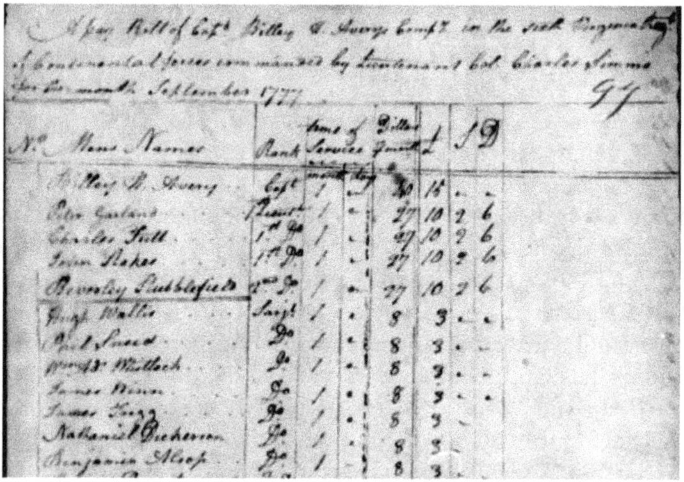

Figure 7.2: A 1777 monthly payroll including a payment of 3 pounds and 8 Continentals to Benjamin Alsop, in the bottom row.[587]

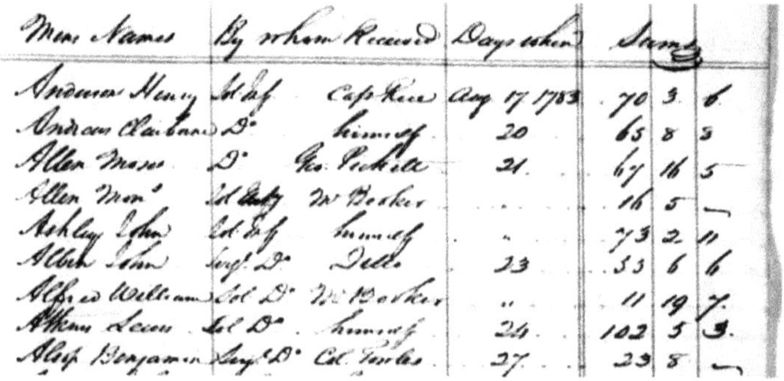

Figure 7.3: A 1783 military payroll including a payment of 23 pounds, 8 shillings to Benjamin Alsop, in the bottom row.[588]

Chapter 8

Jones

David Jones (11-1322),
Winifred (11-1323)

We only know of the Jones family through Spotsylvania legal records, dependent mostly on references to their daughter, Sarah *10-661*, the mother of Benjamin Alsop *9-330*.

On 4 Jul 1768, a £500 "administration bond" was given by "Winifred Jones, admx. of David Jones, decd."[589]—this means David was dead by this time, though unfortunately it is also the only evidence we have that Winifred was his wife. It was common for wives to serve as the administrator ("administratrix," for women of the time) of their husbands' estates—in 1778, for example, their daughter Sarah served as the executrix of the estate of her deceased husband, William Alsop.[590]

Their other appearance in available records is two years earlier, when David recorded a gift to his daughter's family on 7 Jul 1766: "David x Jones of Spts. Co. to his son-in-law,

Wm. Allsup, and Sarah, his wife, dau. of the sd. David Jones. Deed of Gift. 5 slaves, etc." This transaction is referenced later, when Sarah and William then give the slaves to the other daughters of David (and, presumably, Winifred).[591] We have evidence of David (and possibly Winifred) having three daughters:

- **SARAH** *10-661*,[592] b. 1735. See "Alsop" chapter for more.
- **Martha**, married William Leathers bef 27 Apr 1767.[593]
- **Catharine**[594]

Chapter 9

Wigglesworth

John Wiglesworth (10-664), Mary

This generation is as sparse as most of the other colonial-era ancestors and is based mostly on property records: On 3 Apr 1750, a bond was given by a Mary Wiglesworth, the administrator of "John Wiglesworth, decd."[595] Two years later, Mary posted two more bonds, as guardian of the four "orphans"[i] of John Wiglesworth: a £1,000 bond for Esther, Sarah, and John, and another £1,000 bond for William.

At the time, guardians were required to post a bond as a guarantee that they would protect the property of the minors in their care until the children were old enough to take legal ownership. Most property passed directly from a father to his children—a widow was often granted a fraction of her husband's estate, but from the documents currently available,

---

[i]Historically, an "orphan" was simply a child without a father.

we have little insight into the details in this particular case. There are a few clues, though: We can assume Mary had access to at least £2,000 to post as bond, money she may have either inherited from a relative or received personally from John's estate. We can also infer from this that all four of these children were under the age of 21 at the time of their father's death, otherwise they would not have needed a guardian.

There is also a separate bond for William, making his security as large as the one required for his other three siblings commbined. The most plausible explanation of this is that he was the oldest child, which means he would have been much more likely to have inherited his father's land and thus hold a much higher proportion of the estate. However, there is evidence of an older brother: On 24 Feb 1757, 200 acres of land in Spotsylvania County was sold to William Wiglesworth by "James Wiglesworth of Spts. Co. and Mary, his wife." The land is described as "formerly belonging to John Wiglesworth, Decd., and fell to the sd. James, as heir at law to the Decd."[596] If the land fell to James, this implies several possibilities: First, that James Wiglesworth is the oldest sibling in the family; second, but less definitely, that John died without a written will. Given that he left behind four young children, we can guess that he may not have been old nor sick when he died. The other puzzle piece from this transaction is that in 1757, William Wiglesworth would have been old enough to purchase land, meaning he turned 21 at some point between 1750 and 1757. Given this, we can get a rough sketch of the children of Mary and John:

- **James**, b. bef 1730. Married Mary.
- **William**, b. 1729–1736.
- **Esther**, b. aft 1729
- **Sarah**, b. aft 1729.
- **JOHN** *9-332*, b. aft 1729.

Mary's last name appears in various family histories as either "Lindsay" or "Holladay," the latter being the one most frequently corroborated by other genealogies: In 1939, for example, Emily Griffith Roberts described her as "Mary, daughter of William and Mary Holladay,"[597] but did not offer any evidence. There are records of Holladays living in Spotsylvania County at this time, but no discernible connection between them and Mary has been found.

In addition, the origins of the couple remain a mystery: There is a record of a John Wiglesworth arriving in Virginia in 1738,[598] but a (presumably different) John Wiglesworth is recorded in a municipal transaction 10 years earlier in Spotsylvania County.[599]

John Wiglesworth (9-332), Philadelphia C. Fox (9-333)

There is little information available about John and Philadelphia Wigglesworth, despite their position along the family line that extends back dozens of generations—all information about them has been gleaned from their mention in documents mostly about other people. We know, for example, that this Philadelphia was the daughter of Thomas Fox *10-666* because his will mentions "John Wiglesworth and Philadelphia, his wife",[600] a phrase by which they are referred in multiple records of the time.[601]

The most precarious link in their personal history is John and Philadelphia's connection to their son, Thomas. The most readily available source connecting Thomas to his parents is unsourced DAR lineage books, which claim the connection but are not necessarily based on contemporary sources. There is only one another known connection: An 1834 court filing in

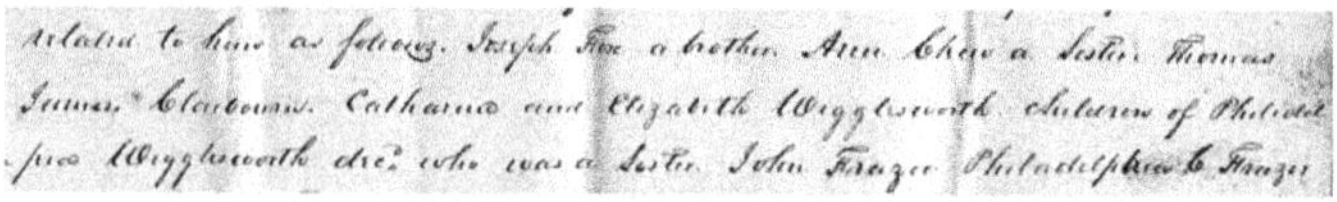
related to him as follows. Joseph Fox a brother. Ann Chew a sister. Thomas
James, Claibourne, Catharine and Elizabeth Wigglesworth children of Philadelphia Wigglesworth dec'd who was a sister. John Frazer Philadelphia Frazer

Figure 9.1: The children of Philadelphia and John Wigglesworth, enumerated in an 1834 lawsuit.[614]

Shenandoah County, Virginia provides valuable genealogical data in reference to a lawsuit regarding the estate of Thomas Fox Jr., the brother of Philadelphia who died in 1818 without having married. The suit mentions her children explicitly: "Thomas, James, Claibourne, Catharine and Elizabeth Wigglesworth, children of Philadelphia Wigglesworth dec'd, who was a sister [of Thomas Fox]."[602] Given the naming conventions at the time, it's possible this is not a reference to our Thomas, but if he had a cousin or uncle by that name, he has not appeared in any documents reviewed so far.

From this, too, we get a better picture of the children of John and Philadelphia:

- **THOMAS** *8-166*,[603] d. abt 1827.
- **James,**[604] d. Aug 1831. No children; may not have married.[605]
- **Claiborne,**[606] b. 1788, d. 1826.[607] Married Lavinia Ward Farish 26 Oct 1818.[608]
- **Catharine,**[609] known as "Katy."[610]
- **John**[611]
- **Elizabeth C.**[612][613]

The birth and death dates of John and Philadelphia are unknown, but there is one clue: Philadelphia died before about 1835, when she is mentioned as being deceased in the above-mentioned lawsuit;[615] John had no reason to be mentioned in the same suit, so his status at that time is unclear.

Thomas Wigglesworth (8-166), Maria Foster (8-167)

As far as we can tell, Thomas and Maria had seven daughters who survived to adulthood. Unfortunately, all we have is a list of names, pulled together from Thomas's will[ii] and a court case from the early 1840s in which the Wigglesworth family was trying to divide up the estate of Thomas's sister, who died without a will or a family of her own.[616] We don't have any definite indication of the birth dates of their children, though we can make some educated guesses: In Thomas's will, which was probated 5 Jan 1828[iii],[617] he lists his seven daughters in a row: Maria, Mary, Sarah, Philadelphia, Frances, Lucy Jane and Lavinia. He then indicates Maria and Mary are the two oldest, and we know Lucy Jane and Lavinia were the youngest, as they were the only ones younger than 21 in the above-mentioned lawsuit. From this, it seems safe to assume their birth order is as written in the will:

- **MARIA C.** *7-83*, married Benjamin Spindle *7-82* before 1834.
- **Mary L.**
- **Sarah A.**
- **Philadelphia**[iv]
- **Frances E.**
- **Lucy Jane**, born after about 1817.[v]
- **Lavinia**, born after about 1817.

[ii]Transcription available in Appendix B.

[iii]This suggests he most likely died in the final months of 1827.

[iv]In the court case, it appears her middle initials are "C.J.," but this has not been affirmed anywhere else.

[v]The first documents in the suit start around 1838, when she and Lavinia are described as "infants under the age of twenty one years."

Chapter 10

Fox

The basis for much of this chapter derives from an article by Fox descendant George H.S. King called, "Memorial to Henry Fox, Gentleman, Of 'Huntington', King William County, Virginia," published in *Tyler's Quarterly Historical and Genealogical Magazine.* King headed the "Society of Descendants of Henry Fox and Anne West," which was active in the late 1930s.[i] His writing reflects a careful examination of extant Virginia records, but his research is not documented extensively enough to reproduce.

The Fox family, however, has been the subject of a considerable amount of modern research based on DNA examination that has gone a long way in confirming the popularly accepted lineages that have been passed down.

---

[i] And possibly later.

John Fox (13-5328)

Speculation by Fox family researchers places John Fox, a captain who "commanded several trading vessels plying between England and Virginia," as the immigrant ancestor of this line:[618] He reportedly bought 200 acres of land in Gloucester County, Virginia in 1682.[619] King states he had four children:

- **HENRY** *12-2664*, the most well-documented of the siblings.
- **Ann**, married Chillon White.[620]
- **Jane**, married Richard Johns.
- **John**

Henry Fox (12-2664),
Anne West (12-2665)

Henry was born around 1650,[621] which means he was likely born in England and came to America as a teenager.[622] He was mentioned in a 1683 record as the "son and heir" of John Fox,[623] and over the proceeding decades collected considerable landholdings.

He lived at "Huntington," a manor on the Mattaponi River,[624] with Anne, of whom much less is known. They had four children:

- **John**[625]
- **THOMAS** *11-1332*[626]
- **Henry**,[627] b. abt 1674, d. abt 1750.[628] Married Mary Kendrick.[629]
- **Anne**, married Thomas Claiborne.[630]

Henry died in 1714.[631] Anne's parents were John West[632] and Unity Croshaw,[633] who appear in the beginning of Part II.

Thomas Fox (11-1332), Mary Tunstall (11-1333)

Thomas and Mary were married in about 1708.[634]   They lived at an estate named, simply, "Fox's," near the home of Thomas's father. They had at least two children:

- **THOMAS** *10-666*, b. abt 1710, d. 1792.[635]
- **Joseph**, d. abt 1789.[636]

Thomas Fox (10-666), Philadelphia Claiborne (10-667)

Thomas was born about 1710, in King William County, Virginia.[637] It's believed he and Philadelphia were married there before moving to Spotsylvania County, where they lived on a plantation called "Tubal."[638]

We are able to obtain considerable genealogical data from an 1835 lawsuit brought in chancery court regarding Thomas's estate that outlines multiple siblings, children, and grandchildren, from which we can determine the children of Thomas and Philadelphia:

- **Thomas**,[639] d. December 1818, Shenandoah County, Va. Never married.[640]
- **Joseph**[641,642]
- **Ann**,[643] married name "Chew."[644]
- **PHILADELPHIA** *9-333*, b. abt 1758.
- **Elizabeth**,[645] known as "Betty."[646]   Married John Frazer 16 Jan 1783.[647]
- **Nathaniel**,[648] d. bef 1835. Had multiple children, many of whom appear to also have died before 1835 after having children of their own.[649]

There are also two half-siblings of the above children named in the 1835 suit: Barbary Wallace and Edmund Fox,[650] though their exact relation is not clarified.[651]

The most likely explanation is more complicated than it appears: King states neither Thomas nor Philadelphia were married before, but that Thomas remarried *after* Philadelphia (Claiborne) Fox died, to another woman also named Philadelphia, which would explain much of the confusion. This woman's maiden name was Philadelphia Herndon, and King records their children as Barbara Tunstall Fox[652] (presumably the "Barbary Wallace" mentioned in the above suit), Mary and John.[653] No mention of an Edmund Fox appears in his article, but King does say Thomas and his second wife had six children.[654] Thomas died in 1792.[655]

Chapter 11

Claiborne

William Claiborne (14-10672), Elizabeth Butler (14-10673)

William, born about 1600, was among the first settlers of the area around the Chesapeake Bay. He established a lucrative trading post on Kent Island, then part of the Virginia Colony, where he would later serve in various leadership roles. Kent Island was later granted to the Maryland colony (the Calvert family in particular, as they rose to prominence in the colonies). He tried on multiple occasions to retake the island on behalf of Virginia, but retired in 1660 to live on his plantation, "Romancoke."

William Claiborne (13-5336), Elizabeth Wilkes (13-5337)

William served in the Virginia House of Burgesses and was a leader in Bacon's Rebellion; he died in 1682.[656] He and Elizabeth had one son: WILLIAM *12-2668*.[657]

William Claiborne (12-2668)

We know essentially nothing of William, other than that he served in the colonial militia and died in 1705.[658] He had one (known) son, WILLIAM *11-1334*.

William Claiborne (11-1334), Elizabeth Whitehead (11-1335)

Information on Elizabeth Whitehead is sparse, other than that her father was likely Philip Whitehead, and her grandfather Richard Whitehead.[659]

The couple lived at "Romancoke," the Claiborne family plantation. William was appointed sheriff of King William County, Virginia in 1728.[660] He died in summer 1746 after relocating to London, England.[661] They had at least three children:[662]

- **PHILADELPHIA** *10-667*, see "Fox" chapter for more.
- **William**
- **Philip**, d. 1772. Married Elizabeth Dandridge.[663] Elizabeth's first cousin was Martha Dandridge, who would eventually marry George Washington.

Part II

Linkage to Royalty

Methodology

This section takes a different approach than the previous one: For starters, the *Ahnentafel* numbering starts over—person number *1* in the previous section was the author, Richard Abdill III. This section is the ancestry of John West *13-5330*, the author's 10th great grandfather, so John is *1* in Part II.

Here is the path we take to get from Part I to Part II:

Richard Abdill III *1-1*, son of
Richard Abdill Jr. *2-2*, son of
Sally Anne Stone *3-5*, daughter of
Henry T. Stone Jr. *4-10*, son of
Henry T. Stone *5-20*, son of
Maria V. Spindle *6-41*, daughter of
Maria C. Wigglesworth *7-83*, daughter of
Thomas Wiglesworth *8-166*, son of
Philadelphia C. Fox *9-333*, daughter of
Thomas Fox *10-666*, son of
Thomas Fox *11-1332*, son of
Anne West *12-2665*, daughter of
John West *13-5330*

While the aim of Part I was to provide a fully annotated analysis of its subjects based on primary documents, there is no original genealogical research in this section, nor are there citations—it uses only parentage that has been widely accepted and documented by historians, in some cases for hundreds of years. If there is any widely disputed information regarding a person's parents, they were excluded. There are no academic claims made for the contents of this part of the book—this isn't intended to be a source of truth, only a starting point, a summary of the relationships commonly acknowledged to be connected to our family tree. There are numerous weaknesses in the information: The anglicization of names ("Hawise" and

"Elizabeth," for example) is inconsistent, individuals are listed only by one title, when in many cases they had multiple; dates of birth and death are frequently missing or the subject of dispute.

Another change from Part I: While the previous section outlined the children of each ancestor, that has been excluded here; only direct ancestors are documented, arranged by Ahnentafel number (and generation), rather than Part I's use of last name as an organizing paradigm. Because of this, all the people in Part II are grandparents of varying degrees.

To help maintain some connection to the original tree, the chapters here are separated by generation, with the number of the generation reflecting the members' overall position in the family. For example: As stated, John West is the new number *1*, and is the only member of the first chapter. However, the name of that chapter is "Generation 13," because he is 12 generations removed from the author. To find John West's parents, you would go to the next chapter, "Generation 14," and look for numbers *2* and *3*.

To figure out how someone in a chapter is related to the author's generation, the number of "greats" in their grandparent title is equal to that person's generation number minus three. For example, John West is in "Generation 13," which means he is the 10th great grandfather of a person in Generation 1. John's parents are in "Generation 14," so are 11th great grandparents, the people in "Generation 15" are 12th great grandparents, and so on.

Patterns of Note

Individually, there are many noteworthy people in our lineage. As a group, however, even more interesting patterns emerge.

Figure 11.1: The insignia of knights of the Order of the Garter.[664]

The Order of the Garter

The Most Noble Order of the Garter was the first English order of chivalry and remains the highest order today, behind only the Victoria Cross and George Cross in the British honours system. Its membership has been capped at 24 "knights companion"[i] since its founding in about 1348, and only the "Sovereign of the Garter"—the king or queen of England—can induct new knights.

We are descended from 16 knights of the Garter:
- Francis Knollys *10*
- Thomas West *32*
- Thomas Boleyn *46*
- Henry Algernon Percy *48*
- Edmund Beaufort *182*

---

[i] "Companions," in this case, to the king of England and prince of Wales, who are not counted against the membership limit.

- Walter Hungerford *260*
- John Beaufort *364*
- Richard Beauchamp *366*
- Thomas Hoo *370*
- John Beaumont *526*
- John of Gaunt *728*
- Thomas Holland *730*
- Thomas de Beauchamp *732*

The final three knights on our list are among the first inductees of the Order: the 25 Founder Knights.

- Edward III, King of England *1,456*[ii]
- Thomas Holland *1,460*
- Thomas de Beauchamp *1,464*

The Battle of Hastings

The Norman Conquest of 1066 changed the face of England forever: The army of William the Conqueror sailed from France in autumn of that year. Within weeks, the king was dead and William, previously the duke of Normandy, had ascended to the throne. The reign of the Anglo-Saxons was over.

Scholars have compiled a list of 15 "proven companions" of King William I at the Battle of Hastings, the decisive battle that resulted in the death of King Harold Godwinson of England. We are descended from six of them:

- Robert de Beaumont *263,770*
- William de Warenne *374,408*
- Robert of Mortain *527,894*
- Aimery of Thouars *527,898*
- Eustace of Boulogne *528,092*
- Walter Giffard *1,054,978*

[ii]There are technically 26 founders: King Edward, plus the 25 Founder Knights.

We are also directly descended from both King Harold of England *1,491,658*, who was killed at the battle, and from William the Conqueror *263,940*, who probably killed him. The lines of these two kings didn't cross until two centuries after their birth: Both were born in the 1020s; their first shared descendant in our tree is King Philip IV of France *5,826*, who wasn't born until 1268.

Magna Carta

Magna Carta ("The Great Charter") was an agreement between King John of England and barons who rebelled against his rule in 1215. It was a model for countless facets of modern government, including multiple parallels with the U.S. Bill of Rights. A council of 25 barons was appointed to "enforce" the agreement, and was theoretically empowered to seize the king's lands if he failed to abide by it.[iii] We are directly descended from King John *16,496*, plus eight of the 25 "sureties" of the charter:

- William de Mowbray *16,480*
- Gilbert de Clare *16,484*
- Hugh Bigod *23,430*
- Richard de Clare *32,968*
- Robert de Vere *33,696*
- Saer de Quincy *33,698*
- Roger Bigod *46,860*
- William Malet *65,674*

[iii]This clause would quickly lead to the outbreak of the First Barons' War.

106

Chapter 12

Examining Part II

The profiles in Part II extend back to the sixth century AD. When family lines are traced that far back, things are going to get knotted up in odd ways. That said, this chapter is skippable if you're just trying to get to the list of fancy people we're related to. What follows is an in-depth explanation quirks of the tree, why people appear multiple times, why grandparents show up in earlier generations than their own grandchildren—details that some will find interesting, but aren't necessary to get information from the results.

Pedigree collapse

The main oddity of large family trees is a phenomenon called "pedigree collapse," in which relatives appear in the tree multiple times, sometimes in different generations. The simplest way to explain it is with a thought experiment: Our tree's first generation has one person in it. Generation 2 has two people in it—the parents of Generation 1. Both people in Generation

2 have two parents, so Generation 3 has four people. This continues to double for every generation, which means once we get back, say, 40 generations, we would have almost *550 billion* 37th great grandparents.

Clearly, the population of 12th century Europe was not 78 times greater than the current population of the entire planet; because all those parents have to come from *somewhere*, the only possible explanation is that the same people hold multiple places in the tree. This comes about when a person's parents share a set of ancestors: in short, when two cousins get married.

This isn't as unusual as it sounds: These were not (in most cases) first cousins, or even fourth or fifth cousins. There are dozens of places in our tree where a couple shares an ancestor from hundreds of years prior, long past when any concerns about inbreeding and genetic diversity have disappeared. These intersections are easy to spot in the Ahnentafel chart, where they appear as "loops"—most Ahnentafel numbers in the list have a name next to it; some, though, have *another number* there instead. That is a place where a person appears more than once, so, rather than repeat the information, that location redirects back to where the person is already mentioned. (The tree has been rearranged to show, with only a few exceptions, the "latest" place in the tree where a person first appears. For example, if the same person is number *1,000,000* and number *3,502,008*, the person's information will appear at *1,000,000*.)

There are 2,284 entries in Part II, 426 of which are these "loops." This means we have 426 examples over about 1,000 years in which a person (or set of parents) appears more than once—which also means that in 426 cases, a great-great-something grandparent is the sibling of a different great-great-something grandparent.

This numbering scheme also has several interesting effects

on the generation numbers: Because people are listed at the lowest number attributed to them, the tree "ends" sooner than it would if all the numbers were filled in. An example: Carloman *8,648,737,284* appears in "Generation 46." His great-great-grandson, Pepin the Short *270,273,040*, appears in "Generation 41," as you'd expect. However, Pepin appears twice in the tree: He is also listed at number *2,152,181,824*, which is in "Generation 44." We can extrapolate several things from this:

1. We are directly descended from two of Pepin's children. At some point, a descendant of one child married a distant descendant of the other child, making Pepin and his wife the intersection.
2. Pepin the Short is both a 38th great grandfather *and* a 41st great grandfather.
3. We know Carloman is five generations ahead of Pepin— because Pepin is in "Generation 41," Carloman appears five generations back, in "Generation 46." However, Pepin appears again, in "Generation 44," which would mean Carloman is also a member of "Generation 49." This generation does not appear in the list because all of its members already appear earlier in the list.

That last point is one that is critical to understanding why there aren't quite as many gaps in the lineage as it appears: Two different lines crossed in our tree at Pepin the Short, who appears twice. It would make sense, then, that Pepin's father, Charles Martel, would also appear twice—however, he doesn't: *Only the intersection is documented.* Once we get to Pepin's entry in Generation 44, the list directs us to his entry that was added higher up the list, which means Charles Martel doesn't appear in Generation 45 even though he is theoretically there.

It would certainly be possible to extend all lines out to their farthest conclusions. This was not done here for several reasons, the primary one being that it is prohibitively complex to finish in a reasonable amount of time. The most efficient way to do this would be to modify the Ahnentafel chart with software designed to add the extra entries, but this was abandoned because it simply doesn't add very much value: No ancestors are excluded from the list entirely, it is simply that some appear less times than they would have otherwise. Charlemagne *135,136,520* would likely appear a dozen times—the only extra data we would gain from actually doing so would be to count how many.

There is another curiosity borne of this collapse: For Pepin the Short to appear in Generation 41 and Generation 44, that must mean he has a (different) child ahead of him, in both Generation 40 and Generation 43. Because Pepin appears in Generation 41, that means his grandfather would be in Generation 43—meaning an ancestor appears in the same generation as his own great-grandfather.

Carolingian descendants aren't rare

It's a special thing to be able to point to a book and say, "You are descended from all the kings and queens of Europe."

However, so is everyone else.

There is a close corollary to the conclusions drawn above about pedigree collapse: The odds are pretty high that everyone of European ancestry living today has a common ancestor from somewhere in the Middle Ages. Charlemagne is a commonly cited example, and for good reason: There just aren't that many connections from modern humans back to the 8th century. The common assumption at hearing this is to conclude that Charlemagne must have had dozens of children for this to be true, but that isn't the case—it is actually due to a combination of three factors: First, there were simply less people around then; probably somewhere around 210 million. However, the number of possible ancestors at that time is actually far smaller—lines "die out," so lots of those 210 million people have *no* living ancestors. Maybe they didn't have children, or their children didn't have children, or their grandchildren died. For a line to make it from Charlemagne's time to modern day, it would need a family to have an unbroken line of descendants that stretches *1,300 years*. That's simply not a common thing to happen.

However, even if we assume *every* person alive in the 700s has living descendants, there's another important factor: Remember that there are 549 *billion* people in any tree's 40th generation. So yes, 210 million people in the 700s is a lot of people, but we *need* a lot of people. The argument is weakened slightly because not everyone has a child at the exact same age, so "Generation 40" in one section of the tree could be around the year 720, but "Generation 40" in another, distantly connected branch could have ancestors alive 400 years later. However, the point remains: We are quite likely distant cousins with every European living today, in a way we could trace to known people from that time.

In short: It is not particularly unique that we are descended from the likes of Charlemagne and Eleanor of Aquitaine. What *is* rare, though, is that we know *how* we're related.

Chapter 13

The Ancestors of John West

Generation 13

1: **John West**, b. abt 1632 in Virginia, d. abt 1691. Married Unity Croshaw. The oldest known ancestor born in America. Served in Virginia militia, was captured during Bacon's Rebellion of 1676 and in 1685 served as a representative in the House of Burgesses. John and Unity's daughter Anne is in Part I under the number *12-2665*.

Generation 14

2: **John West**, b. 14 Dec 1590 in Hampshire, England, d. abt 1659, in Virginia. Sailed to Virginia in 1618, the earliest known ancestor to immigrate permanently to North America. (George Percy *6* arrived earlier, but did not stay.) Served in the Virginia House of Burgesses 1628–1630, and as (temporarily appointed) colonial governor of Virginia in 1635–1637. His massive Virginian land grant grew into the modern town of West Point.

3: **Anne Percy**

Generation 15

4: **Thomas West, 2nd Baron De La Warr**, abt 1556–24 Mar 1602. Knighted in 1587; member of the English Parliament in 1586 and 1593. A close advisor of Queen Elizabeth I. His son, Thomas West, 3rd Baron De La Warr, is the person for whom the state of Delaware (and the adjoining river and bay) is named.

5: **Anne Knollys**, 19 Jul 1555–30 Aug 1608.

6: **George Percy**, b. 4 Sep 1580. The first ancestor to arrive in America: He was among the 104 original settlers of the Jamestown Colony, and arrived in April 1607. Served for a period as colonial governor, then returned to England in 1612.

Figure 13.1: A portrait of George Percy 5.[665] The missing finger on his left hand was reportedly "lost in battle," likely the Eighty Years' War.[666]

7: **Anne Floyd**

Generation 16

8: **William West, 1st Baron De La Warr**, abt 1520–
30 Dec 1595. Convicted of treason and sentenced to death
in connection with a plot to aid an invasion of England;
pardoned by Queen Mary I (known as "Bloody Mary").
Knighted in 1570.

9: **Elizabeth Strange**

10: **Francis Knollys**,
abt 1511–19 Jul 1596.
One of the guardians of
Mary, Queen of Scots
when she sought protec-
tion from Queen Eliza-
beth I. At some point
installed as a Knight of
the Garter.

11: **Catherine Carey**,
abt 1524–15 Jan 1569.
Served as Lady of the
Bedchamber[i] to Queen
Elizabeth I.

12: **Henry Percy, 8th
Earl of Northumber-
land**, 1532–21 Jun 1585.
Served as a member
of Parliament; was
knighted in 1557. Was

*Figure 13.2: A portrait believed
to be of Catherine Carey 11.*[667]

imprisoned three times in the Tower of London, and died of
a mysterious gunshot wound during the third.

13: **Katherine Neville**, 1546–1596.

---

[i]A personal assistant to the queen.

Generation 17

16: **George West**, d. abt 1538.

17: **Elizabeth Morton**

18: **Thomas Strange**

20: **Robert Knollys**, d. 1521. A courtier of Kings Henry VII and Henry VIII of England.

21: **Lettice Penystone**

22: **William Carey**, abt 1500–22 Jun 1528. One of the private servants of King Henry VIII of England.

23: **Mary Boleyn**, abt 1499–19 Jul 1543. A mistress of King Henry VIII of England before he married (and later beheaded) her sister, the famed Anne Boleyn.

24: **Thomas Percy**, abt 1504–2 Jun 1537. Participated in the Pilgrimage of Grace and Bigod's Rebellion, two popular uprisings against royal authority. His participation in the latter led to his conviction for treason. He was hanged, drawn and quartered by King Henry VIII.

25: **Eleanor Harbottle**

Generation 18

32: **Thomas West, 8th Baron De La Warr**, abt 1457–11 Oct 1525. Knighted by King Henry VII in 1486, installed in the Order of the Bath in 1489; installed in the Order of the Garter by King Henry VIII in 1510. A prominent English military commander at the turn of the 16th century.

34: **Robert Morton**

40: **Robert Knollys**

41: **Elizabeth Troutbeck**

42: **Thomas Penystone**

44: **Thomas Carey**, 1455–1500.

45: **Margaret Spencer**, 1472–1536.

46: **Thomas Boleyn, 1ˢᵗ Earl of Wiltshire**, abt 1477–12 Mar 1539. Installed in both the Order of the Garter and Order of the Bath.

47: **Elizabeth Howard**, abt 1480–3 Apr 1538.

48: **Henry Algernon Percy, 5ᵗʰ Earl of Northumberland**, 13 Jan 1477–19 May 1527. Both a Knight of the Garter and a Knight of the Bath.

49: **Catherine Spencer**

50: **Guiscard Harbottle**

51: **Jane Willoughby**

Generation 19

64: **Richard West, 7ᵗʰ Baron De La Warr**, 28 Oct 1430–10 Mar 1476. Fought for the House of Lancaster in the Wars of the Roses.

65: **Katherine Hungerford**

80: **Richard Knollys**

81: **Margaret D'Oyley**

82: **John Troutbeck**

83: **Margaret Hulse**

88: **William Cary**, 1437–6 May 1471. Beheaded after the Battle of Tewkesbury.

89: **Alice Fulford**

90: **Robert Spencer**, d. 1510.

91: **Eleanor Beaufort**, 1431–16 Aug 1501.

92: **William Boleyn**, 1451–10 Oct 1505.

93: **Margaret Butler**, abt 1454–1539.

98: 90

99: 91

Generation 20

128: **Reginald West, 6ᵗʰ Baron De La Warr**, Sep 1395–27 Aug 1450. Knighted before 1416.

129: **Margaret Thorley**

130: **Robert Hungerford, 2ⁿᵈ Baron Hungerford**, 1409–1459. Fought in the Hundred Years' War.

131: **Margaret de Botreaux**

176: **Philip Cary, Member of Parliament**, d. 1437.

177: **Christiana de Orchard**

178: **Baldwin Fulford**, d. abt 1476.

Figure 13.3:   An interpretation of the coat of arms of Philip Cary 176.   "Argent, on a bend Sable, three roses of the first."[668]

182: **Edmund Beaufort, 2ⁿᵈ Duke of Somerset**, 1406–22 May 1455. Installed as a Knight of the Garter during the Hundred Years' War; also participated in the Wars of the Roses.

183: **Eleanor Beauchamp, Duchess of Somerset**, 1408–6 Mar 1467.

184: **Geoffrey Boleyn, Lord Mayor of London**, 1406–1463.

185: **Anne Hoo**, 1424–1484.

186: **Thomas Butler, 7ᵗʰ Earl of Ormond**, 1426–3 Aug 1515. A close advisor to King Henry VII.

187: **Anne Hankford**, abt 1431–13 Nov 1485.

Generation 21

256: **Thomas West, 1st Baron West**, abt 1365–19 Apr 1405. Knighted in 1399.

257: **Joan La Warre**

258: **Robert Thorley**

259: **Anne de la Pole**

260: **Walter Hungerford, Treasurer of England**, 1378–9 Aug 1449. Fought in the Hundred Years' War, including at the Battle of Agincourt made famous in Shakespeare's *Henry V*. Installed as a Knight of the Garter in 1421.

261: **Catherine Peverell**

262: **William de Botreaux, 3rd Baron Botreaux**, 20 Feb 1389–1462.

263: **Elizabeth Beaumont**

352: **Robert Cary, Member of Parliament**, d. abt 1431.

353: **Margaret Courtenay**

354: **William de Orchard**

364: **John Beaufort, 1st Earl of Somerset**, abt 1373–16 Mar 1410. Served with the Teutonic Knights in Lithuania. Was installed in the Order of the Garter in 1397, but eventually died imprisoned in the Tower of London.

365: **Margaret Holland, Duchess of Clarence**, 1385–31 Dec 1439.

366: **Richard Beauchamp, 13th Earl of Warwick**, 1382–30 Apr 1439. A prominent military commander under King Henry IV *1,055,902*; installed into the Order of the Garter in 1403.

370: **Thomas Hoo, 1st Baron Hoo**, abt 1396–1455. Made a Knight of the Garter in 1445.

371: **Elizabeth Wychingham**

Generation 22

512: **Thomas West**, d. 3 Sep 1386.

513: **AliceFitzherbert**, d. 1395.

514: **Roger La Warr**

515: **Eleanor Mowbray**

518: **Michael de la Pole, Lord Chancellor of England**, abt 1330– 5 Sep 1389. Accused of treason and fled to Paris just before the beginning of the "Merciless Parliament" session of 1388, in which many supporters of King Richard II were executed.

519: **Catherine Wingfield**

520: **Thomas Hungerford, Speaker of the House of Commons**, d. 3 Dec 1397. The first person recorded in the rolls of Parliament as speaker, though he was not the first one.

521: **Joan Hussey**, d. 1 Mar 1412.

524: **William de Botreaux, 2ⁿᵈ Baron Botreaux**, 1367–25 May 1395.

525: **Elizabeth St. Lo**

526: **John Beaumont, 4ᵗʰ Baron Beaumont**, 1361–1396. Fought in the Hundred Years' War; later installed into the Order of the Garter.

527: **Catherine Everingham**

704: **John Cary, Chief Baron of the Exchequer**, d. 1395. Also served in Parliament.

705: **Margaret Holleway**

706: **Philip Courtenay**, abt 1355–29 Jul 1406.

707: **Anne Wake**

Figure 13.4: An interpretation of the coat of arms of Michael de la Pole 518. "Azure, a fess between three leopard's faces or."[669]

728: **John of Gaunt, 1ˢᵗ Duke of Lancaster**, 6 Mar 1340–
3 Feb 1399. A prominent military commander and Knight
of the Garter; a brother-in-law to author Geoffrey Chaucer.

729: **Katherine Swynford, Duchess of Lancaster**,
25 Nov 1350–10 May 1403.

730: **Thomas Holland 2ⁿᵈ Earl of Kent**, abt 1354–
25 Apr 1397. Installed in the Order of the Garter in 1375.

731: **Alice FitzAlan, Countess of Kent**, abt 1350–
17 Mar 1416.

732: **Thomas de Beauchamp, 12ᵗʰ Earl of Warwick**,
16 Mar 1338–1401. Fought
closely with John of Gaunt *728*.
A Knight of the Garter.

733: **Margaret Ferrers**

740: **Thomas Hoo**, abt 1370–
23 Aug 1420.

741: **Eleanor de Felton**, 1378–
8 Aug 1400.

*Figure 13.5: An inter-
pretation of the coat of
arms of John de Mow-
bray 1,030. "Gules,
a lion rampant ar-
gent."*[670]

Generation 23

1,026: **Reginald FitzHerbert**

1,027: **Joan**

1,030: **John de Mowbray, 3ʳᵈ
Baron Mowbray**, 29 Nov 1310–
4 Oct 1361. Died of the black
plague.

1,031: **Joan of Lancaster, Baroness of Mowbray**,
abt 1312–7 Jul 1349.

1,036: **William de la Pole**

1,037: **Catherine Norwich**

1,038: **John de Wingfield**, d. abt 1361. Chief administrator to Edward the Black Prince.

1,040: **Walter de Hungerford**. Served three terms in Parliament.

1,041: **Elizabeth FitzJohn**

1,042: **Edmund Hussey**

1,048: **William de Botreaux, 1ˢᵗ Baron Botreaux**, 1337–10 Aug 1391.

1,049: **Elizabeth Daubeny**, d. 29 May 1433.

1,050: **John St. Lo**

1,051: **Margaret Clyvedon**

1,052: **Henry Beaumont, 3ʳᵈ Baron Beaumont**, 1340–1369.

1,053: **Margaret de Vere**, d. 16 Jun 1398.

1,054: **Thomas Everingham**

1,408: **John Cary**

1,409: **Jane de Brian**

1,410: **Robert Holleway**

1,412: **Hugh de Courtenay, Earl of Devon**, 12 Jul 1303–2 May 1377.

1,413: **Margaret de Bohun, Countess of Devon**, 3 Apr 1311–16 Dec 1391.

1,414: **Thomas Wake**

1,415: **Alice de Pateshulle**

1,456: **Edward III, King of England**, 13 Nov 1312–21 Jun 1377. Became king after his mother deposed his father, King Edward II. The most recent known royal ancestor; buried in Westminster Abbey. Founded the Order of the Garter.

1,457: **Philippa of Hainaut, Queen of England**, 24 Jun 1314–15 Aug 1369. Died at Windsor Castle. Queen's College, Oxford is named after her.

1,458: **Paon de Roet**, abt 1310–1380. A knight of otherwise

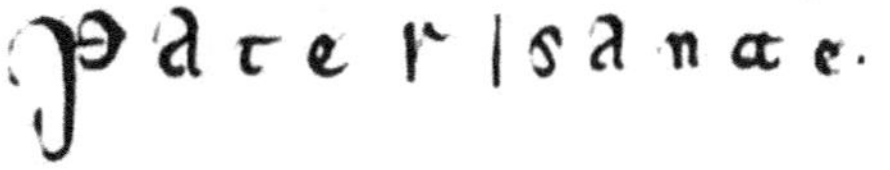

p a t e r | s a n c e.

Figure 13.6: The signature of King Edward III 1,456, the earliest known handwriting to survive from a post-Conquest king of England. It reads, "Pater sancte."[671]

unremarkable birth, who became the ancestor of the modern royalty of England (descendants include Kings Henry IV, Henry V and Henry VI). His tomb was destroyed in London's Great Fire of 1666.

1,460: **Thomas Holland, 1st Earl of Kent**, abt 1314–26 Dec 1360. The 13th of the 25 Founder Knights of the Order of the Garter.

1,461: **Joan of Kent, Princess of Wales**, 29 Sep 1328–7 Aug 1385. Became Welsh royalty by her marriage to Edward, the Black Prince.

1,462: **Richard FitzAlan, 10th Earl of Arundel**, d. 24 Jan 1376. Served as Admiral of the Western Fleet in the Hundred Years' War, and was one of the three main commanders of the English troops at the Battle of Crécy.

1,463: **Eleanor of Lancaster, Countess of Arundel**, 11 Sep 1318–11 Jan 1372.

1,464: **Thomas de Beauchamp, 11th Earl of Warwick**, abt 1313–13 Nov 1369. A commander at the English victories at the Battle of Crécy. The third of the 25 Founder Knights of the Order of the Garter.

1,465: **Katherine Mortimer, Countess of Warwick**, 1314–4 Aug 1369.

(a) Thomas Holland 1,460[672]

(b) Thomas de Beauchamp 1,464[673]

Figure 13.7: Portraits from the Bruges Garter Book, which contains portraits of the founding knights of the Order of the Garter. It was made about 80 years after the deaths of most founders.

Generation 24

2,052: **Herbert FitzReginald**

2,053: **Lucy Peverell**

2,060: **John de Mowbray, 2nd Baron Mowbray**, 4 Sep 1286–23 Mar 1322. Fought under King Edward I *5,654*. Captured during a rebellion and hanged at York.

2,061: **Aline de Braose**, 1291–abt 1331.

2,062: **Henry, 3rd Earl of Lancaster**, abt 1281–22 Sep 1345. Was blind for the final 15 years of his life, during which time he founded a hospital for the poor inside his castle.

2,063: **Maud Chaworth**, 2 Feb 1282–3 Dec 1322.

2,082: **Adam FitzJohn**

2,096: **William de Botreaux**, d. 22 Jul 1349.

2,097: **Isabel de Moels**

2,098: **Ralph Daubeny**

2,102: **John Clyvedon**

2,104: **John Beaumont, 2nd Baron Beaumont**, d. 1342.

2,105: 1,463

2,106: **John de Vere, 7th Earl of Oxford**, abt 1312–24 Jan 1360. Fought in the first two English victories of the Hundred Years' War, at Crécy and Poitiers. Was fighting under Edward the Black Prince, likely in Burgundy, when he was killed in battle.

2,107: **Maud de Badlesmere, Countess of Oxford**, 1310–1366.

2,818: **Guy de Brian**, d. abt 1349.

2,824: **Hugh de Courtenay, Earl of Devon**, 14 Sep 1276–23 Dec 1340.

2,825: **Agnes de Saint John**

2,826: **Humphrey de Bohun, Constable of England**, 1276–16 Mar 1322. Killed in battle in Yorkshire.

2,827: **Elizabeth of Rhuddlan**, 7 Aug 1282–5 May 1316.

2,830: **John de Pateshulle**

2,912: **Edward II, King of England**, 25 Apr 1284–21 Sep 1327. Abdicated the throne because of a plot led by his wife; was imprisoned in Berkeley, where he died, likely of murder.

2,913: **Isabella of France, Queen of England**, 1295– 22 Aug 1358.

2,914: 11,656

2,915: 11,657

2,920: **Robert de Holland, 1st Baron Holand**, abt 1283–1328. Beheaded in the woods by a political enemy.

Figure 13.8: The seal of Humphrey de Bohun 2,826. The drawing is based on a wax seal from a 1301 letter to Pope Boniface VIII.[674]

2,921: **Maud la Zouche**

2,922: **Edmund of Woodstock, 1st Earl of Kent**, 5 Aug 1301–19 Mar 1330. Sentenced to death for treason; when the authorities could not find an executioner willing to kill the son of a king, they had him beheaded by a convicted murderer who wanted a pardon.

2,923: **Margaret Wake, Countess of Kent**, abt 1297– 29 Sep 1349.

2,924: **Edmund FitzAlan, 9th Earl of Arundel**, 1 May 1285–17 Nov 1326. Executed for treason, reportedly with a specifically ordered blunt sword.

2,925: **Alice de Warenne, Countess of Arundel**, 15 Jun 1287–23 May 1338.

2,926: 2,062

2,927: 2,063

2,928: **Guy de Beauchamp, 10th Earl of Warwick**, abt 1272–12 Aug 1315. Fought against William Wallace at the Battle of Falkirk.

2,929: **Alice de Toeni**

2,930: **Roger Mortimer, 1st Earl of March**, 25 Apr 1287–29 Nov 1330. Executed by hanging.

2,931: **Joan de Geneville**

Generation 25

4,104: **Reginald FitzReginald**

4,105: **Joan Martel**

4,106: **Andrew Peverell**

4,120: **Roger de Mowbray, 1st Baron Mowbray**, 1254–21 Nov 1297.

4,121: **Rose de Clare**

4,122: **William de Braose, 2nd Baron Braose**, abt 1260–1326. Held hostage during the Second Barons' War.

4,123: **Agnes**

4,124: **Edmund Crouchback, Earl of Leicester**, 16 Jan 1245–5 Jun 1296. A soldier well-known for his ferocity. His name is believed to have originated in his participation in the Ninth Crusade, where he would have had a metaphorical cross on his back.

4,125: **Blanche of Artois, Queen of Navarre**, abt 1248–2 May 1302.

4,126: **Patrick de Chaworth, Baron of Kidwelly**

4,127: **Isabella de Beauchamp**, b. abt 1263.

4,212: **Alphonse de Vere**

4,213: **Joan Foliot**

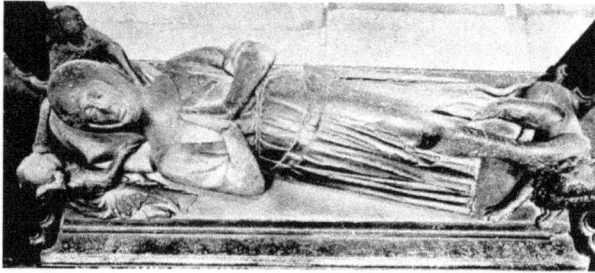

Figure 13.9: An effigy of Edmund Crouchback 4,124 atop his tomb in Westminster Abbey, London.[675]

4,214: **Bartholomew de Badlesmere, 1st Baron Badlesmere**, 18 Aug 1275–14 Apr 1322. Waged a rebellion against King Edward II of England; was eventually arrested, dragged behind a horse for three miles, hanged and beheaded. His body may have been left hanging from the gallows for as long as two years before he was buried.

4,215: **Margaret de Clare**, abt 1287–abt 1334. The first woman prisoner in the Tower of London. While her husband was leading a rebellion against King Edward II, his wife, Queen Isabella, came to the castle in which Margaret was ruling. Margaret denied Isabella entrance, then ordered her archers to fire at the queen when she tried to enter anyway.

5,648: **Hugh de Courtenay**, 25 Mar 1251–28 Feb 1292.

5,652: **Humphrey de Bohun, 3rd Earl of Hereford**, abt 1249–31 Dec 1298.

5,654: **Edward I, King of England**, 1239–7 Jul 1307. Also known as "Edward Longshanks."

5,655: **Eleanor of Castile, Queen of England**, 1241–28 Nov 1290.

5,824: 5,654

5,825: 5,655

5,826: **Philip IV, King of France**, 1268–29 Nov 1314. Arrested hundreds of Knights Templar and had them burned at the stake for heresy.

5,827: **Joan I of Navarre, Queen of France**, 14 Jan 1273–1305. Personally led an army against invaders of Champagne, of which she was countess.

5,828: **William I, Count of Hainaut**, abt 1286–7 Jun 1337.

5,829: **Joan of Valois, Countess of Hainaut**, abt 1294–7 Mar 1342.

5,840: **Robert de Holland**

5,841: **Elizabeth de Samlesbury**

5,842: **Alan la Zouche, 1st Baron la Zouche**, 9 Oct 1267–1314. Fought in the Battle of Falkirk, the English victory that led to the downfall of Scottish leader William Wallace.

5,843: **Eleanor de Segrave**

5,844: 5,654

5,845: **Margaret of France, Queen of England**, abt 1279–14 Feb 1318. Was never technically crowned queen. Her tomb was destroyed during the Reformation.

5,846: **John Wake, 1st Baron Wake of Liddell**

5,847: **Joan de Fiennes**

5,848: **Richard FitzAlan, 8th Earl of Arundel**, 3 Feb 1267–9 Mar 1302.

5,849: **Alice of Saluzzo, Countess of Arundel**, d. 25 Sep 1292.

5,850: **William de Warenne**, 9 Feb 1256–15 Dec 1286. Killed, ostensibly by accident, in a tournament.

5,851: **Joan de Vere**

5,856: **William de Beauchamp, 9th Earl of Warwick**, 1237–1298. Led multiple successful military campaigns against the Welsh.

5,857: **Maud FitzJohn, Countess of Warwick**, abt 1238–1301.

5,860: **Edmund Mortimer, 2nd Baron Mortimer**, 1251–17 Jul 1304.

5,861: **Margaret Fiennes**

Generation 26

8,208:   **Reginald FitzPiers**

8,209: **Joan de Forz**

8,240: **Roger de Mowbray**

8,242: **Richard de Clare, 6th Earl of Gloucester**, 4 Aug 1222–14 Jul 1262. Rumored to have been poisoned.

8,243: **Maud de Lacy, Countess of Gloucester**, 25 Jan 1223–10 Mar 1289.

8,244:   **William de Braose, 2nd Baron Braose**, d. 1326.

8,245: **Aline de Multon**

Figure 13.10: *An interpretation of the coat of arms of William de Braose 8,244. "Azure crusilly of crosses crosslet a lion double queued rampant or."*[676]

8,248:   **Henry III, King of England**, 1 Oct 1207–16 Nov 1272. Ascended to the throne at the age of nine, during the First Barons' War. The rebels were eventually defeated by his troops, who were led by William Marshall *32,970*.

8,249: **Eleanor of Provence, Queen of England**, abt 1223–1291.

8,250: **Robert I, Count of Artois**, 25 Sep 1216–8 Feb 1250. Killed leading a raid during the Seventh Crusade.

8,251: **Matilda of Brabant, Countess of Artois**, 14 Jun 1224–29 Sep 1288.

8,254: 5,856

8,255: 5,857

8,424: **Robert de Vere, 5th Earl of Oxford**, abt 1240–1296. Fought in the Second Barons' War.

8,425: **Alice de Sanford**

8,428: **Gunselin de Badlesmere**, d. abt 1301.

8,429: **Joan FitzBernard**

8,430: **Thomas de Clare, Governor of London**, abt 1245–29 Aug 1287. A close advisor to King Edward I of England *5,654* who accompanied him on the Ninth Crusade.

8,431: **Juliana FitzGerald, Lady of Thomond**, abt 1266–29 Sep 1300.

11,296: **John de Courtenay**

11,297: **Isabel de Vere**

11,304: **Humphrey de Bohun**

11,305: **Eleanor de Braose**, abt 1228–1251.

11,308: 8,248

11,309: 8,249

11,310: **Saint Ferdinand III, King of Castile**, abt 1201–30 May 1252. Canonized in 1671.

11,311: **Joan of Ponthieu, Queen of Castile**, abt 1220–16 Mar 1279.

11,652: **Philip III, King of France**, 30 Apr 1245–5 Oct 1285. Fought in the Eighth Crusade. Appears briefly in Dante's *Divine Comedy*.

11,653: **Isabella of Aragon, Queen of France**, 1248–28 Jan 1271. Buried in the Basilica of St. Denis, where her tomb was raided during the French Revolution.

11,654: **Henry I the Fat, King of Navarre**, abt 1244–22 Jul 1274. Also appears briefly in *The Divine Comedy*.

11,655: 4,125

11,656: **John II, Count of Holland**, 1247–22 Aug 1304.

11,657: **Philippa of Luxembourg, Countess of Holland**, 1252–6 Apr 1311.

11,658: **Charles, Count of Valois**, 12 Mar 1270–16 Dec 1325.

11,659: **Margaret, Countess of Anjou**, 1272–31 Dec 1299.

11,682: **William de Samlesbury**

11,684: **Roger La Zouche**

11,685: **Ela Longespee**, b. 1244.

11,686: **Nicholas de Segrave, 1st Baron Segrave**, abt 1238–1295.

11,687: **Matilda de Lucy**

11,690: 11,652

11,691: **Marie of Brabant, Queen of France**, 13 May 1254–12 Jan 1322.

11,692: **Baldwin Wake**

11,693: **Hawise de Quincy**

11,696: **John FitzAlan, 7th Earl of Arundel**, 14 Sep 1246–18 Mar 1272.

11,697: **Isabella Mortimer**

11,698: **Thomas I, Marquess of Saluzzo**, 1239–1296.

11,699: **Luigia di Ceva**

11,700: **John de Warenne, 6th Earl of Surrey**, 1231–1304. Led the English forces at the Battle of Stirling Bridge, where they were defeated by the Scottish troops under William Wallace.

11,701: **Alice de Lusignan, Countess of Surrey**, 1224–9 Feb 1256. Died in childbirth.

11,702: 8,424

11,703: 8,425

11,712: **William de Beauchamp, Sheriff of Worcestershire**, abt 1215–1268.

11,713: **Isabel Mauduit**

11,714: **John Fitzgeoffrey, Justiciar of Ireland**, d. 23 Nov 1258.

11,715: **Isabel Bigod**

11,720: 23,394

11,721: 23,395

Generation 27

16,418: **William de Forz, 2nd Count of Albemarle**, d. 1195.

16,419: **Maud de Ferrers**, d. 12 Mar 1298.

16,480: **William de Mowbray, 4th Baron Mowbray**, d. abt 1222. One of the rebel barons who resisted the rule of King John of England *16,496* in an uprising that was ended by the ratification of Magna Carta. Was named to the "Council of 25 Barons" charged with enforcing the agreement.

16,481: **Avice**

16,484: **Gilbert de Clare, 5th Earl of Gloucester**, 1180–25 Oct 1230. One of the sureties of Magna Carta.

Figure 13.11: The coat of arms of Gilbert de Clare 16,484. "Or, three chevrons gules."[677]

16,485: **Isabel Marshal**, 9 Oct 1200–17 Jan 1240. Requested to be buried with Gilbert, her first husband, but her second husband had her interred at Beaulieu Abbey, in England; he had her heart sent in a small casket to be with Gilbert instead.

16,486: **John de Lacy, 2nd Earl of Lincoln**, abt 1192–22 Jul 1240. One of the sureties of Magna Carta.

16,487: **Margaret de Quincy, Countess of Lincoln**, abt 1206–1266.

16,488: **John de Braose, Lord of Bramber**, abt 1198–18 Jul 1232. Died after falling off a horse.

16,489: **Margaret Ferch Llywelyn**, b. abt 1202.

16,490: **Thomas de Multon**

16,496: **John Lackland, King of England**, 24 Dec 1166–19 Oct 1216. Concluded an ongoing dispute with rebel barons by signing Magna Carta.

16,497: **Isabella of Angouleme, Queen of England**, abt 1188–4 Jun 1246.

16,498: **Ramon Berenguer IV, Count of Provence**, 1198–19 Aug 1245.

16,499: **Beatrice of Savoy, Countess of Provence**, d. abt 1267.

16,500: **Louis VIII the Lion, King of France**, 5 Sep 1187–8 Nov 1226. Was also briefly titled king of England, though not at the same time as his rule over France.

16,501: **Blanche of Castile, Queen of France**, 4 Mar 1188–27 Nov 1252.

16,502: **Henry II, Duke of Brabant**, 1207–1 Feb 1248.

16,503: **Maria of Swabia, Duchess of Brabant**, 3 Apr 1201–29 Mar 1235.

16,848: **Hugh de Vere, Master Chamberlain of England**, abt 1208–1263. Knighted by King Henry III *8,248*.

16,849: **Hawise de Quincy**

16,860: 8,242

16,861: 8,243

16,862: **Maurice FitzGerald, Justiciar of Ireland**, b. abt 1238.

16,863: **Emmeline Longespee**

22,594: 16,848

22,610: **William de Braose**, abt 1197–2 May 1230. Executed by the husband of Joan of Wales *32,979* after William was caught having an affair with her.

22,611: **Eva Marshal**, 1203–1246.

22,620: **Alfonso IX, King of León**, 15 Aug 1171–1230.

22,621: **Berengaria, Queen of Castile**, abt 1180– 8 Nov 1246. Ruled Castile after her father died until her brother was of age.

22,622: **Simon, Count of Ponthieu**, 1180–21 Sep 1239.

22,623: **Marie, Countess of Ponthieu**, 17 Apr 1199– 21 Sep 1250.

23,304: **Saint Louis IX, King of France**, 25 Apr 1214– 25 Aug 1270. Participated in the Seventh and Eighth Crusades; during the latter, he contracted dysentery and died. Built the Sainte-Chapelle in Paris to house his collection of relics, including what was at the time supposed to be the crown of thorns of Jesus Christ.

23,305: **Margaret of Provence, Queen of France**, 1221– 20 Dec 1295.

23,306: **James I, King of Aragon**, 2 Feb 1208–27 Jul 1276. Claimed in his autobiography to have been shot in the face with a crossbow; his mummified head, exhumed in the 19th century, shows plain evidence of the story's accuracy.

23,307: **Violant of Hungary, Queen of Aragon**, abt 1215– abt 1251.

23,308: **Theobald I, King of Navarre**, 30 May 1201– 8 Jul 1253. Prime leader of the Barons' Crusade of 1239.

23,309: **Margaret of Bourbon, Queen of Navarre**, abt 1217–12 Apr 1256.

23,312: **John I, Count of Hainaut**, 1 May 1218–24 Dec 1257.

23,313: **Adelaide of Holland, Countess of Hainaut**, abt 1230–1284.

23,314: **Henry V, Count of Luxembourg**, 1216–24 Dec 1281.

23,315: **Margaret of Bar, Countess of Luxembourg**, 1220–1275.

23,316: 11,652

23,317: 11,653

23,318: **Charles II, King of Naples**, 1254–5 May 1309.

23,319: **Mary of Hungary, Queen of Naples**, abt 1261–25 Mar 1323.

23,370: **Stephen Longespee**

23,371: **Emmeline de Ridelsford**

23,382: **Henry III, Duke of Brabant**, abt 1230–28 Feb 1261.

23,383: **Adelaide of Burgundy, Duchess of Brabant**, abt 1233–23 Oct 1273.

23,392: **John FitzAlan, 6th Earl of Arundel**, 1223–1267.

23,393: **Maud de Verdun**

23,394: **Roger Mortimer, 1st Baron Mortimer**, 1231–30 Oct 1282. A well-known knight.

23,395: **Maud de Braose**, b. 1224.

23,396: **Manfred III, Marquess of Saluzzo**, d. 1244.

23,397: **Beatrice of Savoy, Marchioness of Saluzzo**, b. abt 1223.

23,400: **William de Warenne, 5th Earl of Surrey**, d. 27 May 1240.

23,401: **Maud Marshal, Countess of Norfolk**, 1192–27 Mar 1248.

23,402: **Hugh X, Seigneur of Lusignan**, d. abt 1249. Was also count of La Marche and Angouleme.

23,403: 16,497

23,424: **Walter de Beauchamp**, abt 1197–1236. Served as a judge.

23,425: **Joan de Mortimer**

23,426: **William de Maudit, Chamberlain of the Exchequer**

23,427: **Alice de Beaumont**

23,428: **Geoffrey Fitz Peter, 1ˢᵗ Earl of Essex**, abt 1162–1213.

23,429: **Aveline de Clare, Countess of Essex**, abt 1178–1225.

23,430: **Hugh Bigod, 3ʳᵈ Earl of Norfolk**, abt 1182–18 Feb 1225. One of the sureties of Magna Carta.

23,431: 23,401

Generation 28

32,836: **Hugh de Vivonia**, served as Sheriff of Somerset and Dorset in 1240.

32,837: **Mabel Malet**

32,838: **William III de Ferrers, 5ᵗʰ Earl of Derby**, abt 1193–28 Mar 1254.

32,839: **Sybil Marshal**

32,960: **Nigel de Mowbray, 5ᵗʰ Baron Thirsk**

32,961: **Mabel**

32,962: **William d'Aubigny, 3ʳᵈ Earl of Arundel**, d. 1 Feb 1221. Fought in the Fifth Crusade but died on the return trip, near Rome.

32,963: **Mabel of Chester**, b. abt 1173.

32,968: Richard de Clare, 6th Lord of Clare, d. 1217. Was named, along with his son, a member of the Council of 25 Barons enforcing Magna Carta.

32,969: Amice FitzWilliam, 4th Countess of Glouces-ter, d. abt 1220.

32,970:   William   Marshal,   1st   Earl   of   Pembroke, abt 1147–14 May 1219.   Knighted in 1166 and became a legendarily successful tournament fighter.

32,971: Isabel de Clare, 4th Countess of Pembroke, abt 1172–1220.

32,972:   Roger   de   Lacy,   High Sheriff of Cumberland, 1170–1211. Fought in the Third Cru-sade under King Richard the Li-onheart, including at the Siege of Acre.

32,973: Maud de Clere

32,974:   Robert   de   Quincy,   d. abt 1217.   Poisoned accidentally by a monk.

32,975: Hawise of Chester, 1180–abt 1243.

32,976:   William   de   Braose,   d. 1210.   After his parents began an (unexplained) feud with King John *16,496*, he and his mother were imprisoned in a dungeon and starved to death.

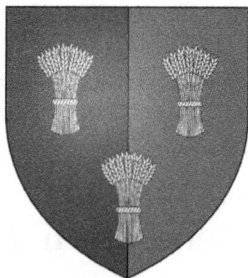

Figure 13.12:   An in-terpretation of the coat of arms of Roger de Lacy 32,972.   "Party per pale gules and azure,   three   garbs or."[678]

32,978:   Llywelyn   the   Great,   Prince   of   Gwynedd, abt 1173–11 Apr 1240. Greatly consolidated power in Wales and, after several military campaigns, ruled essentially the entire region. Had William de Braose *22,610* hanged after discovering him with Joan *32,979*.

32,979: **Joan, Lady of Wales**, abt 1191–2 Feb 1237.

32,992: **Henry Plantagenet, King of England**, 5 Mar 1133–6 Jul 1189. Eventually came to rule much of the land that would eventually make up the United Kingdom: England, Wales, some of Ireland, and about half of France. The king who ordered the murder of Thomas Becket, Archbishop of Canterbury.

32,993: **Eleanor of Aquitaine, Queen of France and England**, abt 1122–1 Apr 1204. Her two marriages, to France's King Louis VII and then to Henry II, made her the queen consort of two of Europe's largest powers. Led troops in the Second Crusade.

32,994: **Aymer, Count of Angouleme**, abt 1160–16 Jun 1202.

32,995: **Alice of Courtenay, Countess of Angouleme**, 1160–12 Feb 1218.

32,996: **Alfonso II, Count of Provence**, 1174–1209.

32,997: **Garsenda, Countess of Forcalquier**, abt 1180–abt 1242.

32,998: **Thomas, Count of Savoy**, d. 1 Mar 1233. Named after Saint Thomas Becket.

32,999: **Margaret of Geneva, Countess of Savoy**, d. abt 1252. Was betrothed to King Philip of France, but was kidnapped by Thomas on the way to France.

33,000: **Philip II, King of France**, 21 Aug 1165–14 Jul 1223. The first to abandon the title "King of the Franks" in favor of the modern title. A leader of the Third Crusade.

33,001: **Isabella of Hainaut, Queen of France**, b. 5 Apr 1170, d. 15 Mar 1190. Believed to have been at least 5 feet, 8 inches tall; died after giving birth to twin boys, who also died several days later. Buried in the Cathedral of Notre Dame in Paris.

33,002: **Alfonso VIII, King of Castile**, 11 Nov 1155–
5 Oct 1214.

33,003: **Eleanor Plantagenet, Queen of Castile**,
13 Oct 1161–31 Oct 1214. Married Alfonso VIII when
she was 12; died within weeks of him, supposedly out of
grief.

33,004: **Henry I, Duke of Brabant**, 1165–5 Sep 1235.

33,005: **Matilda of Boulogne, Duchess of Brabant**, 1170–
16 Oct 1210.

33,006: **Philip of Swabia, King of Germany**, 1177–
21 Jun 1208. Assassinated at the wedding of his niece.

33,007: **Irene Angelina, Queen of Germany**, abt 1181–
27 Aug 1208.

33,696: **Robert de Vere, Master Chamberlain of England**. One of the sureties of Magna Carta.

33,697: **Isabel de Bolebec, Countess of Oxford**, abt 1164–
1245.

33,698: **Saer de Quincy, 1st Earl of Winchester**, abt 1170–
3 Nov 1219. One of the chief authors of Magna Carta.
Fought in the Fifth Crusade, during which he died of an
unspecified illness.

33,699: **Margaret de Beaumont**

33,724: **Maurice FitzGerald, Justiciar of Ireland**,
abt 1194–20 May 1257. Knighted in 1217, but later criticized by King Henry III *8,248* as executing his duties too
harshly.

33,725: **Juliana**

33,726: 23,370

33,727: 23,371

45,220: **Reginald de Braose**, d. 1228. Participated in the
baronial rebellion against King John *16,496*, but refused to
participate in the dealings that resulted in the signing of
Magna Carta.

Figure 13.13: A painting of the assassination of King Philip of Swabia 33,006 from the 13th century history Saxon World Chronicle.[679]

45,222: 32,970

45,223: 32,971

45,240: **Ferdinand II, King of León**, abt 1137–22 Jan 1188.

45,241: **Urraca of Portugal, Queen of León**, 1148–1211.

45,242: 33,002

45,243: 33,003

45,244: **Alberic III, Count of Dammartin**, d. 1200.

45,245: **Mathildis of Clermont**

45,246: **William IV, Count of Ponthieu**, 1179–4 Oct 1221. A leader in the Anglo–French War in the early 1200s.

45,247: **Alys of France, Countess of the Vexin**, 4 Oct 1160–abt 1220.

46,608: 16,500

46,609: 16,501

46,610: 16,498

46,611: 16,499

46,612: **Peter II, King of Aragon**, 1178–12 Sep 1213. Killed at the Battle of Muret.

46,613: **Maria of Montpellier, Queen of Aragon**, 1182–21 Apr 1213.

46,614: **Andrew of Jerusalem, King of Hungary and Croatia**, abt 1177–21 Sep 1235. A leader of the Fifth Crusade.

46,615: **Yolanda de Courtenay, Queen of Hungary**, abt 1200–1233.

Figure 13.14: A 16th century imagining of the appearance of Count Floris IV 46,626.[680]

46,616: **Theobald III, Count of Champagne**, 13 May 1179–24 May 1201. Was elected to lead the Fourth Crusade, but died before it began.

46,617: **Blanche of Navarre, Countess of Champagne**, d. 1229. Ruled Champagne as regent after her husband died, and over the kingdom of Navarre after her brother retired.

46,618: **Archambaud VIII of Bourbon**, 1189–1242.

46,619: **Alix de Forez**

46,624: **Bouchard IV, Lord of Avesnes**, 1182–1244. Fought in multiple military engagements. Was captured in battle and held in Ghent; after his release, his former sister-in-law ordered him beheaded.

46,625: **Margaret II, Countess of Flanders**, 2 Jun 1202–10 Feb 1280.

46,626: **Floris IV, Count of Holland**, 24 Jun 1210–19 Jul 1234.

46,628: **Waleran III, Duke of Limburg**, abt 1165–2 Jul 1226. Fought in the Third Crusade.

46,629: **Cunigunda of Lorraine**

46,630: **Henry II, Count of Bar**, 1190–13 Nov 1239. Killed in the Barons' Crusade.

46,631: **Philippa of Dreux**, 1192–1242.

46,636: **Charles I, King of Naples**, 21 Mar 1227–7 Jan 1285. Also conquered or declared himself king of Albania, Jerusalem, and Sicily.

46,637: **Beatrice of Provence, Queen of Naples**, abt 1234–23 Sep 1267. Accompanied King Charles I on the Seventh Crusade.

46,638: **Stephen V, King of Hungary and Croatia**, d. 6 Aug 1272. At one point, declared war on his father because of allegations he was to be disinherited.

46,639: Elizabeth the Cuman, Queen of Hungary, abt 1244–1290.

46,764: 16,502

46,765: 16,503

46,766: Hugh IV, Duke of Burgundy, 9 Mar 1213–1272.

46,767: Yolande of Dreux, Duchess of Burgundy, 1212–1248.

46,784: John Fitzalan, 3rd Lord of Oswestry, 1200–1240.

46,785: Isabel d'Aubigny

46,786: Theobald le Botiller, Chief Butler of Ireland, 1200–19 Jul 1230.

46,787: Rohese de Verdon

46,788: Ralph de Mortimer

46,789: Gwladus Ddu, d. 1251.

46,790: 22,610

46,791: 22,611

46,792: Boniface of Saluzzo, d. 1212.

46,793: Maria di Torres

46,794: Amadeus IV, Count of Savoy, 1197–24 Jun 1253.

46,795: Marguerite of Burgundy, Countess of Savoy, 1192–1243.

46,800: Hamelin de Warenne, Earl of Surrey, abt 1128–7 May 1202.

46,801: Isabel de Warenne, Countess of Surrey, abt 1137–abt 1203.

46,802: 32,970

46,803: 32,971

46,804: Hugh IX, Seigneur of Lusignan, d. 5 Nov 1219.

46,805: Mathilde of Angouleme, 1181–abt 1233.

46,848: William de Beauchamp

46,849: Amice de Beauchamp

46,850: Roger Mortimer

46,854: **Waleran de Beaumont, 4ᵗʰ Earl of Warwick**, 1153–12 Dec 1204.

46,855: **Alice de Harcourt**

46,856: **Piers de Lutegareshale**

46,858: 65,936

46,859: 65,937

46,860: **Roger Bigod, 2ⁿᵈ Earl of Norfolk**, d. 1221. Was, along with his son Hugh *23,430*, one of the sureties of Magna Carta.

46,861: **Ida de Tosny**

Generation 29

65,674: **William Malet**, one of the 25 executors of Magna Carta.

65,676: **William II de Ferrers, 4ᵗʰ Earl of Derby**, abt 1168–abt 1247. A well-liked ally of King John of England *65,958*.

65,677: **Agnes of Chester**

65,678: 32,970

65,679: 32,971

65,920: **Roger de Mowbray**, d. abt 1188. Fought in the Second Crusade under King Louis VII of France *66,000*. Was later captured at the Battle of Hattin and ransomed by the Knights Templar, but died soon afterward.

65,921: **Alice de Gant**, d. abt 1181.

65,924: **William d'Aubigny, 2ⁿᵈ Earl of Arundel**, d. 24 Dec 1193.

65,925: **Matilda Saint Hilary de Harcouét**

65,926: **Hugh de Kevelioc, 5ᵗʰ Earl of Chester**, 1147–30 Jun 1181. Participated in the Revolt of 1173–74 against King Henry II of England; captured at Battle of Alnwick.

65,927: **Bertrade de Montfort**

65,936: **Roger de Clare, 2ⁿᵈ Earl of Hertford**, 1116–1173.

65,937: **Maud**

65,938: **William Fitz Robert, 2ⁿᵈ Earl of Gloucester**, d. abt 1183.

65,939: **Hawise de Beaumont**

65,940: **John FitzGilbert, Marshal of the Horses**, d. 1165. Served as royal marshal to King Henry I *1,050,836*, managing the king's horses and coordinating guards.

65,941: **Sibyl of Salis-bury**

65,942: **Richard de Clare, 2ⁿᵈ Earl of Pembroke**, d. 20 Apr 1176.

65,943: **Aoife MacMur-rough**, d. abt 1188.

65,944: **John FitzRichard, Con-stable of Chester**

65,945: **Alice**

65,948: 33,698

65,949: 33,699

65,950: 65,926

65,951: 65,927

65,952: **William de Braose, 4ᵗʰ Lord of Bramber**, d.

Figure 13.15:   A 16ᵗʰ century painting of William Fitz Robert 65,938.[681]

9 Aug 1211.   Nicknamed the "Ogre of Abergavenny" after he invited Welsh leaders to a Christmas feast at Abergavenny Castle, then had them murdered. After falling out of favor with King John *16,496*, he was forced to flee to France disguised as a beggar.

65,953: **Maud de St. Valery**, d. 1210. Reportedly accused King John *16,496* of murder; though she and her family fled, she was eventually imprisoned with one of her sons in Corfe Castle, where they were both starved to death.

65,956: **Iorwerth Drwyndwn**, 1130–1174.

65,957: **Marared ferch Madog**

65,958: 16,496

65,959: **Clemence**, a mistress of the king.

65,984: **Geoffrey Plantagenet, Count of Anjou**, 24 Aug 1113– 7 Sep 1151.

65,985: **Matilda, Holy Roman Empress**, abt 1102–10 Sep 1167. Before marrying Geoffrey, she was married in the early 1100s to to Henry V, Holy Roman Emperor.

65,986: **William X, Duke of Aquitaine**, abt 1099–9 Apr 1137. Died on a pilgrimage to Spain.

Figure 13.16: A drawing of Count Baldwin V 66,002 from the 19th century.[682]

65,987: **Aenor de Chatellerault, Duchess of Aquitaine**, abt 1103–1130. Her mother ran away with William IX *131,972*, Aenor's father-in-law, before Aenor married his son.

65,988: **William VI, Count of Angouleme**, d. 1179.

65,989: **Marguerite de Turenne**

65,990: **Peter I of Courtenay**, 1126–10 Apr 1183.

65,991: **Elizabeth de Courtenay**, abt 1127–1205.

65,992: **Alfonso II, King of Aragon**, 1157–25 Apr 1196.

65,993: **Sancha of Castile, Queen of Aragon**, abt 1155–9 Nov 1208.

65,994: **Rainou of Sabran**

65,995: **Garsenda of Forcalquier**

65,996: **Umberto III, Count of Savoy**, 1136–4 Mar 1188.

65,997: **Beatrice of Vennois, Countess of Savoy**, 1160–1230.

65,998: **William I, Count of Geneva**, abt 1132–25 Jul 1195.

65,999: **Marguerite Beatrice de Faucigny**

66,000: **Louis VII, King of the Franks**, 1120–18 Sep 1180.

66,001: **Adela of Champagne, Queen of the Franks**, abt 1140–4 Jun 1206.

66,002: **Baldwin V, Count of Hainaut**, 1150–17 Dec 1195.

66,003: **Margaret I, Countess of Flanders**, d. 15 Nov 1194.

66,004: **Sancho III, King of Castile**, 1134–31 Aug 1158.

66,005: **Blanche of Navarre, Queen of Castile**, d. 12 Aug 1156.

66,006: 32,992

66,007: 32,993

66,008: **Godfrey III, Count of Louvain**, 1142–21 Aug 1190.

66,009: **Margaret of Limburg**

66,010: **Matthew, Count of Boulogne**, abt 1137–1173. Rose to power over Boulogne by abducting Marie and forcibly marrying her.

66,011: **Marie I, Countess of Boulogne**, 1136–25 Jul 1182.

66,012: **Frederick I, Holy Roman Emperor**, 1122–10 Jun 1190. Known as "Frederick Barbarossa"; recognized as one of the most successful rulers of medieval Europe.

66,013: **Beatrice of Burgundy, Holy Roman Empress**, 1143–15 Nov 1184.

66,014: **Isaac II Angelos, Emperor of the Byzantine Empire**, 1156–1195. Was blinded and imprisoned for eight years by his brother before retaking the throne.

67,392: **Aubrey de Vere, 1st Earl of Oxford**, abt 1115–26 Dec 1194. After his wife's father was publicly disgraced, Aubrey tried unsuccessfully to have his marriage to her annulled, then kept her locked away for almost a decade before the pope forced him to free her under threat of excommunication.

67,393: **Agnes of Essex, Countess of Oxford**, abt 1151–abt 1212.

67,394: **Hugh de Bolebec II**

67,395: **Margaret de Montfichet**

67,396: **Robert de Quincy**

67,397: **Orabilis de Mar**

67,448: **Gerald FitzMaurice, 1st Lord of Offaly**, abt 1150–15 Jan 1204. Fought at the Siege of Dublin in 1171.

67,449: **Eve de Bermingham, Lady of Offaly**, d. abt 1226.

90,440: 65,952

90,441: 65,953

90,480: **Alfonso VII, Emperor of All Spain**, 1 Mar 1105–21 Aug 1157. King of León, Galicia and Castile.

90,481: **Berengaria of Barcelona, Queen of León**, 1116–15 Jan 1149.

90,482: **Afonso I, King of Portugal**, 25 Jul 1109–6 Dec 1185. "Founded" the country of Portugal by breaking it out of the rule of the Kingdom of Galicia.

90,483: **Matilda of Savoy, Queen of Portugal**, abt 1125–abt 1158.

90,488: **Alberic II, Count of Dammartin**

90,489: **Clémence de Bar**

90,490: **Renaud II, Count of Clermont**, 1075–1152.

90,492: **John I, Count of Ponthieu**, abt 1140–1191.

90,493: **Beatrice de St. Pol**

90,494: 66,000

90,495: **Constance of Castile, Queen of the Franks**, abt 1140–4 Oct 1160. Died giving birth to Alys *45,247*.

93,224: 65,992

93,225: 65,993

93,226: **William VIII, Lord of Montpellier**, d. 1202.

93,227: **Eudokia Komnene**, abt 1160–abt 1203.

93,228: **Béla III, King of Hungary and Croatia**, abt 1148–23 Apr 1196. Stood 6 feet, 3 inches tall, a giant at the time.

93,229: **Agnes of Antioch, Queen of Hungary**, 1154–abt 1184.

93,230: **Peter II of Courtenay, Emperor of Latin Constantinople**, d. 1219. Fought in the Third Crusade. Was later captured on his way to take power in Constantinople and died in prison two years later.

Figure 13.17: An interpretation of the coat of arms of Lord Guy II of Dampierre 93,236. "Or, a lion gules accompanied by eight shells azure."[683]

93,231: **Yolanda of Flanders, Empress Regent of Latin Constantinople**, 1175–1219. Ruled Constantinople until her son was of age, after her husband was imprisoned before he could assume the throne.

93,232: **Henry I, Count of Champagne**, 1127–16 Mar 1181. Fought in the Second Crusade.

93,233: **Marie of France, Countess of Champagne**, 1145–11 Mar 1198.

93,234: **Sancho VI, King of Navarre**, 21 Apr 1132–27 Jun 1194.

93,235: **Sancha of Castile, Queen of Navarre**, abt 1139–1179.

93,236: **Guy II, Constable of Champagne**, d. 18 Jan 1216. Fought in the Third Crusade as one of the first attackers during the Siege of Acre.

93,237: **Mathilde, Lady of Bourbon**, d. 18 Jun 1228.

93,248: **James, Lord of Avesnes**, 1152–7 Sep 1191.

93,249: **Adela of Guise**, d. 1185.

93,250: **Baldwin I, Emperor of Latin Constantinople**, 1172–abt 1205. A main leader of the Fourth Crusade, later elected to lead the newly acquired Byzantine kingdom.

93,251: **Marie of Champagne**, abt 1174–9 Aug 1204. Was not aware her husband was going to be named emperor, and died before she could join him in Constantinople.

93,252: **William I, Count of Holland**, abt 1167–4 Feb 1222. Fought in the Fifth Crusade.

93,253: **Adelaide of Guelders, Countess of Holland**, abt 1182–1218.

93,256: **Henry III, Duke of Limburg**, abt 1140–21 Jun 1221.

93,257: **Sophie of Saarbrücken**

93,258: **Frederick I, Duke of Lorraine**, abt 1143–7 Apr 1206.

93,260: **Theobald I, Count of Bar**, abt 1158–13 Feb 1214.

93,261: **Ermensinde de Bar-sur-Seine**

93,262: **Robert II, Count of Dreux**, 1154–28 Dec 1218. Fought in the Third Crusade, including the Siege of Acre.

93,263: **Yolande de Coucy**

93,272: 16,500

93,273: 16,501

93,274: 16,498

93,275: 16,499

93,276: **Béla IV, King of Hungary and Croatia**, 1206–3 May 1270.

93,277: **Maria Laskarina**, abt 1206–1270.

93,278: **Seyhan**. A chieftain of a nomadic tribe of Cumans.

93,532: **Odo III, Duke of Burgundy**, 1166–6 Jul 1218.

93,533: **Alice of Vergy, Duchess of Burgundy**, 1182–1252. Ruled as regent until her son was of age.

93,534: **Robert III, Count of Dreux**, 1185–1234.

93,535: **Alianor de St. Valery**

93,568: **William FitzAlan, 1ˢᵗ Lord of Oswestry**, d. 1210.

93,570: 32,962

93,571: 32,963

93,572: **Theobald Walter, Chief Butler of Ireland**, 1165–1206. Also served as sheriff of Lancaster.

93,573: **Maud le Vavasour**

93,574: **Nicholas de Verdon**

93,575: **Joan de Lacy**

93,576: **Roger de Mortimer**

93,578: 32,978

93,588: 32,998

93,589: 32,999

93,590: 187,064

93,591: **Beatrice of Albon**, 1161–1228.

93,600: 65,984

93,602: **William de Warenne, 3ʳᵈ Earl of Surrey**, 1119–6 Jan 1148. Fought in the Second Crusade; killed at the Battle of Mount Cadmus.

93,603: **Adela**

93,610: **Wulgrin III, Count of Angouleme**

93,700: **Hugh de Mortimer**, d. abt 1181.

93,701: **Matilda Le Meschin**

93,708: **Roger de Beaumont, 2ⁿᵈ Earl of Warwick**, 1102–
    12 Jun 1153.

93,709: **Gundred de Warenne**

93,710: **Robert de Harcourt**

93,720: **Hugh Bigod, 1ˢᵗ Earl of Norfolk**, 1095–1177.

93,721: **Juliana de Vere**, d. abt 1199.

Generation 30

131,352: **William I de Ferrers, 3rd Earl of Derby**, d. 1190. Member of the Knights Templar. Fought in the Third Crusade under King Richard I of England ("Richard the Lionheart") and died at the Siege of Acre.

131,353: **Sybil de Braose**

131,354: 65,926

131,355: 65,927

131,840: **Nigel de Daubeney, 1st Baron Mowbray**, 1070–21 Nov 1129. A favored ally of King Henry I of England *131,970*.

131,841: **Gundred de Gournay**, 1097–1155.

131,842: **Walter de Gant**

131,848: **William d'Aubigny, 1st Earl of Arundel**, d. 12 Oct 1176. Built a castle in England that is still standing in the Norfolk village of Castle Rising.

131,849: **Adeliza of Louvain, Queen of England**, abt 1103–30 Jan 1121. Her first husband was King Henry I of England *131,970*, whom she married when she was about 18 and he was about 53. After his death, she married William d'Aubigny and had seven children.

131,852: **Ranulf II, 4th Earl of Chester**, 1099–16 Dec 1153. Heavily involved in the military wrangling of the mid-1100s involving King Stephen of England and Empress Matilda. Died after being poisoned by William Peverell *525,410*.

131,853: **Maud of Gloucester, Countess of Chester**, d. 29 Jul 1189.

131,854: **Simon III de Montfort**

131,872: **Richard Fitz Gilbert, 3rd Lord of Clare**, d. 15 Apr 1136. Was assassinated on his way home from war, at a spot that was marked with the "Garreg Dial" (Welsh for "The Stone of Revenge") that is still visible today.

131,873: **Alice de Gernon**

131,874: **James de St. Hillary**

131,876: **Robert Fitzroy, 1st Earl of Gloucester**, d. 31 Oct 1147. Illegitimate son of King Henry I of England. A major supporter of his half-sister, Empress Matilda *65,985*, during her unsuccessful attempt to take the throne.

131,877: **Mabel FitzRobert, Countess of Gloucester**, 1090–29 Sep 1157.

131,880: **Gilbert, Marshal of the Horses**, d. 1129. His son John was the first to inherit the title of royal marshal.

131,881: **Margaret**

131,884: **Gilbert fitz Gilbert de Clare, Earl of Pembroke**, d. 6 Jan 1148.

131,885: **Isabel de Beaumont**

131,886: **Diarmait Mac Murchada, King of Leinster**, d. abt 1171. Ruled over the Irish kingdom of Leinster backed by the military muscle of his close ally, King Henry II.

131,887: **Mor O'Toole**, d. abt 1191.

131,904: **William de Braose, 3rd Lord of Bramber**. An English military leader associated with kings Stephen and Henry II.

131,905: **Bertha of Hereford**, b. abt 1130.

131,906: **Bernard de St. Valéry**

131,907: **Matilda**

Figure 13.18: A woodcarving based on a portrait of King Diarmait Mac Murchada 131,886 believed to have been drawn from his actual appearance.[684]

131,912: **Owain ap Gruffudd, King of Gwynedd**, d. 1170. The first "Prince of Wales."

131,913: **Gwladys ferch Llywarch**

131,914: **Madog ap Meredudd, Prince of Wales**, d. 1160.

131,968: **Fulk the Younger, King of Jerusalem**, d. 13 Nov 1143. His second wife, Melisende, was queen of Jerusalem; his power derived from marrying her. Died after his skull was crushed in a fall from his horse.

131,969: **Ermengard, Countess of Maine**, abt 1096–1126.

131,970: **Henry I, King of England**, d. 1 Dec 1135. Seized power in 1100. His death sparked "The Anarchy," a 19-year civil war in England caused by Henry's lack of legitimate heir.

131,971: **Matilda of Scotland, Queen of England**, d. 1 May 1118. Buried at Westminster Abbey.

131,972: **William IX, Duke of Aquitaine**, 22 Oct 1071–11 Feb 1127. The earliest documented troubadour, a songwriter using the Occitan language.

Figure 13.19: An interpretation of the coat of arms of Viscount Aimery I 131,974. "Argent a lion gules, on a bordure sable eight bezants or."[685]

131,973: **Philippa, Countess of Toulouse**, abt 1073–28 Nov 1118. Studied religion at the Abbey of Fontevrault, where the women were in charge of the men.

131,974: **Aimery I, Viscount of Chatellerault**, abt 1075–7 Nov 1151.

131,975: **Dangereuse de l'Isle Bouchard, Viscountess of Chattellerault**, 1079–abt 1151. Historians believe her first name was likely a nickname, and that her first name may have been "Amauberge."

131,976: **Wulgrin II, Count of Angouleme**, d. 16 Nov 1140.

131,977: **Pontia de la Marche**

131,980: **Louis VI the Fat, King of the Franks**, 1 Dec 1081–1 Aug 1137.

131,981: **Adelaide of Savoy, Queen of the Franks**, 1092–18 Nov 1154. Buried at the Church of St. Pierre at Montmartre, where her grave was destroyed during the French Revolution.

131,982: 372,922

131,983: 372,923

131,984: **Ramon Berenguer IV, Count of Barcelona**, abt 1114–6 Aug 1162. A leader in the Second Crusade.

131,985: **Petronilla, Queen of Aragon**, 1136–15 Oct 1173.

131,986: 90,480

131,987: **Richeza of Poland, Queen of Castile**, abt 1140–16 Jun 1185.

131,990: **William IV, Count of Forcalquier**, abt 1130–abt 1208.

131,991: **Adelaide de Beziers**

131,992: **Amadeus III, Count of Savoy**, 1095–1148. A leader in the Second Crusade, during which he fell ill and died.

131,993: **Mahaut of Albon, Countess of Savoy**, 1112–1148.

131,994: **Géraud I, Count of Macon**

131,995: **Maurette de Salins**

131,996: **Amadeus I, Count of Geneva**, 1098–1178.

131,997: **Matilde of Cuiseaux**

132,000: 131,980

132,001: 131,981

132,002: **Theobald II, Count of Champagne**, 1090–1152.

132,003: **Matilda of Carinthia, Countess of Champagne**, d. abt 1161.

132,004: **Baldwin IV, Count of Hainaut**, 1108–8 Nov 1171.

132,005: **Alice of Namur**, d. 1169.

132,006: **Thierry of Alsace, Count of Flanders**, abt 1099–17 Jan 1168. Went on multiple military campaigns, including participation in the Second Crusade.

132,007: **Sibylla of Anjou, Countess of Flanders**, abt 1112–1165. Ruled as regent of Flanders while Count Thierry was away fighting.

132,008: 90,480

132,009: 90,481

132,010: **García Ramírez, King of Navarre**, abt 1112–21 Nov 1150.

132,011: **Margaret of L'Aigle, Queen of Navarre**, d. 25 May 1141.

132,016; **Godfrey II, Count of Louvain**, abt 1110–13 Jun 1142.

132,017: **Lutgarde of Sulzbach**

132,018: **Henry II, Duke of Limburg**, abt 1111–1167.

132,019: **Mathilda of Saffenberg**

132,020: 132,006

132,021: 132,007

132,022: **Stephen, King of England**, d. 25 Oct 1154.

132,023: **Matilda of Boulogne, Queen of England**, d. 3 May 1152.

132,024: **Frederick II, Duke of Swabia**, 1090–6 Apr 1147.

132,025: **Judith of Bavaria, Duchess of Swabia**, 19 May 1100–27 Aug 1130.

132,026: **Reginald III, Count of Burgundy**, abt 1093–1148.

132,027: **Agatha of Lorraine, Countess of Burgundy**, abt 1120–1147.

132,028: **Andronikos Doukas Angelos**, b. abt 1122.

132,029: **Euphrosyne Kastamonitissa**, b. abt 1125.

134,784: **Aubrey de Vere II, Chamberlain of the King**, abt 1085–1141. Served under kings Henry I *131,970* and Stephen *132,022* of England.

134,785: **Adeliza**

134,786: **Henry of Essex**, d. abt 1170. A royal constable under kings Stephen *132,022* and Henry II, a position that required he carry the royal standard in battle to indicate the location of the king. After he dropped it during a battle, he was sentenced to trial by combat, which he lost and was almost killed. Spent the rest of his life in a monastery.

134,787: **Alice de Montford**

134,792: **Saer I de Quincy**

134,793: **Matilda of St. Liz**

134,896: **Maurice FitzGerald, Lord of Llanstephan**, abt 1105–1176. Fought in the Norman invasion of Ireland to help Diarmait Mac Murchada *131,886* regain the throne of Leinster.

134,898: **Robert de Bermingham**

180,960: **Raymond, Count of Galicia**, abt 1070–24 May 1107. A mercenary adventurer before he came to rule.

180,961: **Urraca, Queen of León**, 1079–8 Mar 1126. Married to Raymond at age 8.

180,962: **Ramon Berenguer III, Count of Barcelona**, d. 1131.

180,963: **Douce I, Countess of Provence**, abt 1090–1127.

180,964: **Henry, Count of Portugal**, 1066–1112.

(a) Count Raymond of Galicia 180,960[686]

(b) Queen Urraca 180,961[687]

Figure 13.20: Two signatures from a 1097 charter. In the time before many monarchs could read or write, it was common for them to sign documents with a signum manus, or small drawing.

Figure 13.21: The signature of Ramon Berenguer III.[688]

180,965: **Theresa de León, Countess of Portugal**, 1080–11 Nov 1130.

180,966: 131,992

180,967: 131,993

180,978: **Reginald I, Count of Bar**, abt 1080–10 Mar 1149.

180,979: **Gisele de Vaudémont**

180,980: **Hugh I, Count of Clermont**, 1030–1101.

180,981: **Marguerite de Ramerupt**

180,984: **Guy II, Count of Ponthieu**, abt 1120–25 Dec 1147. Fought in the Second Crusade.

180,985: **Ida**

180,990: 90,480

180,991: 90,481

186,452: **William VII, Lord of Montpellier**, abt 1131–abt 1172.

186,453: **Matilda of Burgundy**

186,456: **Géza II, King of Hungary and Croatia**, 1130–31 May 1162.

186,457: **Euphrosyne of Kiev, Queen of Hungary**, abt 1130–abt 1193.

186,458: **Raynald of Chatillon, Prince of Antioch**, abt 1125–4 Jul 1187. Fought in the Second Crusade. Captured and imprisoned in Aleppo for 15 years. Later captured

Figure 13.22: A 15th century illustration of the execution of Prince Raynald 186,458.[689]

while waging war against Saladin, who may have personally executed him.

186,459: **Constance of Hauteville, Princess of Antioch**, 1128–1163. Died while her husband was in prison.

186,460: 65,990

186,461: 65,991

186,462: 66,002

186,463: 66,003

186,464: 132,002

186,465: 132,003

186,466: 66,000

186,467: 32,993

186,468: 132,010

186,469: 132,011

186,470: 90,480

186,471: 90,481

186,472: **William I, Lord of Dampierre**

186,473: **Ermengarde of Mouchy**

186,474: **Archambault of Bourbon**

186,475: **Alix of Burgundy**

186,496: **Nicholas d'Oisy, Lord of Avesnes**, abt 1130– abt 1170. Built several castles.

186,497: **Matilda de la Roche**

186,498: **Bouchard of Guise**

186,500: 66,002

186,501: 66,003

186,502: 93,232

186,503: 93,233

186,504: **Floris III, Count of Holland**, 1141–1 Aug 1190. A leader of the Third Crusade, during which he died of illness.

186,505: **Ada of Huntingdon, Countess of Holland**, b. abt 1146.

186,506: **Otto I, Count of Guelders**, 1150–1207. Fought in the Third Crusade.

186,507: **Richardis of Bavaria, Countess of Guelders**, 1173–7 Dec 1231.

186,512: 132,018

186,513: 132,019

186,516: **Matthias I, Duke of Lorraine**, abt 1119–13 May 1176.

186,517: **Judith of Swabia, Duchess of Lorraine**

186,520: **Reginald II, Count of Bar**, d. 25 Jul 1170.

186,521: **Agnes of Champagne**, d. 1207.

186,522: **Guy II of Brienne**

186,523: **Petronille de Chancenay**

186,524: **Robert I, Count of Dreux**, abt 1123–11 Oct 1188.

186,525: **Agnes de Baudemont, Countess of Braine**

186,552: 46,614

186,553: **Gertrude of Merania**, 1185–28 Sep 1213. Assassinated by Hungarian magnates because of a perceived unfairness in her granting of lands.

186,554: **Theodore I Laskaris**, abt 1175–abt 1222.

186,555: **Anna Komnene Angelina, Empress of Nicaea**, abt 1176–1212

187,064: **Hugh III, Duke of Burgundy**, 1142–25 Aug 1192. Fought in the Third Crusade; died at the Siege of Acre.

187,065: **Alice of Lorraine**

187,066: **Hugh of Vergy**

187,067: **Gillette de Trainel**

187,068: 93,262

187,069: 93,263

187,136: **William FitzAlan, Lord of Oswestry**, 1105–1160.

187,137: **Christiana**

187,144: **Hervey Walter**

187,145: **Maud de Valoignes**

187,146: **Robert le Vavasour**

187,152: 93,700

187,153: 93,701

187,182:   **Guigues V, Count of Albon**, abt 1125–29 Jul 1162.

187,204: **William de Warenne**, d. 11 May 1138.

187,205: **Elizabeth of Vermandois**, abt 1085–13 Feb 1131.

187,206: **William III, Count of Ponthieu**, abt 1093–1172.

187,207: **Helie of Burgundy**, abt 1080–28 Feb 1141.

187,220: 65,988

187,221: 65,989

187,400: **Hugh de Mortimer**, d. abt 1150.

187,402: **William Meschin**, d. abt 1135. Fought in the First Crusade, including the 1097 Siege of Nicaea.

187,403: **Cecily de Rumily**

187,416: **Henry de Beaumont, 1st Earl of Warwick**, d. 20 Jun 1119.

187,417: **Margaret of Perche**

187,418: 187,204

187,419: 187,205

187,440: **Roger Bigod**, d. abt 1107.

187,441: **Adeliza de Tosny**

187,442: 134,784

187,443: 134,785

Generation 31

262,704: **Robert II de Ferrers, 2nd Earl of Derby**, d. 1162. Funded the establishment of a small abbey in Merevale, in Warwickshire, England.

262,705: **Margaret Peverell, Countess of Derby**

262,706: 131,904

262,707: 131,905

263,680: **Roger d'Aubigny**, abt 1036–1104.

263,681: **Alice de Grandmesnil**, abt 1055–1100.

263,682: **Gerard de Gournay, Baron of Gournay**, 1066–1104.

263,696: **William d'Aubigny**, d. 1139. An Anglo-Norman nobleman also known as "Pincerna," which means "butler." He apparently was a butler to King Henry I *131,970*.

263,697: **Maud Bigod**

263,698: **Godfrey I, Duke of Lower Lorraine**, abt 1060– 25 Jan 1139.

263,699: **Ida of Chiny**, 1078–abt 1117.

263,704: **Ranulf le Meschin, 3ʳᵈ Earl of Chester**, 1070– 1129. One of three commanders under King Henry I of England at the Battle of Tinchebray in 1106.

263,705: **Lucy of Bolingbroke, Countess of Chester**, d. abt 1138. A significant religious patron; outlived all three of her husbands.

263,706: 131,876

263,707: 131,877

263,708: **Amaury III of Montfort, Count of Evreux**, d. abt 1137.

263,744: **Gilbert Fitz Richard, 2ⁿᵈ Lord of Clare**, d. abt 1117.

263,745: **Adeliza de Claremont**

263,752: 131,970

263,754: **Robert Fitzhamon**, d. 1107. Co-founded Tewkes-bury Abbey, in Gloucestershire, England.

263,755: **Sybil de Montgomery**

263,768: 263,744

263,769: 263,745

Figure 13.23: A portrait of Count Godfrey I 263,698.[690]

Figure 13.24: A 16th century depiction of Robert Fitzhamon 263,754 and Sybil de Montgomery 263,755 holding Tewkesbury Abbey.[691]

263,770: **Robert de Beaumont, 1ˢᵗ Earl of Leicester**, d. 5 Jun 1118. One of the proven companions of William the Conqueror. Was on the hunting trip where William's grandson, King William the Red, was accidentally killed.

263,771: 187,205

263,772: **Donnchad mac Murchada, King of Leinster**

263,773: **Orlaith ingen O'Braenain**

263,808: **Philip de Braose, 2ⁿᵈ Lord of Bramber.** May have fought in the last years of the First Crusade.

263,809: **Aenor de Totnes**

263,810: **Miles of Gloucester, 1ˢᵗ Earl of Hereford**, abt 1097–24 Dec 1143. Appears to have died after being shot in the head with an arrow during a hunting trip.

263,811: **Sibyl de Neufmarché**, born at Brecon Castle in Wales and inherited large estates and much land from her father. Moved into a monastery after her husband's death.

263,812: **Reginald de St. Valéry**, d. abt 1162.

263,824: **Gruffudd ap Cynan, King of Gwynedd**, abt 1055–1137. After multiple attempts to seize power in Gwynedd, he was captured and imprisoned for at least a decade. He then escaped, and, at the time of his death, was once again ruler of Wales.

263,825: **Angharad**, d. 1162, supposedly at the age of 97.

263,828: **Maredudd ap Bleddyn, King of Powys**

263,829: **Hunedd ferch Einudd**

263,936: **Fulk IV, Count of Anjou**, 1043–14 Apr 1109. May have written a history of Anjou and a genealogical study of his ancestry.

263,937: **Bertrade de Montfort, Queen of the Franks**, abt 1070–14 Feb 1117. Eventually left Fulk to marry King Philip I of France *263,960*, despite Bertrade and Philip both having living spouses.

263,938: **Elias I, Count of Maine**, d. 11 Jul 1110.

263,939: **Matilda**

263,940: **William the Conqueror, King of England**, abt 1028–9 Sep 1087. Reigned as Duke of Normandy starting in 1035, and claimed his (heavily contested) right to the English throne during the Norman Invasion of 1066, which crested with the Battle of Hastings on 14 Oct.

263,941: **Matilda of Flanders, Queen of England**, abt 1031–2 Nov 1083. Descended from the kings of France; gave to her husband William the ship *Mora*, which he sailed to England during his army's conquest in 1066.

263,942: **Malcolm III, King of Alba**, abt 1031–13 Nov 1093. Ruled part of modern-day Scotland and is the historical basis for the character of the same name in Shakespeare's *Macbeth*. Was killed by Roger de Mowbray, the father-in-law of Nigel de Daubeney *131,840*.

263,943: **Saint Margaret, Queen of Scotland**, d. 16 Nov 1093. Her skull was kept at one point by Mary, Queen of Scots, but was then taken to France, where it was lost during the French Revolution.

263,944: **William VIII, Duke of Aquitaine**, abt 1025–25 Sep 1086.

263,945: **Hildegarde of Burgundy, Duchess of Burgundy**, d. abt 1104.

263,946: **William IV, Count of Toulouse**, abt 1040–1094.

263,947: **Emma of Mortain**

263,948: **Boson II de Chatellerault**

263,949: **Aleanor de Thouars**

263,950: **Bartholomew de l'Isle Bouchard**

263,952: **William V, Count of Angouleme**, d. abt 1120.

263,954: **Roger the Poitevin**

263,955: **Almodis**

263,960: **Philip I, King of the Franks**, 23 May 1052–

29 Jul 1108. Later ran away with Bertrade de Montfort *263,937.*

263,961: **Bertha of Holland, Queen of the Franks**, abt 1055–15 Oct 1094.

263,962: **Umberto II, Count of Savoy**, 1065–19 Oct 1103.

263,963: **Gisela of Burgundy, Marchioness of Montferrat**, 1075–1135.

263,968: 180,962

263,969: 180,963

263,970: **Ramiro II, King of Aragon**, 24 Apr 1086–16 Aug 1157.

263,971: **Agnes of Aquitaine, Queen of Aragon**, abt 1105–abt 1159.

Figure 13.25: The signum regis of King Ramiro II 263,970.[692]

263,974: **Władysław II, High Duke of Poland**, 1105–30 May 1159. Deposed in 1146 and died in exile.

263,975: **Agnes of Babenberg, Duchess of Poland**, d. 1163.

263,980: **Bertrand I, Count of Forcalquier**

263,981: **Josserande de Flotte**

263,982: **Raymond I Trencavel, Viscount of Carcassonne**, d. 1167. Murdered by the citizens of Béziers after publicly unpopular decisions. As punishment, Raymond's son, Viscount Roger II, allowed besieging troops from Aragon to enter the city and massacre the civilians.

263,983: **Adelaide de Beziers**

263,984: 263,962

263,985: 263,963

263,986: **Guigues III, Count of Albon**, d. 21 Dec 1133.

263,987: **Matilda**

263,992: **Aymon I, Count of Geneva**

263,993: **Ida Faucigny**

263,994: **Hugo I, Count of Cuiseaux**

264,004: **Stephen II Henry, Count of Blois**, abt 1045–19 May 1102. A leader of the First Crusade; killed later in the Crusade of 1101.

264,005: **Saint Adela of Normandy, Countess of Blois**, abt 1067–8 Mar 1137.

264,006: **Engelbert II, Duke of Carinthia**, d. 13 Apr 1141.

264,007: **Uta of Passau**

264,008: **Baldwin III, Count of Hainaut**, 1088–1120.

264,009: **Yolande of Guelders**

264,010: **Godfrey I, Count of Namur**, d. 19 Aug 1139.

264,011: **Ermesinde of Luxembourg, Countess of Namur**, abt 1080–24 Jun 1143.

264,012: **Theodoric II, Duke of Lorraine**, d. 30 Dec 1115.

264,013: 528,109

264,014: 131,968

264,015: 131,969

264,020: **Ramiro Sánchez, Lord of Monzón**, 1070–1116.

264,021: **Cristina Rodríguez**

264,022: **Gilbert of L'Aigle**

264,023: **Juliana du Perche**

264,032: 263,698

264,033: 263,699

264,034: **Berengar II, Count of Sulzbach**, d. 3 Dec 1125.

264,035: **Adelheid of Wolfratshausen, Countess of Sulzbach**, d. 1126.

264,036: **Waleran II, Duke of Lower Lorraine**, abt 1085–1139.

264,037: **Jutta von Wassenberg**

264,044: 264,004

264,045: 264,005

264,046: **Eustace III, Count of Boulogne**, d. abt 1125. Fought in the First Crusade.

264,047: **Mary of Scotland, Countess of Boulogne**, 1082–1116.

264,048: **Frederick I, Duke of Swabia**, b. abt 1050.

264,049: 527,951

264,050: **Henry IX, Duke of Bavaria**, 1075–13 Dec 1126.

264,051: **Wulfhilde of Saxony, Duchess of Bavaria**, 1072–29 Dec 1126.

264,052: **Stephen I, Count of Burgundy**, 1065–1102. Fought in the Crusade of 1101; later died at the Battle of Ramla.

264,053: **Beatrix of Lorraine, Countess of Burgundy**

264,054: **Simon I, Duke of Lorraine**, 1076–13 Apr 1138. Buried at Saint-Dié-des-Vosges, where his descendant Henry Stone Jr. would fight in the first world war 780 years later.

264,055: **Adelaide of Leuven**, d. abt 1158.

264,056: **Constantine Angelos**

264,057: **Theodora Komnene Angelina**, b. 15 Jan 1096.

269,568: **Aubrey de Vere I**, d. abt 1113.

269,569: **Beatrice**

269,570: 263,744

269,571: 263,745

269,572: **Robert fitz Swein**

269,586: **Simon I de Senlis, Earl of Northampton**, d. abt 1111.

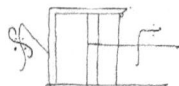

Figure 13.26: The signum regis of Emperor Alfonso VI 361,922, from a 1097 charter.[693]

269,587: **Maud of Huntingdon, Queen of Scotland**, abt 1074–abt 1131. Her second marriage was to King David I of Scotland *746,020*.

269,792: **Gerald de Windsor**, abt 1075–1135.

269,793: **Nest ferch Rhys**, b. abt 1085.

361,920: **William I, Count of Burgundy**, 1020–12 Nov 1087.

361,921: **Stephanie**

361,922: **Alfonso VI, Emperor of All Spain**, abt 1047–1109. Known as "Alfonso the Brave," believed to have been married at least five times.

361,923: **Constance of Burgundy, Queen of León**, 8 May 1046–1093.

361,924: **Ramon Berenguer II, Count of Barcelona**, abt 1054–5 Dec 1082. Murdered while on a hunting trip, a move believed to have been orchestrated by his twin brother, Berenguer Ramon.

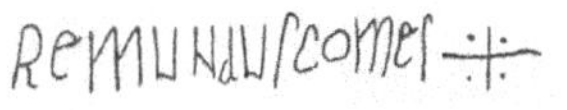

Reymundu[comef —+—

Figure 13.27: The signature of Count Ramon Berenguer II 361,924.[694]

361,925: **Maud, Countess of Barcelona**, abt 1059–abt 1112.

361,926: **Gilbert I, Count of Gévaudan**, d. 1108. Participated in the Crusades.

361,927: **Gerberga, Countess of Provence**, d. 1115.

361,928: **Henry of Burgundy**, abt 1035–abt 1074.

361,930: 361,922

361,931: **Jimena Muñoz**

361,956: **Theodoric I, Count of Montbéliard**, abt 1045–2 Jan 1105.

361,957: **Ermentrude of Burgundy, Countess of Montbéliard**, 1055–1105.

361,958: **Gérard I, Count of Vaudémont**

361,959: **Heilwig von Egisheim**

361,960: **Renaud I, Count of Clermont**, 1042–1088.

361,962: **Hilduin IV, Count of Montdidier**, d. 1063. May have served as an ambassador to Rome.

361,963: **Alice de Roucy**

361,968: 187,206

361,969: 187,207

372,904: **William VI, Lord of Montpellier**, d. 1161.

372,905: **Sibylla**

372,906: **Hugh II, Duke of Burgundy**, 1084–1143.

372,907: **Felicia-Matilda of Mayenne, Duchess of Burgundy**

372,912: **Béla II, King of Hungary and Croatia**, abt 1109–13 Feb 1141. His uncle, King Coloman, had him blinded as a child after Béla's father repeatedly schemed to take the crown of Hungary from Coloman.

372,913: **Helena of Serbia, Queen of Hungary**. Reportedly pushed successfully for the execution of dozens of Hungarian leaders who had played a role in blinding Béla II. Later ruled as regent after her husband's death.

372,914: **Mstislav I, Grand Prince of Kiev**, 1 Jun 1076–14 Apr 1132.

372,915: **Ljubava Saviditsch, Grand Princess of Kiev**

372,916: **Hervé of Donzy**

372,918: **Bohemond II, Prince of Antioch**, abt 1108–1130. Killed in battle against Turkish forces.

372,919: **Alice, Princess of Jerusalem**, b. abt 1110.

372,920: 131,980

372,921: 131,981

372,922: **Renaud de Courtenay**, d. 27 Sep 1194. Fought in the Second Crusade.

372,923: **Elizabeth du Donjon**

372,992: **Walter I, Lord of Avesnes**

372,993: **Ada of Tournai, Lady of Avesnes**

373,008: **Dirk VI, Count of Holland**, abt 1114–5 Aug 1157.

373,009: **Sophia of Rheineck, Countess of Holland**, abt 1120–26 Sep 1176. Died and was buried in Jerusalem.

373,010: **Henry of Scotland, Earl of Huntingdon**, 1114–12 Jun 1152.

373,011: **Ada de Warenne**, abt 1120–1178.

373,012: **Henry I, Count of Guelders**, 1117–1182.

373,013: **Agnes of Arnstein**

373,014: **Otto I the Redhead, Duke of Bavaria**, 1117–11 Jul 1183.

373,015: **Agnes of Loon, Duchess of Bavaria**, 1150–1191.

373,032: 264,054

373,033: 264,055

373,034: 132,024

373,035: 132,025

373,040: 180,978

373,041: 180,979

373,042: 132,002

373,043: 132,003

373,048: 131,980

373,049: 131,981

373,106: **Berthold, Duke of Merania**, abt 1159–12 Aug 1204. A standard-bearer in the Third Crusade.

373,107: **Agnes of Rochlitz, Duchess of Merania**, d. 1195.

373,108: **Manuel Laskaris**

373,109: **Ioanna Karatzaina**

373,110: **Alexios III Angelos, Emperor of the Byzantine Empire**, abt 1153–1211. Came to power by blinding his brother Isaac *66,014*.

373,111: **Euphrosyne Doukaina Kamatera, Empress of the Byzantine Empire**, abt 1155–1211.

374,128: **Odo II, Duke of Burgundy**, 1118–1162.

374,129: 93,251

374,130: 186,516

374,131: 186,517

374,272: **Alan fitz Flaad**, b. abt 1078.

374,364: **Guigues IV, Count of Albon**, d. 28 Jun 1142. Died of wounds received in battle.

374,365: **Margaret of Macon**

374,408: **William de Warenne, 1st Earl of Surrey**, d. 1088. One of the documented companions of William the Conqueror.

374,409: **Gundred, Countess of Surrey**, d. 27 May 1085.

374,412: **Robert of Belleme, 3rd Earl of Shrewsbury**, b. abt 1056. Was at one point imprisoned as part of an elaborate power play against King William II of England. Later put down a peasant rebellion in Rouen by throwing them into dungeons en masse.[695]

374,413: **Agnes, Countess of Ponthieu**, b. abt 1080.

374,414: **Odo I, Duke of Burgundy**, 1060–1102. Fought in the Crusade of 1101.

374,415: **Sibylla, Duchess of Burgundy**, 1065–1103.

374,800: **Ranulph de Mortimer**, d. abt 1104.

374,804: **Ranulf de Briquessart**, d. abt 1089. One of the most powerful landholders in the Bessin region of Normandy.

374,805: **Margaret Goz**

374,806: **Robert de Rumily**

374,832: **Roger de Beaumont**, abt 1015–29 Nov 1094. A close advisor of William the Conqueror; known as "The Bearded," as his full beard was unusual for Norman culture of the time. Is believed to be the bearded figure at a feast depicted in the Bayeux Tapestry, a 230-foot embroidery depicting the Norman Conquest.

374,833: **Adeline of Meulan**, d. 1081.

374,834: **Geoffrey II, Count of Perche**, d. 1100.

374,835: **Beatrix de Ramerupt**

Generation 32

525,408: **Robert I de Ferrers, 1ˢᵗ Earl of Derby**, d. 1139.

525,409: **Hawise**

525,410: **William Peverell**, d. 1155.

525,411: **Oddona**

527,392: **Roger d'Aubigny**

527,393: **Amice**

527,394: 187,440

527,395: 187,441

527,396: **Henry II, Count of Louvain**, d. abt 1071.

527,398: **Otto II, Count of Chiny**, b. abt 1065. Ruled a county in what is now Belgium.

527,399: **Adelaide of Namur**, 1068–abt 1124.

527,416: **Simon I de Montfort**, abt 1025–1087.

527,417: **Agnes d'Evreux**, b. abt 1030.

527,488: **Richard Fitz Gilbert, 1ˢᵗ Lord of Clare**, d. abt 1090. Prominently involved in the Norman invasion of 1066, was granted dozens of titles and land grants. The eighth richest landowner in England at the time, according to the Domesday Book.

527,489: **Rohese Giffard**, d. aft 1113.

527,490: **Hugh, Count of Clermont**, d. abt 1101.

527,491: **Margaret de Roucy**

527,508: **Hamo Dapifer, Sheriff of Kent**, d. abt 1100. One of five known royal stewards during the reign of King William II of England, alongside Roger Bigod *527,394*.

527,540: 374,832

527,541: 374,833

527,542: **Hugh Magnus, Count of Vermandois**, 1057– 18 Oct 1101. One of the leaders of the First Crusade, but was not at the siege of Jerusalem—a departure that almost got him excommunicated. Later died of wounds received in the minor Crusade of 1101.

527,543: Adelaide, Countess of Vermandois, d. abt 1124. The last member of the Carolingian dynasty.

527,616: William de Braose, 1ˢᵗ Lord of Bramber, d. abt 1096. Granted lands by William the Conqueror after the Norman Invasion.

527,618: Juhel de Totnes, d. abt 1130. A leader of Breton (French) forces in the wake of the Norman Invasion, granted lands by William the Conqueror.

527,620: Walter of Gloucester, d. abt 1129. Served as a constable under King Henry I of England *131,970*.

527,621: Bertha

527,622: Bernard de Neufmarché, abt 1050–abt 1125. Participated in the Rebellion of 1088, and played a role in the Norman conquest of Wales in the latter half of the 11ᵗʰ century.

527,623: Nest ferch Osbern

527,648: Cynan ab Iago, King of Gwynedd, abt 1014–1063. His father, then the king, died when Cynan was about 15; if he held the throne himself, it was only for a brief time before power was seized by the Saxons.

527,649: Ragnhilda of Dublin

527,650: Owain ab Edwin, Lord of Tegingl, d. abt 1105. May have ruled for a short period as king of Gwynedd.

527,656: Bleddyn ap Cynfyn, King of Powys, d. 1073. Killed by King Rhys ab Owain of Dyfed.

527,872: Geoffrey II, Count of Gatinais, d. abt 1046.

527,873: Ermengarde of Anjou, Duchess of Burgundy, d. abt 1076.

527,874: 527,416

527,875: 527,417

527,876: Jean de la Fleche

527,877: **Paula of Maine**

527,878: **Gervais II, Lord of Chateau-du-Loir**, d. abt 1095.

527,880: **Robert I, Duke of Normandy**, 22 Jun 1000–Jul 1035. Died returning from a pilgrimage to Jerusalem.

527,881: **Herleva**, d. abt 1050.

527,882: **Baldwin V, Count of Flanders**, 19 Aug 1012–1 Sep 1067. Ruled France as regent for seven years with Anne of Kiev *1,055,085* while his nephew, King Philip I, was too young to rule.

527,883: **Saint Adela of France, Countess of Flanders**, abt 1009–8 Jan 1070. Became a nun after the death of her husband, was later sainted by the Roman Catholic Church.

527,884: **Duncan I, King of Alba**, abt 1001–14 Aug 1040. The basis for the character of the same name in Shakespeare's *Macbeth*, in which he is murdered by the title character. In real life, he was killed in battle against the historical Macbeth.

527,885: **Suthen**

527,886: **Edward the Exile**, 1016–1057. The Danish conquerors of England sent the infant Edward to King Olof Skötkonung of Sweden *4,220,342*, presumably to be murdered. He was spared, however, and was called back to England in the late 1050s as the strongest heir to the English throne. Instead, he died immediately after arriving.

527,887: **Agatha**

527,888: **William the Great, Duke of Aquitaine**, abt 969–31 Jan 1030. Declined the crown of Italy in 1024.

527,889: **Agnes of Burgundy, Duchess of Aquitaine**, d. 10 Nov 1068.

527,890: **Robert I, Duke of Burgundy**, 1011–18 Mar 1076. After repudiating his first wife, Helie *187,207*, he killed her brother and her father, Lord Dalmace I *1,447,694*.

527,891: 527,873

527,892: **Pons, Count of Toulouse**, 991–1060.

527,893: **Almodis de la Marche**, abt 1020–16 Oct 1071. Kidnapped in about 1053 and was married to her captor.

527,894: **Robert, Count of Mortain**, abt 1031–1090. One of the proven companions of William the Conqueror *263,940* at the Battle of Hastings.

527,895: **Matilda de Montgomery**

527,896: **Hugues I de Chatellerault**

527,897: **Gerberge**

527,898: **Aimery IV, Viscount of Thouars**, abt 1024– abt 1094. One of the proven companions of William the Conqueror *263,940*.

527,899: **Aremgarde de Mauleon**, d. abt 1070.

527,900: **Archimbaud Borel de Bueil**

527,901: **Agnes de l'Isle Bouchard**

527,904: **Fulk, Count of Angouleme**, d. abt 1089.

527,908: **Roger de Montgomerie, 1ˢᵗ Earl of Shrewsbury**, d. 1094. One of the chief advisors to William the Conqueror, including a presence at the Council of Lillebonne before the Invasion of 1066.

527,909: **Mabel de Belleme, Countess of Shrewsbury**, d. 2 Dec 1079. Accrued a lifelong reputation of cruelty and pettiness; was eventually beheaded by a noble whose lands she had taken.

527,910: **Aldebert II, Count of La Marche**

527,920: **Henry I, King of the Franks**, 4 May 1008– 4 Aug 1060.

527,921: **Anna Yaroslavna of Kiev, Queen of the Franks**, d. 1075. Could read and write, a rarity among women at the time.

527,922: **Floris I, Count of Holland**, d. 28 Jun 1061. Ambushed during a minor war and died in battle.

527,923: **Gertrude Billung, Countess of Holland**, abt 1030–4 Aug 1113.

527,924: **Amadeus II, Count of Savoy**, abt 1050–26 Jan 1080.

527,926: 361,920

527,927: 361,921

527,940: **Sancho Ramírez, King of Aragon**, abt 1042–4 Jun 1094. Lost a conflict early in his reign involving two of his cousins, both also named "Sancho"; the conflict was known as the "War of the Three Sanchos."

527,941: **Felicia of Roucy, Queen of Aragon**, abt 1060–3 May 1123.

527,942: 131,972

527,943: 131,973

527,948: **Bolesław III Wrymouth, High Duke of Poland**, 20 Aug 1086–28 Oct 1138.

527,949: **Zbyslava of Kiev, Duchess of Poland**, d. abt 1114.

527,950: **Saint Leopold III, Margrave of Austria**, 1073–15 Nov 1136. Founded Klosterneuburg Monastery, where he is buried and his skull is on display wearing a crown.

527,951: **Agnes of Germany, Duchess of Swabia**, abt 1073–24 Sep 1143.

527,960: **William III, Count of Toulouse**, abt 970–1037.

527,961: **Emma of Provence, Countess of Toulouse**

527,962: **Arnould de Flotte**

527,963: **Adelaide de Comps**

527,964: **Bernard Ato IV, Viscount of Nimes**, d. 1129.

527,965: **Cecilia of Provence**

527,972: **Guigues II, Count of Albon**

527,973: **Petronel of Turin**

527,986: **Luís of Faucigny**

528,008: **Theobald III, Count of Blois**, 1012–1089.

528,009: **Gersende of Maine**

528,010: 263,940

528,011: 263,941

528,012: **Engelbert I, Count of Sponheim**, d. 1096.

528,013: **Hedwig**

528,016: **Baldwin II of Mons, Count of Hainaut**, b. abt 1056. Fought in the First Crusade; presumed dead after he disappeared during a battle in Anatolia.

528,017: **Ida, Countess of Hainaut**, d. 1139. Led an unsuccessful search for her husband after his disappearance.

528,018: **Gerard I, Count of Guelders**, abt 1060–8 Mar 1129.

528,020: **Albert III, Count of Namur**, abt 1027–29 Jul 1102.

528,021: **Ida of Saxony, Countess of Namur**

528,022: **Conrad I, Count of Luxembourg**, abt 1040–8 Aug 1086. Died returning from a pilgrimage to Jerusalem.

528,023: **Clementia of Aquitaine, Countess of Luxembourg**, 1060–4 Jan 1142.

528,024: **Gerard, Duke of Lorraine**, abt 1030–14 Apr 1070.

528,025: **Hedwige of Namur, Duchess of Lorraine**

528,026: **Robert I, Count of Flanders**, abt 1035–1093.

528,027: **Gertrude of Saxony, Countess of Flanders**, abt 1030–4 Aug 1113. Ruled Holland as regent after her husband's death.

Figure 13.28: The signature of El Cid, Prince Rodrigo Díaz 528,042. It reads, "ego ruderico," or "I, Rodrigo" in Latin.[696]

528,040: **Sancho Garcés, Lord of Uncastillo**, abt 1038–6 Jan 1083. Died in battle alongside his brother, Ramiro.

528,041: **Constanza**

528,042: **Rodrigo Díaz de Vivar, Prince of Valencia**, abt 1040–10 Jun 1099. The Castilian military leader known as "El Cid." Buried at the Cathedral of Saint Mary of Burgos in Spain.

528,043: **Jimena Díaz**

528,044: **Richer of L'Aigle**

528,045: **Judith d'Avranches**

528,046: 374,834

528,047: 374,835

528,070: **Otto II, Count of Wolfratshausen**

528,071: **Justizia**

528,072: **Henry I, Duke of Lower Lorraine**, d. abt 1119.

528,073: **Adelaide of Pottenstein, Duchess of Lower Lorraine**

528,074: 528,018

528,092: **Eustace II, Count of Boulogne**, abt 1015–abt 1087. One of the proven companions of William the Conqueror at the Battle of Hastings.

528,093: **Ida of Lorraine, Countess of Boulogne**, abt 1040–13 Apr 1113.

528,094: 263,942

528,095: 263,943

528,096: **Frederick von Büfren**

528,097: **Hildegard of Egisheim-Dagsburg**

528,098: 1,055,902

528,099: 1,055,903

528,100: **Welf I, Duke of Bavaria**, d. 6 Nov 1101. Fought in the Crusade of 1101; died on his way home.

528,101: **Judith of Flanders, Duchess of Bavaria**, d. 5 Mar 1095.

528,102: **Magnus, Duke of Saxony**, abt 1045–23 Aug 1106. The last member of the House of Billung.

528,103: **Sophia of Hungary, Duchess of Saxony**, abt 1050–18 Jun 1095.

528,104: 361,920

528,105: 361,921

528,106: 528,024

528,107: 528,025

528,108: 264,012

528,109: **Gertrude of Flanders, Duchess of Lorraine**, abt 1070–1117.

528,110: **Henry III, Count of Louvain**, d. abt 1095.

528,111: 528,109

528,112: **Manolis Angelos.** A man of lowly birth from the Turkish city of Alasehir, known in the Middle Ages as Philadelphia.

Figure 13.29: A portrait of Duke Magnus 528,102 from the late 1500s.[697]

528,114: **Alexios I Komnenos, Emperor of the Byzantine Empire**, d. 15 Aug 1118.

528,115: **Irene Doukaina, Empress of the Byzantine Empire**, abt 1066–19 Feb 1138.

539,144: **Swein**

539,172: **Laudri de Senlis**

539,173: **Ermengarde**

539,174: **Waltheof, Earl of Northumbria**, 1050–31 May 1086. Was alleged to have participated in the Revolt of the Earls against King William I of England *263,940*; he was beheaded near Winchester and eventually buried in a church. Several years later, his coffin was moved, and it was reportedly discovered that his severed head had become reattached.

539,175: **Judith of Lens**

539,584: **Walter FitzOther, Constable of Windsor Castle**, d. abt 1116

539,586: **Rhys ap Twedwr, King of Deheubarth**, d. 1093. Killed by Normans in Brycheiniog.

539,587: **Gwladys ferch Rhiwallon**

723,840: **Reginald I, Count of Burgundy**, d. abt 1057.

723,841: **Alice of Normandy, Countess of Burgundy**, abt 1002–1038.

723,844: **Ferdinand I, Emperor of All Spain**, abt 1015–24 Dec 1065.

723,845: **Sancha, Empress of All Spain**, d. 27 Nov 1067. Her husband became king after killing her brother, Bermudo III, in battle.

723,846: 527,890

723,847: **Helie de Semur-en-Brionnais**

723,848: **Ramon Berenguer I, Count of Barcelona**, 1023–1076.

Figure 13.30: The signature of Count Ramon Berenguer I 723,848.[698]

723,849: 527,893

723,850: **Robert Guiscard, Duke of Sicily**, abt 1015–17 Jul 1085. A warrior who appears as a character in Dante's *Divine Comedy*.

723,851: **Sikelgaita, Duchess of Sicily**, 1040–16 Apr 1090. Commanded troops in battle, wearing a suit of armor.

723,854: **Geoffrey I, Count of Provence**, d. abt 1063.

723,855: **Etiennette**

723,856: 527,890

723,857: 723,847

723,912: **Louis, Count of Montbéliard**

723,913: **Sophie, Countess of Bar**, d. 1093.

723,914: 361,920

723,915: 361,921

723,924: **Hilduin III, Count of Montdidier**

723,926: **Ebles I, Count of Roucy**, d. 11 May 1033.

723,927: **Beatrix of Hainaut**

745,808: **William V, Lord of Montpellier**, d. 1121. Fought in the First Crusade.

745,809: **Ermensenda**

745,812: 374,414

745,813: 374,415

745,814: **Gauthier, Count of Mayenne**

745,815: **Adelina de Presles**

745,824: **Álmos, Duke of Hungary**, d. abt 1129. Blinded by his brother after conspiring to seize the throne from him.

745,825: **Predslava of Kiev**, b. abt 1090.

745,826: **Uros I, Grand Prince of Serbia**

745,827: **Anna Diogenissa, Grand Princess of Serbia**, abt 1074–1145.

745,828: **Vladimir II Monomakh, Grand Prince of Kievan Rus'**, 1053–19 May 1125. Ruled over the tribal federation in eastern Europe that would eventually become Belarus, Ukraine, and parts of Russia.

745,829: **Gytha of Wessex**, d. abt 1107.

745,836: **Bohemond I, Prince of Antioch**, abt 1054–3 Mar 1111. A leader of the First Crusade.

745,837: **Constance of France, Princess of Antioch**, 1078–14 Sep 1125.

745,838: **Baldwin II, King of Jerusalem**, d. 21 Aug 1131. Fought in the First Crusade.

745,839: **Morphia of Melitene**, d. abt 1127.

745,844: **Milo de Courtenay**

746,016: **Floris II, Count of Holland**, abt 1085–2 Mar 1121.

746,017: **Petronilla of Lorraine, Countess of Holland**, abt 1082–1144. Ruled as regent after the death of Floris II.

746,018: **Otto I, Count of Salm**, abt 1080–1150. Built Reineck Castle, still standing today.

746,019: **Gertrude of Nordheim**

746,020: **David I, King of the Scots**, abt 1084–24 May 1153. Founded or endowed many monasteries, several of which are still extant, albeit in ruins.

746,021: 269,587

746,022: 187,204

746,023: 187,205

746,024: **Gerard II, Count of Guelders**, d. 24 Oct 1131.

746,025: **Ermengarde, Countess of Zutphen**, d. 1138.

746,026: **Louis III of Arnstein**

746,028: **Otto IV, Count of Scheyern**, abt 1083–4 Aug 1156.

746,029: **Heilika of Pettendorf-Ligenfeld**

746,030: **Louis I, Count of Loon**, d. 11 Aug 1171.

746,031: **Agnes of Metz**

746,212: **Berthold I, Margrave of Istria**, abt 1110–14 Dec 1188.

746,213: **Hedwig of Wittelsbach**

746,214: **Dedi III, Margrave of Lusatia**, abt 1130–16 Aug 1190.

746,215: **Matilda of Heinsberg**

746,220: 132,028

746,221: 132,029

746,222: **Andronikos Kamateros**, b. abt 1110.

748,256: 372,906

748,257: 372,907

748,728: 263,986

748,729: 263,987

748,816: **Ranulf I de Warenne**

748,817: **Beatrice**

748,824: 527,908

748,825: 527,909

748,826: **Guy I, Count of Ponthieu**, d. 13 Oct 1100.
Appears multiple times in the Bayeux Tapestry because
of his encounters with King Harold Godwinson of England
1,491,658.

748,828: 361,928

748,830: 361,920

748,831: 361,921

749,600: **Roger I of Mortemer**

749,601: **Hadewisa**

749,610: **Richard Goz**

749,664: **Humphrey de Vieilles**, d. abt 1050. A prominent
Norman nobleman.

749,665: **Albreda de la Haye Auberie**

749,666: **Waleran III, Count of Meulan**

749,668: **Rotrou I, Viscount of Chateaudun**, d. 1080.

749,669: **Adelise de Belleme**

749,670: 361,962

749,671: 361,963

Generation 33

1,050,816: **Henry de Ferrers**, d. abt 1100. Born in Normandy, France; believed to have fought at the Battle of
Hastings in 1066 under William the Conqueror, who subse-
quently awarded him huge swaths of land in England after
war's end. Lived for at least some time in Tutbury Castle,
in Staffordshire, England.

1,050,820 **William Peverell**, abt 1040–abt 1115. A soldier
likely involved in the Norman Conquest of England.

1,054,792: **Lambert II, Count of Louvain**, d. 19 Jun 1054.

1,054,793: **Oda of Verdun**

1,054,796: **Arnold I, Count of Chiny**, d. 16 Apr 1106.

1,054,797: **Adelaide of Montdidier**

1,054,798: 528,020

1,054,799: 528,021

1,054,832: **Amaury I, Lord of Montfort**

1,054,833: **Bertrade**

1,054,834: **Richard, Count of Evreux**, d. 1067.

1,054,835: **Godechildis**

1,054,976: **Gilbert de Brionne, 2nd Count of Eu**, d. abt 1040. A powerful landowner in Normandy and one of the guardians of a young Duke William II, who had been orphaned. (Duke William II became King William I, the Conqueror.)

1,054,978: **Walter Giffard, Lord of Longueville**. A powerful Norman landowner and one of the 15 proven companions of William the Conqueror *263,940* in the Norman invasion. Was also present at the Council of Lillebonne, where the invasion was decided upon.

1,054,979: **Ermengarde**

1,054,980: **Renaud I, Count of Clermont**

1,054,982: 361,962

1,054,983: 361,963

1,055,016: **Hamon Dentatus, Lord of Torigni-sur-Vire**, d. abt 1047.

1,055,084: 527,920

1,055,085: 527,921

1,055,086: **Herbert IV, Count of Vermandois**, d. abt 1080.

1,055,087: **Adele of Valois**

1,055,240: **Roger de Pitres**. Served as sheriff of Gloucester under William the Conqueror.

1,055,246: **Osbern FitzRichard**

1,055,247: **Nest ferch Grufydd**

1,055,296: **Iago ab Idwal ap Meurig, Prince of Gwynedd**, d. 1039. Believed to have been killed by his own soldiers.

1,055,298: **Olaf Sigtryggsson**, d. 1034. Reportedly killed by Anglo-Saxon soldiers during a pilgrimage to Rome.

1,055,300: **Edwin, Lord of Tegeingl**, d. 1073.

1,055,301: **Iwerydd**

1,055,312: **Cynfyn ap Gwerystan**, b. abt 990.

1,055,313: **Angharad**

1,055,744: **Hugues du Perche**

1,055,745: **Beatrice de Macon**

1,055,746: **Fulk the Black, Count of Anjou**, abt 970–1040. One of the first prolific castle-builders.

1,055,747: **Hildegarde of Sundgau**

1,055,754: **Herbert I, Count of Maine**, d. 13 Apr 1035. At one point captured by Fulk the Black *1,055,746* and held captive for two years.

1,055,760: **Richard II, Duke of Normandy**, 23 Aug 963–28 Aug 1026.

1,055,761: **Judith of Brittany, Duchess of Normandy**, 982–28 Aug 1017. The sarcophagus of a woman believed to be Judith was discovered in the foundation of a church in northern France in the 1800s.

1,055,764: **Baldwin IV, Count of Flanders**, abt 980–30 May 1035.

1,055,766: **Robert II of France, King of the Franks**, 27 Mar 972–20 Jul 1031. Revived the Roman custom of burning heretics at the stake. Known as "Robert the Pious."

1,055,767: **Constance of Arles, Queen of the Franks**, abt 986–28 Jul 1032. After her husband died, she engaged in military battles against troops commanded by her sons.

1,055,768: **Crínán of Dunkeld**, d. abt 1045. Killed in battle against the troops of Macbeth.

1,055,769: **Bethóc**

1,055,772: **Edmund Ironside, King of England**, d. 30 Nov 1016. Is believed to have been buried at Glastonbury Abbey, which was looted and destroyed during King Henry VIII's Dissolution of the Monasteries; his remains, along with countless others, were lost.

1,055,776: **William IV, Duke of Aquitaine**, 937–3 Feb 994. Refused to recognize the authority of King Hugh Capet *2,111,532* (who may have been his brother-in-law) and went to war against him, ultimately to no effect. Retired to a monastery.

1,055,777: **Emma of Blois, Duchess of Aquitaine**, abt 950–27 Dec 1003. Ruled Aquitaine as regent until her son was old enough to assume the throne.

1,055,778: **Otto-William, Count of Burgundy**, abt 962–21 Sep 1026.

1,055,779: **Ermentrude de Roucy, Countess of Burgundy**

1,055,780: 1,055,766

1,055,781: 1,055,767

1,055,784: 527,960

1,055,785: 527,961

1,055,786: **Bernard I, Count of Marche**

1,055,787: **Amélie**

1,055,788: **Herluin de Conteville**, 1001–1066. Died in the burning of Mantes, in north-central France.

1,055,790: 527,908

1,055,791: 527,909

1,055,796: **Geoffrey II of Thouars**

1,055,797: **Agnes de Blois**

1,055,798: **Geoffrey de Mauleon**

1,055,808: **Geoffrey, Count of Angouleme**, d. 1048.

1,055,809: **Petronille**

1,055,818: **William I Talvas**, d. abt 1052. Allegedly invited a rival to his second wedding, then had the man mutilated and blinded when he attended.

1,055,819: **Hildeburg**

1,055,840: 1,055,766

1,055,841: 1,055,767

1,055,842: **Yaroslav the Wise, Grand Prince of Kiev**, d. 20 Feb 1054. One of the more successful rulers of Kiev and Novgorod. Likely hobbled by an arrow wound, he appears in Norse sagas as "Jarisleif the Lame." His body was exhumed in 1939 for examination and reportedly re-interred in 1964, but in 2009 when his sarcophagus was opened, his body was missing.

1,055,843: **Irene Olofsdotter, Grand Princess of Kiev**, abt 1001–10 Feb 1050. Her Swedish birth name was "Ingegerd," changed in favor of the Greek "Irene" when she married Yaroslav I.

1,055,844: **Dirk III, Count of Holland**, abt 989–27 May 1039.

Figure 13.31: A painting of Count Otto I 1,055,848 by an unknown artist.[699]

1,055,845: **Othelindis**

1,055,846: **Bernard II, Duke of Saxony**, d. 29 Jun 1059.

1,055,847: **Eilika of Schweinfurt**, b. abt 1005.

1,055,848: **Otto I, Count of Savoy**, abt 1023–abt 1060.

Figure 13.32: A representation of Duke Bernard II 1,055,846, drawn about 500 years after his death.[700]

1,055,849: **Adelaide of Susa, Marchioness of Turin**, d. 19 Dec 1091. When the city of Asti rebelled against her rule, she had it recaptured and burned.

1,055,873: 527,893

1,055,880: **Ramiro I, King of Aragon**, d. 8 May 1063.

1,055,881: **Ermesinda of Bigorre, Queen of Aragon**, 1015–1 Dec 1049. Birth name was "Gerberga."

1,055,882: 361,962

1,055,883: 361,963

1,055,894: 527,890

1,055,895: 723,847

1,055,896: **Władysław I Herman, Duke of Poland**, abt 1044–4 Jun 1102. Openly received a large Jewish population at the end of the 11th century.

1,055,897: **Judith of Bohemia, Duchess of Poland**, abt 1058–25 Dec 1086.

1,055,898: **Sviatopolk II, Grand Prince of Kiev**, 1050–16 Apr 1113.

1,055,900: **Leopold II, Margrave of Austria**, 1050–12 Oct 1095.

1,055,901: **Ida of Austria**, abt 1055–1101. Commanded an army in the Crusade of 1101, where she is believed to have died.

1,055,902: **Henry IV, Holy Roman Emperor**, 11 Nov 1050–7 Aug 1106. His second wife, Adelaide, accused him of joining a Satanist sect and attempting a black mass in his palace.

1,055,903: **Bertha of Savoy, Holy Roman Empress**, 21 Sep 1051–27 Dec 1087.

1,055,922: **Rotbold II, Count of Provence**, d. abt 1015.

1,055,923: **Ermengarde de Maurienne**

1,055,928: **Raymond Bernard, Viscount of Nimes**

1,055,929: **Ermengarde of Carcassonne**

1,055,930: **Bertrand II, Count of Provence**, d. 1093.

1,055,931: **Matilda**

1,056,016: **Odo II, Count of Blois**, 983–15 Nov 1037.

1,056,017: **Ermengarde of Auvergne**

1,056,018: 1,055,754

1,056,024: **Siegfried I, Count of Sponheim**, abt 1010–
7 Feb 1065.

1,056,025: **Richgard, Countess of Lavant Valley**

1,056,032: **Baldwin VI, Count of Hainaut**, abt 1030–
17 Jul 1070.

1,056,033: **Richilde, Countess of Hainaut**, abt 1018–
15 Mar 1086.

1,056,034: **Henry II, Count of Louvain**, d. abt 1078.

1,056,035: **Adela of Thuringa**

1,056,036: **Theodoric of Wassenberg**

1,056,040: **Albert II, Count of Namur**, d. 1067.

1,056,041: **Regelinde**, d. 1067.

1,056,042: 1,055,846

1,056,043: 1,055,847

1,056,044: **Giselbert, Count of Luxembourg**, abt 1007–
14 Aug 1059.

1,056,048: **Gerard de Bouzonville**

1,056,049: **Gisela**

1,056,050: 1,056,040

1,056,051: 1,056,041

1,056,052: 527,882

1,056,053: 527,883

1,056,054: 1,055,846

1,056,055: 1,055,847

1,056,080: **García Sánchez III, King of Navarre**, 1016–
1 Sep 1054.

1,056,084: **Diego Laínez**

1,056,142: **Berthold I, Count of Diessen**

1,056,144: **Waleran I, Count of Limburg**, d. 1082.

1,056,145: **Jutta**

1,056,146: **Botho of Pottenstein**

1,056,147: **Judith**

1,056,184: **Eustace I, Count of Boulogne**, d. 1049.

1,056,185: **Matilda of Louvain**

1,056,186: **Godfrey III, Duke of Lower Lorraine**, abt 997–24 Dec 1069.

1,056,187: **Doda**

1,056,200: **Albert Azzo II, Margrave of Milan**, d. 20 Aug 1097.

1,056,201: **Kunigunde of Altdorf**, abt 1020–31 Aug 1054.

1,056,202: 1,055,764

1,056,203: **Eleanor of Normandy, Countess of Flanders**, 1010–1071.

1,056,204: **Ordulf, Duke of Saxony**, abt 1022–28 Mar 1072.

1,056,205: **Wulfhild, Princess of Norway**, 1020–24 May 1071.

1,056,206: **Béla I, King of Hungary**, d. 11 Sep 1063. Killed when his throne collapsed onto him.

1,056,207: **Adelaide of Poland, Queen of Hungary**

1,056,220: 527,396

1,056,228: **John Komnenos**, abt 1015–12 Jul 1067.

1,056,229: **Anna Dalassene**, abt 1030–abt 1102. Governed the Byzantine Empire during the military absences of her son.

1,056,230: **Andronikos Doukas**, d. 14 Oct 1077.

1,056,231: **Maria of Bulgaria**

1,078,288: **Robert FitzWimarc Sheriff of Essex**. One of four advisors present at the deathbed of King Edward the Confessor.

1,078,348: **Siward, Earl of Northumbria**. Waged a war against the Scots that may have deposed King Macbeth.

1,078,349: **Ælfflæd**

1,078,350: **Lambert II, Count of Lens**, d. 1054. Killed at the Battle of Lille.

1,078,351: **Adelaide of Normandy, Countess of Aumale**, b. abt 1030.

1,079,168: **Othere**

1,079,174: **Rhiwallon ap Cynfyn, King of Wales**, abt 1020–abt 1069. Killed at the Battle of Mechain.

1,447,680: 1,055,778

1,447,681: 1,055,779

1,447,682: 1,055,760

1,447,683: 1,055,761

1,447,688: **Sancho III, King of Pamplona**, abt 990–18 Oct 1035.

1,447,689: **Muniadona of Castile, Queen of Pamplona**, d. 1066.

1,447,690: **Alfonso V, King of León**, 994–7 Aug 1028.

1,447,691: **Elvira Menéndez, Queen of León**, abt 996–2 Dec 1022.

1,447,694: **Delmace I, Lord of Semur**, d. abt 1048.

1,447,696: **Berenguer Ramon I, Count of Barcelona**, 1005–26 May 1035.

1,447,697: **Sancha Sánchez**

1,447,700: **Tancred of Hauteville**, d. abt 1041

1,447,701: **Fressenda**

1,447,702: **Guaimar IV, Prince of Salerno**, abt 1013–1052. Assassinated by four of his brothers-in-law.

1,447,703: **Gemma**

1,447,708: **William II, Count of Provence**, abt 981–1018.

1,447,709: **Gerberga of Burgundy**

1,447,826: **Frederick II, Duke of Upper Lorraine**, abt 995–1026.

1,447,827: **Matilda of Swabia, Duchess of Upper Lorraine**, abt 989–abt 1032.

1,447,848: **Hilduin II, Count of Arcis-sur-Aube**

1,447,854: **Reginar IV, Count of Mons**, d. 1013.

1,447,855: **Hedwig of France, Countess of Mons**, b. abt 970.

1,491,616: **William IV, Lord of Montpellier**, d. 1068.

1,491,617: **Ermengarde**

1,491,618: **Peter, Count of Mauguio**

1,491,648: **Géza I, King of Hungary**, abt 1040–25 Apr 1077.

1,491,650: 1,055,898

1,491,652: **Marko, Prince of Rascia**

1,491,654: **Constantine Diogenes**, d. 1073. Killed in battle.

1,491,655: **Theodora Komnene**

1,491,656: **Vsevolod I, Grand Prince of Kiev**, 1030–13 Apr 1093.

1,491,657: **Anastasia of Byzantium**

1,491,658: **Harold Godwinson, King of England**, abt 1022–14 Oct 1066. The last Anglo-Saxon king; killed by the troops of the invading William the Conqueror *263,940* at the Battle of Hastings.

1,491,659: **Edith Swanneck, Queen of England**, abt 1025–abt 1086.

1,491,672: 723,850

1,491,673: **Alberada of Buonalberto**

1,491,674: 263,960

1,491,675: 263,961

1,491,676: **Hugh I, Count of Rethel**, 1040–1118.

1,491,677: **Melisende of Crécy**

1,491,678: **Gabriel of Melitene**, d. abt 1103.

1,492,032: **Dirk V, Count of Frisia**, 1052–17 Jun 1091.

1,492,033: **Othelhilde**

1,492,034: 264,012

1,492,035: **Hedwige of Formbach**

1,492,036: **Hermann, Count of Salm**, abt 1035–28 Sep 1088. Elected German anti-king in 1081; died in battle.

1,492,037: **Sophia of Formbach**

1,492,038: **Henry, Margrave of Frisia**, abt 1055-1101.

1,492,039: **Gertrude of Brunswick, Margravine of Meissen**, abt 1060–9 Dec 1117.

1,492,040: 263,942

1,492,041: 263,943

1,492,048: **Gerard I, Count of Guelders**, abt 1060–8 Mar 1129.

1,492,050: **Otto II, Count of Zutphen**

1,492,051: **Judith of Arnstein**

1,492,056: **Otto III, Count of Scheyern**

1,492,058: **Frederick III of Pettendorf**

1,492,059: **Heilika of Swabia**

1,492,060: **Arnold II, Count of Looz**, d. 1146.

1,492,061: **Aleide**

1,492,062: **Folmar V, Count of Metz**

1,492,063: **Matilda of Dagsburg**

1,492,424: **Berthold II, Count of Andechs**, d. 27 Jun 1151.

1,492,425: **Sophia of Istria**

1,492,426: 746,028

1,492,427: 746,029

1,492,428: **Conrad, Margrave of Meissen**, abt 1097–5 Feb 1157.

1,492,429: **Luitgard of Elchingen-Ravenstein**

1,492,444: **Gregory Kamateros**

1,492,445: **Irene Doukaina**

1,497,652: **Hugh II, Count of Ponthieu**

1,499,200: **Hugh, Bishop of Coutances**

1,499,332: **Hugh I, Count of Meulan**, d. 1081.

1,499,336: **Geoffrey II, Viscount of Chateaudun**, d. 1040. Killed after a riot broke out on his arrival in Chartres.

1,499,337: **Elizabeth de Corbon**

1,499,338: **Guérin de Domfront**

Generation 34

2,101,632: **Vauquelin de Ferrers**, d. abt 1040. A prominent baron in Normandy, France.

2,101,641: **Maud Ingelrica**

2,101,652: **Alfred**, of northwestern France.

2,109,584: **Lambert I, Count of Louvain**, d. 12 Sep 1015. Killed by Godfrey II, the brother of Frederick, Count of Verdun *4,219,186*.

2,109,585: **Gerberga of Lower Lorraine, Countess of Louvain**

2,109,586: **Gothelo I, Duke of Lorraine**, d. 19 Apr 1044.

2,109,592: **Louis II, Count of Chiny**, b. abt 1025.

2,109,593: **Sophie**, b. abt 1010. Her uncle, Gothelo *2,109,586*, killed her father-in-law, Louis I *4,219,184*.

2,109,594: 361,962

2,109,595: 361,963

2,109,664: **William de Hainaut**

2,109,668: **Robert II, Archbishop of Rouen**, d. 1037.

2,109,669: **Herleva**

2,109,952: **Geoffrey of Brionne, 1ˢᵗ Count of Eu**, d. abt 1010. Given the county of Eu and the castle at Brionne by his half-brother, Richard the Good, duke of Normandy.

2,109,956: **Osbern de Bolebec**

2,109,958: **Gerard Flaitel**. A Norman knight who accompanied Duke Robert I *527,880* on his pilgrimage to Jerusalem.

When the duke fell fatally ill on the return trip, he entrusted a relic (an alleged finger bone of Saint Stephen) to Gerard to be brought to a monastery. Gerard brought it to the Abbey of St. Wandrille, then stayed there as a monk.

2,110,172: **Otto, Count of Vermandois**, 29 Aug 979–25 May 1045.

2,110,173: **Pavia, Countess of Vermandois**, b. abt 990.

2,110,174: **Raoul III of Valois**

2,110,175: **Adele de Bar-sur-Aube**

2,110,492: **Richard Fitz Scrob**. Granted lands by King Edward the Confessor of England and built Richard's Castle, in western England.

2,110,494: **Gruffydd ap Llywelyn, King of Wales**, d. 1063. Reportedly killed by his own men while fleeing the troops of King Harold II of England.

2,110,495: **Ealdgyth, Queen of England**. Married King Harold II after her first husband, Gruffydd ap Llywelyn, was killed trying to flee him.

2,110,592: **Idwal**

2,110,596: **Sigtrygg Silkbeard, King of Dublin**, abt 970–1042.

2,110,597: **Sláine ingen Briain**

2,110,624: **Gwerystan ap Gwaithfoed**

2,110,625: **Nest ferch Cadell**

2,111,488: **Fulcuich, Count of Montagne**, died some time in the early 1000s.

2,111,489: **Melisende, Viscountess of Chateaudun**

2,111,492: **Geoffrey I, Count of Anjou**, d. 21 Jul 987.

2,111,493: **Adele of Meaux**, d. abt 982.

2,111,508: **Hugh III, Count of Maine**, d. abt 1015. Waged war against both King Hugh Capet *2,111,532* and King Robert II of France.

2,111,520: Richard the Fearless, Count of Rouen, 28 Aug 933–20 Nov 996.

2,111,521: Gunnora, Duchess of Normandy

2,111,522: Conan I of Rennes, Duke of Brittany, d. 27 Jun 992. Died at the Battle of Conquereuil fighting the troops of Fulk the Black *1,055,746*, his brother-in-law.

2,111,523: Ermengarde of Anjou, Countess of Rennes, d. abt 1024.

2,111,528: Arnulf II, Count of Flanders, abt 961–30 Mar 987.

2,111,532: Hugh Capet, King of the Franks, abt 941–24 Oct 996. The first to hold the title "King of the Franks," and the originator of the Capetian dynasty; brought Paris into the center of government and presided over what is considered the birth of modern France.

2,111,533: Adelaide of Aquitaine, Queen of the Franks, d. 1004.

2,111,534: William I, Count of Provence, b. abt 950.

2,111,538: Malcolm II, King of the Scots, abt 954–25 Nov 1034.

2,111,544: Æthelred II, King of England, d. 23 Apr 1016. After years of conflict with the Danish, he ordered the "St. Brice's Day massacre" of 1002, ordering all the Danish men in England to be killed. The Danes invaded western England the following year.

2,111,552: William III, Duke of Aquitaine, 915–3 Apr 963.

2,111,553: Gerloc, d. 14 Oct 962.

2,111,554: Theobald I, Count of Blois, abt 913–975. Battled against Richard the Fearless *2,111,520*.

2,111,555: Luitgarde of Vermandois, Duchess of Normandy, d. 9 Feb 978. Her first marriage, to William Longsword *4,223,040*, produced no descendants.

2,111,556: **Adalbert, King of Italy**, abt 936–abt 975.

2,111,557: **Gerberga of Macon**

2,111,558: **Renaud, Count of Roucy**, d. 10 May 967. A Viking invader; buried in the Abbey of Saint-Remi.

2,111,559: **Alberade of Lorraine**

2,111,594: **Odo I, Count of Blois**, abt 950–12 Mar 996.

2,111,595: **Bertha of Burgundy, Queen of the Franks**, 964–16 Jan 1010.

2,111,616: **William II, Count of Angouleme**, abt 952–1028.

2,111,636: **William of Belleme**, abt 965–1028. Led a brief and unsuccessful revolt against Duke Robert I of Normandy *527,880*.

2,111,637: **Mathilde of Condé-sur-Noireau**

2,111,684: **Saint Vladimir the Great, Grand Prince of Kiev**, abt 958–15 Jul 1015. Observed Slavic paganism until his baptism in the late 900s, after which the Kievan Rus' was Christianized.

2,111,686: **Olof Skótkonung, King of Sweden**, abt 980–abt 1022.

2,111,687: **Estrid of the Obotrites, Queen of Sweden**, d. 1035. Likely offered in marriage to King Olof after a treaty between his forces and the Polabian Obotrite tribes.

2,111,688: **Arnulf, Count of Holland**, d. 18 Sep 993.

2,111,689: **Lutgardis of Luxembourg, Countess of Holland**, b. abt 955.

2,111,692: **Bernard I, Duke of Saxony**, abt 950–9 Feb 1011.

2,111,693: **Hildegarde von Stade**, d. 3 Oct 1011.

2,111,694: **Henry of Schweinfurt**, d. 18 Sep 1017.

2,111,695: **Gerberga of Gleiberg**, b. abt 970.

2,111,696: **Humbert the White-Handed, Count of Savoy**

2,111,698: **Ulric Manfred II, Count of Turin**, d. abt 1034.

2,111,699: **Bertha of Milan, Countess of Turin**

2,111,760: 1,447,688

2,111,761: **Sancha de Aibar**

2,111,762: **Bernard-Roger, Count of Bigorre**, abt 962–abt 1034.

2,111,763: **Garsenda of Bigorre**

2,111,792: **Casimir I the Restorer, Duke of Poland**, 25 Jul 1016–28 Nov 1058. Reunited the disparate pieces of the Polish kingdom under one rule.

2,111,793: **Maria Dobroniega of Kiev, Duchess of Poland**, d. 1087.

2,111,794: **Vratislaus II, King of Bohemia**, d. 14 Jan 1092. The first king of Bohemia.

2,111,795: **Adelaide of Hungary, Queen of Bohemia**, abt 1040–2 Jan 1062.

2,111,796: **Iziaslav I, Grand Prince of Kiev**, 1024–3 Oct 1078.

2,111,800: **Ernest, Margrave of Austria**, 1027–10 Jun 1075.

2,111,801: **Adelaide of Eilenburg**, abt 1030–26 Jan 1071.

2,111,802: **Rapoto IV of Cham**

2,111,803: **Mathilde**

2,111,804: **Henry III, Holy Roman Emperor**, 27 Oct 1016–5 Oct 1056.

2,111,805: **Agnes of Poitou, Holy Roman Empress**, abt 1025–14 Dec 1077. Ruled the empire after her husband's death.

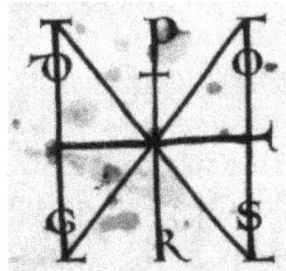

Figure 13.33: The signum manus of Emperor Henry III 2,111,804 from a 1049 charter.[701]

2,111,806: 1,055,848

2,111,807: 1,055,849

2,111,844: **Rotbold I, Count of Provence**, d. 1008.

2,111,845: **Emilde**

2,111,860: **Fulk Bertrand, Margrave of Provence**, d. 27 Apr 1051.

2,112,048: **Eberhard I, Count of Spanheim**

2,112,049: **Hedwig, Countess of Nellenburg**

2,112,064: 527,882

2,112,065: 527,883

2,112,068: 1,054,792

2,112,069: 1,054,793

2,112,080: **Albert I, Count of Namur**, c.abt 1011.

2,112,082: 2,109,586

2,112,088: **Frederick of Luxembourg, Count of Moselgau**, 965–6 Oct 1019.

2,112,160: 1,447,688

2,112,288: **Waleran, Count of Arlon**

2,112,290: **Frederick, Duke of Lower Lorraine**, abt 1003–18 May 1065.

2,112,294: **Otto III, Duke of Swabia**, d. 28 Sep 1057.

2,112,295: **Immilla of Turin, Duchess of Swabia**, abt 1020–1078.

2,112,368: **Baldwin II, Count of Boulogne**, d. abt 1027. Died in battle, though details are unknown.

2,112,369: **Adelina of Holland, Countess of Boulogne**

2,112,370: 2,109,584

2,112,371: 2,109,585

2,112,372: 2,109,586

2,112,400: **Albert Azzo I, Margrave of Milan**, d. 1029.

2,112,401: **Adelaide**

2,112,402: **Welf II, Count of Swabia**, d. 10 Mar 1030.

2,112,403: **Imiza of Luxembourg, Countess of Swabia,**
d. 1055.

2,112,406: 1,055,760

2,112,407: 1,055,761

2,112,408: 1,055,846

2,112,409: 1,055,847

2,112,410: **Saint Olaf II, King of Norway,** 995–29 Jul 1030. Posthumously titled *Rex Perpetuus Norvegiae,* "the eternal king of Norway." Represented by the axe still displayed in the country's coat of arms.

2,112,411: **Astrid Olofsdotter, Queen of Norway,** d. 1035.

2,112,412: **Vazul.** Possibly the duke of Nyitra; was at one point imprisoned and blinded there.

2,112,414: **Mieszko II Lambert, King of Poland,** abt 990–1034. Fled to Bohemia in 1031 to escape Yaroslav I *1,055,842,* where he was imprisoned by Oldrich *8,447,176.*

2,112,415: **Richeza of Lotharingia, Queen of Poland,** d. 21 Mar 1063.

2,112,456: **Manuel Erotikos Komnenos**

2,112,458: **Alexios Charon**

2,112,460: **John Doukas,** d. abt 1088.

2,112,461: **Irene Pegonitissa**

2,112,462: **Troian of Bulgaria**

2,156,698: **Ealdred II, Earl of Bernicia,** d. 1038. Killed a magnate named Thurbrand to avenge his father's death; he was later murdered by Thurbrand's son.

Figure 13.34: A rendering of the Norwegian national coat of arms. The axe was added in the 1400s to symbolize King Olaf II 2,112,410.[702]

2,156,700: 1,056,184

2,156,701: 1,056,185

2,156,702: 527,880

2,158,348: 1,055,312

2,158,349: 2,110,603

2,895,376: **García Sánchez II, King of Pamplona**, d. abt 1000.

2,895,377: **Jimena Fernández, Queen of Pamplona**

2,895,378: **Sancho García, Count of Castile**, d. 1017.

2,895,379: **Urraca Gómez**

2,895,380: **Bermudo II, King of León**, abt 953–999.

2,895,381: **Elvira of Castile, Queen of León**, abt 978–1017.

2,895,382: **Menendo González, Duke of Galicia**, d. 6 Oct 1008. Killed in unclear circumstances.

2,895,383: **Toda**

2,895,392: **Ramon Borrell, Count of Barcelona**, 972–1017.

2,895,393: **Ermesinde of Carcassonne, Countess of Barcelona**, abt 972–1 Mar 1058. Ruled as regent until her son was old enough to take the throne, then held power again when he died and her grandson was not yet of age.

2,895,394: 2,895,378

2,895,395: 2,895,379

2,895,404: **Guaimar III, Prince of Salerno**, abt 983–abt 1031.

2,895,405: **Gaitelgrima of Benevento**

2,895,416: 2,111,534

2,895,417: **Arsende de Comminges**

2,895,418: 1,055,778

2,895,419: 1,055,779

2,895,652: **Theodoric I, Duke of Upper Lorraine**, abt 965–abt 1027.

2,895,654: **Herman II, Duke of Swabia**, d. 4 May 1003.

2,895,655: **Gerberga of Burgundy, Duchess of Swabia**, abt 966–abt 1019.

2,895,696: **Hilduin I, Count of Montdidier**

2,895,708: **Reginar III, Count of Hainaut**, abt 920–973. After a power struggle involving King Louis IV of France *8,438,340*, King Otto and Conrad the Red *33,788,864*, Reginar died in exile in Bohemia.

2,895,710: 2,111,532

2,895,711: 2,111,533

2,983,232: **William III, Lord of Montpellier**, d. 1058.

2,983,233: **Beliardis**

2,983,234: **Raymond I, Count of Melgueil**

2,983,296: 1,056,206

2,983,297: 1,056,207

2,983,304: **Petrislav, Prince of Rascia**, d. abt 1083.

2,983,308: **Romanos IV Diogenes, Emperor of the Byzantine Empire**, abt 1030–1072. Captured in battle after being betrayed by one of his commanders, Andronikos Doukas *1,056,230*. Was later ransomed and returned to power.

2,983,312: 1,055,842

2,983,313: 1,055,843

2,983,314: **Constantine IX Monomachos, Emperor of the Byzantine Empire**, abt 1000–11 Jan 1055.

2,983,316: **Godwin, Earl of Wessex**, 1001–15 Apr 1053.

2,983,317: **Gytha Thorkelsdóttir**, abt 997–abt 1069.

2,983,346: 723,840

2,983,347: 723,841

2,983,352: **Manasses III, Count of Rethel**, 1022–1065.

2,983,353: **Judith of Roucy**

2,983,354: **Guy I, Lord of Montlhéry**, d. 1095.

2,983,355: **Hodierna of Gometz**, d. 1108.

2,984,064: 527,922

2,984,065: 527,923

2,984,070: **Frederick, Count of Formbach**

2,984,072: **Giselbert, Count of Luxembourg**, abt 1007–
14 Aug 1059.

2,984,076: **Otto of Nordheim, Duke of Bavaria**, abt 1020–
11 Jan 1083. Played a large role in two Saxon revolts against
Emperor Henry IV *1,055,902*.

2,984,077: **Richenza of Swabia**, b. abt 1025.

2,984,078: **Egbert I, Margrave of Meissen**, d. 11 Jan 1068.

2,984,079: 2,112,295

2,984,096: **Theodoric of Wassenberg**

2,984,100: **Gottschalk, Count of Zutphen**

2,984,101: **Adelheid, Countess of Zutphen**

2,984,112: **Eckhard I, Count of Scheyern**

2,984,113: **Richardis**

2,984,120: **Arnold I, Count of Looz**, 1060–1135.

2,984,121: **Agnes von Mainz, Countess of Looz**

2,984,856: **Thimo I, Count of Wettin**, abt 1015–abt 1100.

2,984,857: **Ida of Nordheim, Countess of Wettin**

2,995,304: **Enguerrand I, Count of Ponthieu**

2,998,664: **Waleran II, Count of Meulan**

2,998,672: 2,111,488

2,998,673: 2,111,489

2,998,674: **Rainard, Lord of Pithiviers**

2,998,675: **Helvise**

Generation 35

4,219,168: 2,895,708

4,219,170: Charles, Duke of Lower Lorraine, 953–993. Waged a war against Hugh Capet *2,111,532* for the throne of France, but was captured and imprisoned, where he died.

4,219,171: Adelaide of Troyes

4,219,172: Godfrey I, Count of Verdun, d. 1002. Captured and held for several years by Herbert III of Vermandois *4,220,344*.

4,219,184: Louis, Count of Verdun, d. 28 Sep 1025. Killed by Gothelo *2,109,586*.

4,219,185: Adélaíde de Saint Varme

4,219,186: Frederick, Count of Verdun, d. 6 Jan 1022. In 1020, he retired to life as a monk in Saint-Vanne Abbey.

4,219,336: 2,111,520

4,219,337: 2,111,521

4,219,904: 2,111,520

4,220,344: Herbert III, Count of Vermandois, abt 953–1015.

4,220,345: Ermengard of Bar-sur-Seine, b. abt 946.

4,220,988: Llywelyn ap Seisyll, King of Gwynedd, Powys and Deheubarth, d. 1023. United several smaller kingdoms that would later make up part of Wales.

4,220,990: Ælfgar, Earl of Mercia, d. abt 1060.

4,221,184: Meurig

4,221,192: Amlaíb mac Sitric, King of Dublin, d. 981. Captured in battle and eventually ransomed in exchange for 1,200 cows.

4,221,193: Gormflaith ingen Murchada

4,221,194: Brian Boru, High King of Ireland, d. 23 Apr 1014. Killed at the Battle of Clontarf and reportedly buried in the north wall of St. Patrick's Cathedral, in Armagh, Ireland.

4,221,206: Maredudd ab Owain, King of Wales

4,222,976: Rotrou

4,222,978: **Hugh I, Viscount of Chateaudun**

4,222,979: **Hildegarde, Viscountess of Chateaudun**

4,222,984: **Fulk II, Count of Anjou**, d. 960.

4,222,986: **Robert of Vermandois, Count of Meaux**

4,222,987: **Adelais of Burgundy**

4,223,016: **Hugh II, Count of Maine**, b. abt 920.

4,223,040: **William Longsword, Ruler of Normandy**, abt 893–17 Dec 942. Ruled before "duke" was a commonly used title; assassinated by followers of Arnulf I *8,446,112*.

4,223,041: **Sprota**, a Breton captive who was either a concubine or wife of William Longsword, though the terms of their relationship remain unclear.

4,223,044: **Judicael Berengar, Count of Rennes**

4,223,045: **Gerberga**

4,223,056: **Baldwin III, Count of Flanders**, abt 940–962.

4,223,064: **Hugh the Great, Duke of the Franks**, 898–16 Jun 956.

4,223,065: **Hedwig of Saxony**, d. 10 May 965. Ruled the Frankish kingdom as regent after her husband died, until her son Hugh Capet was of age.

Figure 13.35: A contemporary painting of King Edgar the Peaceful 4,223,088.[703]

4,223,068: **Boso II of Arles**

4,223,069: **Constance of Vienne**

4,223,076: **Kenneth II, King of the Scots**, abt 925–995. Was assassinated, possibly by a woman named Finella, after attempting to change the rules of succession to favor his heirs.

4,223,088: **Edgar the Peaceful, King of England**, d. 8 Jul 975.

4,223,089: **Ælfthryth, Queen of England**, d. abt 1001. The first queen consort[ii] of England to be officially crowned. Appears as an "evil stepmother" figure in medieval stories.

4,223,104: **Ebalus, Duke of Aquitaine**, d. 935.

4,223,105: **Emilienne**, d. abt 915.

4,223,106: **Rollo, Ruler of Normandy**, abt 846–abt 930. A Viking warrior who came to rule Rouen, in Normandy.

4,223,107: **Poppa of Bayeux**, a prominent member of the Frankish upper class. What historical information exists suggests she was originally abducted by her (future) husband Rollo when his forces invaded Bayeux.

4,223,108: **Theobald le Vieux of Blois, Viscount of Tours**

4,223,109: **Richildis**

4,223,110: **Herbert II, Count of Vermandois**, d. 23 Feb 943. Heavily involved in Frankish politics; captured King Charles the Simple of West Francia *16,876,680* and held him for six years, until the deposed king died.

4,223,112: **Berengar II, King of Italy**, abt 900–4 Aug 966. Revolted against Emperor Otto I *16,899,324* and was imprisoned in Germany, where he died.

4,223,113: **Willa of Tuscany, Queen of Italy**. Was imprisoned in a convent after she was found to have mistreated a political prisoner.

4,223,114: **Lambert, Count of Chalon**, abt 930–22 Feb 978.

[ii] A queen whose title derives from her marriage to a king, not the inheritance of the title.

4,223,115: **Adelaide of Chalon**

4,223,118: **Gilbert, Duke of Lorraine**, d. 2 Oct 939. Drowned in the Rhine while fleeing the forces of Odo of Wetterau *16,876,796* at the Battle of Andernach.

4,223,119: **Gerberga of Saxony**

4,223,188: 2,111,554

4,223,189: 2,111,555

4,223,190: **Conrad the Peaceful, King of Burgundy**, abt 925–19 Oct 993.

4,223,191: **Matilda of France, Queen of Burgundy**, 943–27 Jan 992.

4,223,232: **Arnald II Manzer, Count of Angouleme**

4,223,272: **Yves de Belleme**, d. abt 1005.

4,223,273: **Godeheut**

4,223,368: **Sviatoslav I, Grand Prince of Kiev**, abt 942–Mar 972. A commander of prolific foreign military campaigns who is still a part of Soviet-bloc lore. Was killed by his ally Kurya, a Pecheneg khan, who reportedly had Sviatoslav's skull turned into a chalice.

Figure 13.36: A portrait believed to be of Count Sigfried of Luxembourg 4,223,378.[704]

4,223,372: **Eric the Victorious, King of Sweden**, d. abt 995. The first known Swedish king for whom documentation exists outside of legends and oral myths.

4,223,376: **Dirk II, Count of Holland**, abt 930–6 May 988.

4,223,377: **Hildegard**

4,223,378: **Sigfried, Count of the Ardennes**, d. 28 Oct 998. The first ruler of Luxembourg.

4,223,379: **Hedwig of Nordgau**, b. abt 922.

4,223,384: **Hermann Billung**, d. 27 Mar 973. Founder of the "House of Billung," a dynasty that ruled Saxony for nearly 300 years. (Technically, he never served as duke himself.)

4,223,385: **Oda**

4,223,386: **Henry I the Bald, Count of Stade**, d. 11 May 976. Allegedly tried (and failed) to capture Hermann Billung *4,223,384*.

4,223,387: **Hildegard von Reinhausen**

4,223,388: **Berthold of Schweinfurt**, d. 15 Jan 980.

4,223,389: **Eilika of Walbeck**

4,223,390: **Herbert, Count of Wetterau**, d. 992. One of the survivors of the Battle of Stilo in 982, in which the forces of Emperor Otto II were killed en masse by the Saracens.

4,223,391: **Irmtrud of Avalgau**

4,223,392: **Amadeus**

4,223,396: **Manfred I, Marquis of Susa**, d. abt 1000.

4,223,397: **Prangarda**

4,223,524: **Roger I, Count of Carcassonne**, d. 1012.

4,223,584: 2,112,414

4,223,585: 2,112,415

4,223,586: 2,111,684

4,223,588: **Bretislav I, Duke of Bohemia**, d. 10 Jan 1055. Was not of high enough birth to marry Judith of Schweinfurt, so he kidnapped her from a monastery; whether she was a willing participant is unclear.

4,223,589: **Judith of Schweinfurt, Duchess of Bohemia**, d. 2 Aug 1058.

4,223,590: **Andrew I, King of Hungary**, b. abt 1015.

4,223,591: **Anastasia of Kiev, Queen of Hungary**, b. abt 1023. Retired to a convent.

4,223,592: 1,055,842

4,223,593: 1,055,843

4,223,600: **Adalbert, Margrave of Austria**, abt 985–26 May 1055.

4,223,601: **Frozza Orseolo**, 1015–17 Feb 1071. Eventually came to be known by the name "Adelheid."

4,223,602: **Dedi I, Margrave of Lower Lusatia**, 1004–1075.

4,223,603: **Oda of Lusatia**

4,223,608: **Conrad II, Holy Roman Emperor**, abt 990–4 Jun 1039.

4,223,609: **Gisela of Swabia, Holy Roman Empress**, 11 Nov 990–14 Feb 1043.

4,223,610: 527,888

4,223,611: 527,889

4,223,688: 4,223,068

4,223,689: 4,223,069

4,223,720: 1,447,708

4,223,721: 1,447,709

4,224,160: **Robert I, Count of the Lommegau**, d. abt 981.

4,224,176: 4,223,378

4,224,177: 4,223,379

4,224,580: 2,112,088

4,224,588: 2,111,694

4,224,589: 2,111,695

4,224,590: 2,111,698

4,224,591: 2,111,699

4,224,736: **Arnulf III, Count of Boulogne**, d. abt 990.

4,224,800: **Otbert II, Margrave of Milan**

4,224,801: **Railend**

4,224,804: **Rudolf II, Count of Altdorf**, d. abt 990.

4,224,805: **Ita of Öhningen**

4,224,806: 2,112,088

4,224,822: 2,111,686

4,224,823: **Edla**

4,224,824: **Michael of Hungary**, d. abt 997.

4,224,828: **Bolesław I the Brave, King of Poland**, 967–17 Jun 1025. The first king of Poland.

4,224,829: **Emnilda, Duchess of the Polans**

4,224,830: **Ezzo, Count Palatine of Lotharingia**, abt 955–21 Mar 1034.

4,224,831: **Matilda of Germany**, 979–1025.

4,224,920: **Andronikos Doukas**

4,224,924: **Ivan Vladislav, Tsar of Bulgaria**, d. 1018. His whole family was sentenced to death, but Ivan alone was saved by his cousin, whom he then killed years later. Ivan himself was killed during a siege of Dyrrhachium, under unclear circumstances that may have been an assassination.

4,313,396: **Uhtred the Bold, Ealdorman of All Northumbria**, d. 1016. Defeated an invasion by King Malcolm II of Scotland *2,111,538* and displayed the severed heads of his enemies on pikes. Assassinated by Thurbrand, who would later be killed in return by Uhtred's son.

5,790,752: **Sancho II, King of Pamplona**, abt 938–abt 994.

5,791,753: **Urraca Fernández, Queen of Leon**, d. 1007. Sancho II was her third marriage; the previous two were to Ordoño III *5,790,760* and Ordoño IV, both kings of León.

5,790,754: **Fernando Bermúdez, Count of Cea**, d. abt 978.

5,790,755: **Elvira Díaz**

5,790,756: **García Fernández, Count of Castile**, abt 938–995. Died of wounds suffered while being captured during a hunting trip.

5,790,757: **Ava of Ribagorza**

5,790,758: **Gómez Díaz**

5,790,759: **Muniadona Fernández**

5,790,760: **Ordoño III, King of León**, abt 926–956.

5,790,762: 5,790,756

5,790,763: 5,790,757

5,790,764: 2,895,380

5,790,765: 2,895,381

5,790,784: **Borrel II, Count of Barcelona**, d. 993. Also ruled over Girona and Ausona; retired to a monastery.

5,790,785: **Letgarda of Rouergue**

5,790,786: 4,223,524

5,790,808: **John II, Count of the Palace of Salerno**, d. abt 998. Served as regent of Salerno.

5,790,810: **Pandulf II, Prince of Benevento**, d. 1014.

5,790,834: **Arnaldo of Comminges**

5,790,835: **Arsende of Carcassonne**

5,791,304: **Frederick I, Duke of Upper Lorraine**, abt 912–18 May 978.

5,791,305: **Beatrice of France, Duchess of Upper Lorraine**, abt 938–23 Sep 987.

5,791,308: **Conrad I, Duke of Swabia**, abt 920–20 Aug 997.

5,791,310: 4,223,190

5,791,311: 4,223,191

5,791,416: **Reginar II, Count of Hainaut**, abt 890–932.

5,966,464: **William II, Lord of Montpellier**

5,966,608: **Mihailo Vojislavljević, King of the Slavs**, d. 1081.

5,966,616: **Constantine Diogenes**, d. 1032. A prominent military commander in the Byzantine Empire.

5,966,628: **Theodosios Monomachos**

5,966,634: **Thorgil Sprakling**

5,966,704: **Manasses II, Count of Rethel**, d. 1032.

5,966,705: **Dada**

5,966,706: **Gilbert, Count of Roucy**

5,966,710: **William, Lord of Gometz**

5,968,144: **Frederick of Luxembourg, Count of Mosel-gau**, 965–6 Oct 1019.

5,968,152: **Bernard, Count of Nordheim**

5,968,153: **Eilika**

5,968,156: **Liudolf of Brunswick, Margrave of Frisia**, abt 1003–23 Apr 1038.

5,968,157: **Gertrude of Egisheim**

5,968,224: **Otto I, Count of Scheyern**, b. abt 1020.

5,968,226: **Udalrich, Margrave of Carniola**

5,968,240: **Emmo, Count of Looz**, d. 17 Jan 1078.

5,968,241: **Suanhildis**

5,968,242: **Gerhard I, Count of Rieneck**

5,968,243: **Helwig von Bliescastel**

5,969,712: **Theodoric II, Margrave of Lower Lusatia**, abt 990–19 Nov 1034.

5,969,713: **Mathilda**

5,969,714: 2,984,076

5,969,715: 2,984,077

5,990,608: **Hugh I, Count of Ponthieu**, abt 970–abt 1000.

5,990,609: **Gisela of France, Countess of Ponthieu**, abt 968–1002.

5,997,328: **Waleran I, Count of Meulan**

5,997,344: **Rotrou of Nogent**

5,997,346: **Hugh I, Viscount of Chateaudun**

Generation 36

8,438,340: **Louis IV, King of West Francia**, abt 921–10 Sep 954.

8,438,341: 4,223,119

8,438,344: **Gozlin, Count of the Ardennes**, 911–abt 943.

8,438,345: **Oda of Metz**, d. 10 Apr 963.

8,438,368: **Otto of Vermandois**, d. 987.

8,440,688: **Adalbert I, Count of Vermandois**, d. abt 987.

8,440,689: **Gerberge of Lorraine**, d. 978.

8,441,980: **Leofric, Earl of Mercia**, d. 1057. Founded or otherwise funded several monasteries in England, near the Welsh border.

8,441,981: **Godiva, Countess of Mercia**. The "Lady Godiva" of legend, who allegedly rode naked through the streets of Coventry, England to protest the oppressive taxation of her husband, Leofric.

8,442,368: **Idwal the Bald, King of Gwynedd**, d. abt 942. Killed in battle against Saxon troops.

8,442,386: **Murchad mac Finn, King of Leinster**

8,442,388: **Cennétig mac Lorcáin, King of Tuadmumu**, d. 951. Ruled a region of Gaelic Ireland now located in Counties Clare and Limerick.

8,442,389: **Bé Binn inion Urchadh, Queen of Tuadmumu**

8,442,412: **Owain ap Hywel Dda**, d. abt 987.

8,445,956: **Geoffrey I, Viscount of Chateaudun**

8,445,957: **Ermengarde**

8,445,958: **Hervé I, Count of Perche**. Likely a close ally of Hugh the Great *4,223,064*.

8,445,959: **Mélisende**

8,445,968: **Fulk the Red, Count of Anjou**, d. abt 942.

8,445,969: **Roscilla de Loches**

8,445,972: 4,223,110

8,445,974: **Gilbert, Duke of Burgundy**, d. 8 Apr 956.

8,445,975: **Ermengard**

8,446,032: **Hugh I, Count of Maine**, d. abt 933.

8,446,080: 4,223,106

8,446,081: 4,223,107

8,446,112: **Arnulf I, Count of Flanders**, d. 28 Mar 965. Extended his political influence by taking advantage of warring between King Charles the Simple *16,876,680* and King Robert I of France *8,446,128*.

8,446,113: **Adele of Vermandois, Countess of Flanders**, abt 915–960.

8,446,128: **Robert I, King of the Franks**, 866–15 Jun 923. Seized the throne from King Charles the Simple *16,876,680* in 922. Killed in a battle against the armies of Charles the following year.

8,446,129: **Beatrice of Vermandois**

8,446,130: **Henry the Fowler, King of the East Franks**, d. 2 Jul 936. Elected ruler in 919 of what would become Germany.

8,446,131: **Saint Matilda of Ringelheim, Queen of the East Franks**, abt 897–14 Mar 968.

8,446,152: **Malcolm I, King of the Scots**, abt 895–954. Killed in battle; was likely buried on Iona, a small island off the coast of modern-day Scotland.

8,446,176: **Edmund I, King of England**, 921–26 May 946. Assassinated, possibly during a church service.

8,446,177: **Ælfgifu of Shaftesbury, Queen of England**, d. 944.

8,446,178: **Ordgar, Ealdorman of Devon**, d. 971. Founded Tavistock Abbey.

8,446,208: **Ranulf II, Duke of Aquitaine**, d. 5 Aug 890. Declared himself "King of Aquitaine," a title not used since.

8,446,220: **Herbert I, Count of Vermandois**, d. 907. Ordered the killing of Raoul, son of Baldwin I of Flanders *33,784,448*. Was then likely assassinated by Baldwin II *16,892,224*.

8,446,221: **Bertha de Morvis**

8,446,224: **Adalbert I, Margrave of Ivrea**

8,446,225: **Gisela of Friuli**

8,446,226: **Boso, Margrave of Tuscany**

8,446,227: **Willa of Burgundy**

8,446,228: **Robert of Dijon**

8,446,229: **Ingeltrude**

8,446,230: 8,445,974

8,446,231: 8,445,975

8,446,238: 8,446,130

8,446,239: 8,446,131

8,446,380: **Rudolph II, King of Burgundy**, abt 880–11 Jul 937.

8,446,381: **Bertha of Swabia, Queen of Italy**, b. abt 907.

8,446,382: 8,438,340

8,446,383: 4,223,119

8,446,464: **William Taillefer I, Count of Angouleme**, d. 962.

8,446,736: **Igor I, Prince of Rus'**, d. 945. His life is almost entirely undocumented, but it's believed he was the ruler who led two sieges of Constantinople in the mid-900s.

8,446,737: **Saint Olga of Kiev**, d. 11 Jul 969. According to legend, Olga avenged the death of her husband Igor at the hands of the Drevlian tribe by receiving their messengers, then having them buried alive, then burning their village and killing the fleeing survivors. She converted to Christianity and was sainted by the Roman Catholic and Russian Eastern Orthodox Churches; she is recognized with the title "Holy Equal-to-the-Apostles Olga" by several branches.

8,446,772: **Lothar II, Count of Stade**, 874–929. Killed at the Battle of Lenzen, in which the forces of Henry the Fowler *8,446,130* invaded Slavic territory.

8,446,773: **Swanhilde of Saxony**

8,446,774: **Elli I, Count of Reinhausen**

8,446,778: **Lothar II, Count of Walbeck**, d. 3 Dec 992.

Reportedly aided in the assassination of Otto I the Great *16,899,324* and was imprisoned by his future son-in-law, Berthold of Schweinfurt *4,223,388*.

8,446,779: **Mathilde von Arneburg**

8,446,780: **Odo, Count of Wetterau**, d. 2 Dec 949. Helped Emperor Otto I *16,899,324* crush a rebellion with a decisive victory at the Battle of Andernach against Gilbert of Lorraine *16,881,378*.

8,446,781: **Cunegonda of Vermandois**

8,446,782: **Megingoz the Brown**, d. abt 1001.

8,446,783: **Gerberga of Lorraine**, abt 925–995.

8,446,792; **Arduin Glaber, Margrave of Turin**

8,446,794: **Adalbert Atto, Count of Canossa**

8,446,795: **Hildegard**

8,447,048: **Arnaud I, Count of Couserans**, d. 983.

8,447,049: **Arsinde of Carcassonne**

8,447,176: **Oldrich, Duke of Bohemia**, abt 975–9 Nov 1034.

8,447,178: 2,111,694

8,447,179: 2,111,695

8,447,182: 1,055,842

8,447,183: 1,055,843

8,447,200: **Leopold I, Margrave of Austria**, abt 940–994.

8,447,201: **Richardis of Sualafeldgau**, d. 994.

8,447,202: **Otto Orseolo, Doge of Venice**, abt 992–1032. Was eventually deposed by the people and exiled to Constantinople, where he later died.

8,447,204: 5,969,712

8,447,205: 5,969,713

8,447,216: **Henry of Speyer**, abt 970–abt 992.

8,447,217: **Adelaide of Metz**

8,447,218: 2,895,654

8,447,219: 2,895,655

8,448,739: **Hildegarde, Viscountess of Chateaudun**

8,449,472: **Arnulf II, Count of Boulogne**, d. abt 972.

8,449,600: **Oberto I Obizzo, Count of Milan**, d. 15 Oct 975.

8,449,608: **Rudolf I, Count of Altdorf**

8,449,610: 5,791,308

8,449,648: **Taksony, Grand Prince of the Hungarians**, d. abt 973.

8,449,656: **Mieszko I, Duke of Poland**, abt 930–25 May 992. The first Christian ruler of Poland, though he was a Pagan until his marriage.

8,449,657: **Doubravka of Bohemia, Duchess of the Polans**, abt 945–977.

8,449,658: **Dobromir of Lusatia**

8,449,660: **Herman I, Count Palatine of Lotharingia**, d. 996.

8,449,661: **Heylwig of Dillingen**

8,449,662: **Otto II, Holy Roman Emperor**, 955–7 Dec 983. Known as "Otto the Red," according to one story because he invited political enemies to a banquet, then had them killed.

8,449,663: **Theophanu, Holy Roman Empress**, abt 955–15 Jun 991.

8,449,848: **Aron of Bulgaria**, d. 14 Jun 976. Executed when his plot to seize power was uncovered.

8,626,792: **Waltheof, Ealdorman of Bamburgh**

8,626,793: **Ecgfrida**

8,626,794: **Aldhun, Bishop of Durham**

11,581,504: **García I, King of Pamplona**, abt 919–970. Became king at about age 6, when his father died.

11,581,505: **Andregoto Galíndez**

11,583,506: **Fernán González, Count of Castile**, d. 970.

11,583,507: **Sancha Sánchez, Queen of León**

11,581,508: **Bermudo Núñez, Count of Cea**, d. abt 955.

11,581,509: **Argilo**

11,581,510: **Diego Muñoz, Count of Saldaña**

11,581,511: **Tregidia**

11,581,518: 11,583,506

11,581,519: 11,583,507

11,581,520: **Ramiro II, King of León**, abt 900–1 Jan 951.

11,581,521: **Adosinda Gutiérrez**

11,581,568: **Sunyer, Count of Barcelona**, abt 870–950.

11,581,569: **Richilda, Countess of Barcelona**

11,581,616: **Lampert of Spoleto**

11,581,620: **Landulf III, Prince of Benevento**, d. abt 969.

11,582,608: **Wigeric of Lotharingia, Count of the Bidgau**

11,582,609: **Cunigunda of France**, b. abt 893.

11,582,610: 4,223,064

11,582,611: 4,223,065

11,582,832: **Reginar, Duke of Lorraine**, abt 850–915. May have served as a regent of the Frankish kingdom in 877.

11,933,216: **Stefan Vojislav, Prince of the Serbs**, d. 1043. Was imprisoned in Constantinople after an unsuccessful revolt, but escaped and rose to power around 1018.

11,933,408: **Manasses of Omont**

11,933,409: **Castricia**

11,933,412: 2,111,558

11,933,413: 2,111,559

11,936,288: 4,223,378

11,936,289: 4,223,379

11,936,312: **Brun I, Count of Brunswick**, abt 975–abt 1010. Fought in battles against the forces of Duke Boleslaus II *16,899,314*.

11,936,313: 4,223,609

11,936,448: **Heinrich I, Count in the Pegnitz**

11,936,480: **Giselbert, Count of Looz**, abt 980–abt 1045.

11,936,481: **Erlande of Geldenaken**

11,936,482: 1,055,844

11,936,483: 1,055,845

11,939,424: **Dedo I, Count of Wettin**, abt 950–13 Nov 1009.

11,939,425: **Thietburga of Haldensleben**

11,939,426: **Eckard I, Margrave of Meissen**, abt 960–30 Apr 1002.

11,939,427: **Schwanehilde**

11,981,218: 2,111,532

11,981,219: 2,111,533

Generation 37

16,876,680: **Charles the Simple, King of West Francia**, 17 Sep 879–7 Oct 929. As king, he created the Duchy of Normandy as part of a peace treaty made with the Viking Rollo *4,223,106.*

16,876,681: **Eadgifu of Wessex, Queen of West Francia**, b. 902. Fled to England after her husband's capture and raised her son there until he was called to return to rule.

16,876,688: 11,582,608

16,876,689: 11,582,609

16,876,690: **Gerhard I, Count of Metz**, abt 875–22 Jun 910. Killed in a battle against the Bavarians.

16,876,691: **Oda of Saxony, Queen of Lotharingia**, b. abt 877. Was married first to King Zwentibold of Lotharingia, who died before Oda was 15. Gerhard was her second husband.

16,876,736: 8,440,688

16,876,737: 8,440,689

16,880,178: 8,446,130

16,880,179: 8,446,131

16,881,376: 4,223,110

16,881,377: 4,223,111

16,881,378: 4,223,118

16,881,379: 4,223,119

16,883,960: **Leofwine, Ealdorman of the Hwicce**, d. abt 1023. Chief magistrate of Hwicce, in England.

16,884,736: **Anarawd ap Rhodri, King of Gwynedd**, d. abt 916.

16,884,778: **Urchadh mac Murchadh, King of Maigh Seóla**, d. abt 943.

16,884,824: **Hywel the Good, King of Deheubarth**, d. 950. Consolidated power during his reign and eventually came to rule most of Wales, where he developed the first official Welsh legal codes.

16,891,936: **Ingelger, Count of Anjou**, d. abt 942.

16,891,937: **Adelais of Amboise**

16,891,938: **Warnerius, Seigneur de Loches, de Villentrois, and de la Haye**

16,891,939: **Tecandra**

16,891,944: 8,446,220

16,891,945: 8,446,221

16,891,950: **Richard, Duke of Burgundy**, d. abt 921.

16,891,951: **Adelaide of Auxerre, Duchess of Burgundy**

16,892,064: **Ragenold of Neustria, Count of Maine**, d. 25 Jul 885. Killed while attacking Vikings who had invaded Rouen.

16,892,065: **Rothilde**, d. abt 929.

16,892,224: **Baldwin II, Margrave of Flanders,**

Figure 13.37: A portrait of Baldwin II 16,892,224.[705]

d. 10 Sep 918. Believed to have ordered the assassination of Herbert I *67,255,682*.

16,892,225: **Ælfthryth, Countess of Flanders**, abt 877–7 Jun 929.

16,892,226: 4,223,110

16,892,256: **Robert the Strong, Count of Anjou**, d. 2 Jul 866. Killed at the Battle of Brissarthe fighting against an attack from Breton and Viking invaders.

16,892,257: **Adelaide of Tours**

16,892,258: 8,446,220

16,892,259: 8,446,221

16,892,260: **Otto I, Duke of Saxony**, abt 851–30 Nov 912.

16,892,261: **Hedwiga**, d. 24 Dec 903.

16,892,262: **Dietrich of Ringelheim**

16,892,263: **Reinhild**

16,892,304: **Domnall mac Causantin, King of the Scots**, d. 900.

16,892,352: **Edward the Elder, King of the Anglo-Saxons**, d. 17 Jul 924.

16,892,353: **Eadgifu of Kent, Queen of the Anglo-Saxons**, d. abt 966.

16,892,355: **Wynflaed**

16,892,416: **Ranulf I, Duke of Aquitaine**, abt 820–abt 866. Killed at the Battle of Brissarthe, the same one at which Robert the Strong *16,892,256* died.

16,892,417 **Bilichild of Maine**

16,892,440: **Pepin, Count of Vermandois**, b. 817.

16,892,448: **Anscar I, Margrave of Ivrea**

16,892,450: **Berengar I, Holy Roman Emperor**, d. 7 Apr 924.

16,892,452: **Theobald, Count of Arles**, d. abt 895.

16,892,453: **Bertha**, abt 863–8 Mar 925.

16,892,760: **Rudolph I, King of Upper Burgundy**, 859–25 Oct 912.

16,892,761: **Guilla of Provence**

16,892,762: **Burchard II, Duke of Swabia**, abt 884–29 Apr 926.

16,892,763: **Regelinda of Zurich**

16,892,928: **Alduin I, Count of Angouleme**, d. 27 Mar 916.

16,893,544: **Lothar I, Count of Stade**, 840–880. May have been killed at the Battle of Lúneburg Heath, fighting for King Louis III of France against the "Great Heathen Army" of Norsemen.

16,893,545: **Oda**

16,893,556: **Lothar I, Count of Walbeck**, 902–929. Killed at the Battle of Lenzen with (the unrelated) Lothar II, Count of Slade *8,446,772.*

16,893,558: **Bruno, Count of Arneburg**

16,893,559: **Frederuna**

16,893,560: **Gebhard, Duke of Lorraine**, d. 22 Jun 910. Killed in battle against the Magyars.

16,893,561: **Ida**

16,893,566: **Godfrey, Count Palatine of Lotharingia**, b. abt 905.

16,893,567: **Ermentrude**

16,893,584: **Roger, Count of Auriate**

16,893,588: **Sigifred of Lucca**

16,893,966: 11,583,506

16,893,967: 11,583,507

16,894,082: 11,583,506

16,894,083: 11,583,507

16,894,352: **Boleslaus II, Duke of Bohemia**, abt 930–7 Feb 999.

16,894,356: 4,223,388

16,894,357: 4,223,389

16,894,402: **Ernest IV of Sualafeldgau**

16,894,404: **Pietro II Orseolo, Doge of Venice**, d. 1009.

16,894,405: **Maria Candiano, Dogaressa of Venice**

16,894,432: **Otto I, Duke of Carinthia**, abt 948–4 Nov 1004.

16,898,944: **Adelolf, Count of Boulogne**, d. abt 933.

16,899,296: **Zoltán of Hungary**, d. abt 950. May have been crowned Grand Prince of the Hungarians, as his son was.

16,899,312: **Siemomysł, Duke of the Polans**, d. abt 960.

16,899,314: **Boleslaus I, Duke of Bohemia**, abt 915–15 Jul 967. Known as "Boleslaus the Cruel"; rose to power after killing his older brother, Duke Wenceslaus I, who became the subject of the "Good King Wenceslas" holiday carol.

16,899,320: **Erenfried II, Count of Keldachgau**, d. abt 970.

16,899,321: **Richwara of Zülpichgau**, d. 10 Jul 963.

16,899,324: **Otto the Great, Holy Roman Emperor**, 23 Nov 912–7 May 973.

16,899,325: **Saint Adelaide of Italy, Holy Roman Empress**, 931–16 Dec 999. Ruled the Holy Roman Empire after the death of her husband, then retired to a nunnery.

16,899,696: **Nicholas of Bulgaria**. A local ruler of unclear origins.

16,899,697: **Ripsime of Armenia**

23,163,008: **Sancho I, King of Pamplona**, abt 860–10 Dec 925. Killed Lubb ibn Muhammad, who coincidentally was the man responsible for the death of Count Wilfred I *23,163,136*.

23,163,009: **Toda, Queen of Pamplona**, abt 876–958.

23,163,010: **Galindo Aznárez II, Count of Aragon**, d. 922.

23,163,011: **Sancha Garcés, Countess of Aragon**

23,167,012: **Gonzalo Fernández, Count of Castile**
23,167,013: **Muniadona**
23,167,014: 23,163,008
23,167,015: 23,163,009
23,163,040: **Ordoño II, King of León**, abt 873–924.
23,163,041: **Elvira Menéndez**
23,163,042: **Gutier Osoriz**
23,163,043: **Ildonzia Menéndez**
23,163,136: **Wilfred the Hairy, Count of Barcelona**, d.
  11 Aug 897. Killed in battle against the Muslim troops of
  Lubb ibn Muhammad.
23,163,137: **Guinidilda**
23,163,240: **Landulf II, Prince of Benevento**, d. 961.
  Known as "Landulf the Red."
23,163,241: **Yvantia**
23,165,219: **Ermentrude of France**, b. abt 878.
23,878,848: **Theodoric I of Wettin**, abt 916–abt 976.
23,878,852: **Gunther, Margrave of Merseburg**, d.
  13 Jul 982.
23,878,854: 4,223,384

Generation 38

33,753,360: **Louis the Stammerer, King of West Francia**, 1 Nov 846–Apr 879.
33,753,361: **Adelaide of Paris, Queen of West Francia**,
  abt 853–10 Nov 901.
33,753,362: 16,892,352
33,753,380: **Adalhard, Count of Metz**, abt 840–890.
33,767,920: **Ælfwine**
33,769,472: **Rhodri the Great**, abt 820–abt 878. Ruled
  most of what is now the country of Wales.

33,769,473: **Angharad ferch Meurig**

33,769,556: **Murchadh mac Maenach, King of Maigh Seóla**, d. abt 891.

33,769,648: **Cadell ap Rhodri, King of Seisyllwg**, 854–909.

33,783,900: **Bivin of Gorze**, d. abt 863.

33,783,902: **Conrad II, Count of Auxerre**, d. 876.

33,784,130: **Charles the Bald, Holy Roman Emperor**, 13 Jun 823–6 Oct 877. Reigned as king of the Franks starting in 840, became Holy Roman emperor in 875.

33,784,131: **Richilde of Provence**, d. 2 Jun 910. Oversaw the empire while Charles was away fighting.

33,784,448: **Baldwin I, Margrave of Flanders**, d. abt 879.

33,784,449: **Judith of Flanders, Queen of Wessex**, d. abt 870. Married King Æthelwulf of Wessex *67,568,900*, then married Æthelbald, Æthelwulf's son (and her step-son), after her first husband's death, which means her first two husbands were kings of Wessex. Her third marriage, to Baldwin I of Flanders, was the only to produce children.

33,784,450: **Alfred the Great, King of Wessex**, 849–26 Oct 899. The first monarch to describe his position as "king of the Anglo-Saxons"; his remains were lost after the monastery at which he was buried got demolished; coffins were exhumed in the late 1700s during the construction of a prison, but the bones were scattered and lost.

33,784,451: **Ealhswith, Queen of Wessex**, d. 5 Dec 902. Founded the "Nunnaminster," an abbey in Hampshire, England.

33,784,512: **Robert III, Count of Worms**, d. abt 834.

33,784,513: **Waldrada of Worms**, b. 801.

33,784,514: **Hugh, Count of Tours**, d. 837.

33,784,515: **Ava**

33,784,520: **Liudolf, Duke of Saxony**

33,784,521: **Oda**

33,784,608: **Constantín mac Cináeda, King of the Picts**, abt 836–877. The last ruler of Pictland before it began its transition into Scotland. Killed by invading Vikings, whose raids peaked during his reign.

33,784,704: 33,784,450

33,784,705: 33,784,451

33,784,706: **Sigehelm, Ealdorman of Kent**, d. 902. Killed at the Battle of the Holme.

33,784,880: **Bernard of Italy, King of the Lombards**, 797–17 Apr 818. Ruled Italy in the early 800s; died after his uncle, King Louis the Pious *67,568,260*, had him blinded as punishment for plotting against him.

33,784,881: **Cunigunde**

33,784,900: **Eberhard, Duke of Friuli**, d. 16 Dec 866.

33,784,901: **Gisela**, b. abt 821. Gifted several large mosaics to the cathedral at Aquileia, still present today.

33,784,904: **Hucbert**, d. 864. Served as the lay-abbot of the Abbey of Saint Maurice, now in Switzerland. Killed in battle near the Orbe River.

33,784,906: **Lothair II, King of Lotharingia**, 835–8 Aug 869.

33,784,907: **Waldrada**

33,785,520: 33,783,902

33,785,524: **Burchard I, Duke of Swabia**, d. 911.

33,785,525: **Liutgard of Saxony, Queen of the Franks**, abt 845–17 Nov 885. Her first husband was King Louis the Younger.

33,785,526: **Eberhard I, Count of Zurich**

33,785,856: **Wulgrin I, Count of Angouleme**, abt 830–3 May 886. Built multiple castles as bulwarks against invading Vikings.

33,785,857: **Roselinde**

33,787,090: 33,784,520

33,787,091: 33,784,521

33,787,118: **Volkmar, Count of Harzgau**

33,787,120: **Udo of Neustria**

33,787,121: **Judith**

33,787,132: 16,876,690

33,787,133: 16,876,691

33,787,198: 16,876,680

33,787,199: **Frederuna, Queen of West Francia**, 887–917. The first wife of King Charles the Simple.

33,788,704: 16,899,314

33,788,810: **Vitale Candiano**, d. abt 979.

33,788,864: **Conrad the Red, Duke of Lorraine**, abt 922– 10 Aug 955.

33,788,865: **Liutgarde of Saxony, Duchess of Lorraine**, 931–18 Nov 953.

33,797,888: 16,892,224

33,797,889: 16,892,225

33,798,592: **Árpád**, d. abt 907.

33,798,628: **Vratislaus I, Duke of Bohemia**, abt 888– 13 Feb 921. Died in battle, fighting Hungarian forces.

33,798,629: **Drahomíra, Duchess of Bohemia**. Ruled Bohemia as regent until her son was of age.

33,798,640: **Eberhard I, Count of Bonngau**, d. abt 937.

33,798,648: 8,446,130

33,798,649: 8,446,131

33,798,650: 8,446,380

33,798,651: 8,446,381

33,799,394: **Ashot II, King of Armenia**, d. abt 929.

33,799,395: **Marie**

46,326,016: **García Jiménez**

46,326,017: **Dadidis de Pallars**

46,326,018: **Aznar Sánchez**

46,326,019: **Onneca Fortúnez, Princess of Pamplona**, b. abt 848.

46,326,020: **Aznar Galíndez II, Count of Aragon**, d. abt 893.

46,326,022: **García Jiménez**, d. 882. Killed in battle in Aybar, in northern Spain.

46,326,023: **Oneca**

46,326,080: **Alfonso III, King of León**, abt 848–20 Dec 910. Also ruled over Galicia and Asturias.

46,326,081: **Jimena**

46,326,082: **Hermenegildo Gutiérrez**

46,326,083: **Ermesenda Gatónez**

46,326,264: 33,784,448

46,326,265: 33,784,449

46,326,480: **Landulf I, Prince of Benevento**, d. 10 Apr 943.

46,326,481: **Gemma**

46,330,438: 33,753,360

46,330,439: 33,753,361

Generation 39

67,506,720: 33,784,130

67,506,721: **Ermentrude of Orleans, Queen of the Franks**, 27 Sep 823–6 Oct 869. Moved to a convent after King Charles had her brother William executed.

67,506,722: **Adelard, 8th Count of Paris**, abt 830–abt 890.

67,506,760: **Adalard the Seneschal, Lord Chancellor of West Francia**. Served as head of the national judiciary under King Louis the Pious *67,568,260*.

67,538,944: **Merfyn Frych, King of Gwynedd**. Known as "Merfyn the Freckled."

67,538,946: **Meurig, King of Seisyllwg**

67,567,804: **Conrad I, Count of Auxerre**, d. 876.

67,567,805: 16,892,257

67,568,260: **Louis the Pious, Holy Roman Emperor**, abt 778–20 Jun 840. Served as "co-emperor" with his father, Charlemagne, and then on his own after his father's death. Was also king of the Franks.

67,568,261: **Judith of Bavaria, Empress of the Franks**, d. 19 Apr 843. Heavily involved in the political work of both her husband and son, Charles the Bald.

67,568,262: 33,783,900

67,568,900: **Æthelwulf, King of Wessex**, d. 13 Jan 858. An ornate ring made for him was discovered in a road more than 900 years after his death and is now in a British museum.

67,568,901: **Osburh, Queen of Wessex**

67,568,902: **Æthelred Mucel, Ealdorman of the Gaini**

67,568,903: **Eadburh**

67,569,024: **Robert II, Count of Hesbaye**, d. 12 Jul 807. The earliest known male-line ancestor along the Capetian line, which ruled France for more than 1,000 years after Robert's death.

67,569,216: **Kenneth MacAlpin, King of the Picts**. Recognized in Scotland as the first "king of Scots." Died of cancer.

67,569,760: **Pepin of Italy, King of the Lombards**, Apr 773–8 Jul 810. Named ruler of Italy at age 8 by his father, Charlemagne.

67,569,800: **Unruoch II, Duke of Friuli**, d. abt 853. Witness to the last will of Charlemagne *135,136,520*.

67,569,801: **Engeltrude**

67,569,802: 67,568,260

67,569,803: 67,568,261

67,569,808: **Boso the Elder, Count of Turin**, d. 855.

67,569,809: **Engeltrude**

67,569,812:   **Lothair I, Holy Roman Emperor**, 795–29 Sep 855. His remains were discovered buried in the Prüm monastery in the 19th century.

67,569,813: **Ermengarde of Tours, Holy Roman Emperess**, d. 20 Mar 851.

67,571,050: 33,784,520

67,571,051: 33,784,521

67,571,712: **Vulfard, Count of Flavigny**

67,571,713: **Suzanne**

67,574,240: **Gebhard, Count of the Lahngau**, d. 879.

67,574,398: **Deitrich Theodoric von Ringelheim**

67,574,399: **Gisela of Lotharingia**

67,577,728: **Werner V, Count of Wormsgau**, d. abt 935.

67,577,729: **Hicha of Swabia, Countess of Wormsgau**

67,577,730: 16,899,324

67,577,731: **Edith of England, Queen of Germany**, 910–26 Jan 946. A sarcophagus in the Magdeburg Cathedral with her name on it was believed to be empty, until it was opened and examined in 2008 and her remains were discovered inside, making hers the oldest surviving remains of an English royal.

67,597,184: **Álmos**, d. abt 895. Considered the first ruler of the tribes that would become Hungary.

67,597,256: **Borivoj I, Duke of Bohemia**, abt 852–abt 889.

67,597,257: **Saint Ludmila of Bohemia, Duchess of Bohemia**, abt 860–15 Sep 921. Was murdered at the orders of her daughter-in-law, Drahomíra *33,798,629*. Canonized after her death, and is considered a patron saint of problems with in-laws.

67,597,280: **Erenfried I, Count of Bonngau**

67,597,281: **Adelgunde of Burgundy**, abt 860–902.

Figure 13.38: A 14th century depiction of the murder of Saint Ludmila 67,597,257. She can be seen on the right, being strangled with her own veil.[706]

67,598,788: **Smbat I, King of Armenia**, abt 850–abt 914. Surrendered to a besieging army, which then tortured and beheaded him, then hung his body from a cross.

92,652,038: **Fortún Garcés, King of Pamplona**, d. 922. Retired in the early 900s and spent the last 17 years of his life as a monk.

92,652,039: **Auria**

92,652,040: **Galindo Aznárez I, Count of Aragon**, d. 867.

92,652,160: **Ordoño I, King of Asturias**, abt 821–866.

92,652,161: **Muniadona**

92,652,164: **Gutierre**. A count in Galicia.

92,652,165: **Elvira**

92,652,166: **Gatón**. A count in Galicia.

92,652,960: **Atenulf I, Prince of Benevento**, d. 910. Conquered Benevento in 899, which would be held by his descendants for generations.

92,652,962: **Athanasius, Duke of Naples**, d. 898. As
bishop of Naples, he had his brother Sergius blinded in
order to depose him and make himself duke as well.

Generation 40

135,013,442: **Odo I, Count of Orléans**, d. 834.

135,013,443: **Engeltrude**

135,013,444: **Wulfhard of Flavigny**

135,013,520: **Leuthard I, Count of Paris**, d. abt 816.

135,013,521: **Grimhilda**

135,017,602: 33,784,450

135,017,603: 33,784,451

135,041,282: 33,784,130

135,041,283: 67,506,721

135,077,888: **Gwriad ap Elidyr**

135,077,889: **Ethyllt ferch Cynan**, b. abt 744.

135,135,608: **Welf**

135,136,520: **Charlemagne, Holy Roman Emperor and
King of the Franks**, abt 748–28 Jan 814. Recognized
as the first emperor of Western Europe since the fall of
the Roman Empire after he united what is now France,
Germany, Italy, Belgium and the Netherlands.

135,136,521: **Hildegard of the Vinzgau, Queen of the
Franks**, d. 30 Apr 783. Likely married Charlemagne around
the age of 13.

135,136,522: 135,135,608

135,137,800: **Egbert, King of Wessex**, abt 775–839.

135,137,802: **Oslac**

135,139,520: 135,136,520

135,130,521: 135,136,521

135,139,602: **Beggo, Count of Toulouse**, d. 28 Oct 816.

135,139,624: 67,568,260

135,139,625: **Ermengarde of Hesbaye, Holy Roman Empress**, abt 778–3 Oct 818.

135,139,626: 33,784,514

135,143,426: 135,139,602

135,155,456: **Werner IV**

135,155,458: 16,892,762

135,155,459: 16,892,763

135,155,460: 16,892,352

135,155,461: **Ælfflæd, Queen of Wessex**

135,155,462: 16,892,352

135,155,463: 16,892,353

135,194,562: 33,783,902

135,197,576: **Ashot I, King of Armenia**, abt 820–890.

135,197,577: **Katranide I, Queen of Armenia**

185,304,076: **García Íñiguez, King of Pamplona**, abt 805–882.

185,304,080: **Aznar Galíndez I, Count of Aragon**, d. 839.

185,304,320: **Ramiro I, King of Asturias**, abt 790–1 Feb 850. Buried in the Pantheon of Asturian Kings, in a location that has since been lost.

185,305,920: **Landenulf, Gastald of Teano**

185,305,924: **Gregory III, Duke of Naples**, d. 870.

Generation 41

270,026,884: **Adrian of Orléans.**

270,027,040: **Gerard I, Count of Paris**, d. abt 779.

270,027,041: **Rotrude**, possibly a granddaughter of Charles Martel *540,546,080.*

270,155,778: **Cynan Dindaethwy, King of Gwynedd**, d. abt 817. Was exiled after losing a power struggle with a leader who may have been his brother.

270,155,779: **Matilda of Flintshire**

270,273,040: **Pepin the Short, King of the Franks**, abt 714–24 Sep 768. Ruled the kingdom of Francia with his brother, Carloman, and later as the sole king.

270,273,041: **Bertrada of Laon, Queen of the Franks**, d. 12 Jul 783.

270,273,042: **Gerold of Vinzgau**, d. abt 795.

270,273,043: **Emma**

270,279,204: 270,027,040

270,279,205: 270,027,041

270,279,250: **Ingerman, Count of Hesbaye**, d. abt 818.

270,279,251: **Rotrude**

270,309,442: 33,783,902

270,395,152: **Smbat VIII**

370,608,152: **Íñigo Arista, King of Pamplona**, abt 790–abt 852.

370,608,640: **Bermudo I, King of Asturias**, abt 750–797. Appears to have only ruled for two or three years, after which he abdicated and likely lived out his days as a monk.

370,611,848: **Sergius I, Duke of Naples**, d. 864.

370,611,849: **Drusa**

Generation 42

540,546,080: **Charles Martel, Mayor of the Palace of Austrasia**, abt 686–22 Oct 741. Known as "Charles the Hammer." The "mayor of the palace" was the functional ruler of the Frankish kingdom at this time, with the king essentially a figurehead. His son, Pepin, would later seize the throne as well.

540,546,081: **Rotrude of Hesbaye**

540,546,082: **Charibert, Count of Laon**, d. abt 762.

540,546,086: **Hnabi**, d. abt 788. A duke of the Alemanni tribes in what would become Germany.

540,558,500: **Sigram, Count of Hesbaye**

Generation 43

1,081,092,160: **Pepin of Herstal, Mayor of the Palace of Austrasia**, abt 635–16 Dec 714. Ruled Francia starting in 680; greatly consolidated power in the Frankish realms.

1,081,092,161: **Alpaida**

1,081,092,165: **Bertrada of Prüm**. Co-founded the Prüm Abbey with her son, Charibert, in 721.

1,081,092,172: **Huoching**, d. abt 744. A nobleman in the Alemanni tribes of the upper Rhine River area.

1,081,117,000: **Sigramnus, Count of Hesbaye**

1,081,117,001: **Landrade of Hesbaye**

Generation 44

2,162,184,320: **Ansegisel**. Served as a duke under Frankish King Sigbert III. Killed in the mid-600s.

2,162,184,321: **Saint Begga**, abt 615–17 Dec 693. Became a nun after the death of her husband, founded multiple churches, and went on to be venerated by the Roman Catholic and Eastern Orthodox Churches.

2,162,184,322: **Alberic of Austrasia**

2,162,184,323: **Adéle of Poiters**

Generation 45

4,324,368,640: **Saint Arnulf, Bishop of Metz**, d. abt 647. Prominent official and soldier who later became a priest.

4,324,368,641: **Doda**

4,324,368,642: **Pepin of Landen, Mayor of the Palace of Austrasia**, abt 580–27 Feb 640. Ruled under Frankish kings Dagobert I and Sigebert III.

4,324, 368,643: **Saint Itta of Metz**, abt 592–8 May 652. Became a nun after the death of her husband and founded the Abbey of Nivelles. Canonized by the Catholic Church, as were her two daughters and son, Bavo the hermit.

Generation 46

8,648,737,284: **Carloman**. Nothing of him is known other than his relation to his son, Pepin of Landen, according to an unattributed Frankish document from the 800s now called the *Chronicle of Fredegar*. The oldest known ancestor in the Abdill tree, though his date of birth his unknown. His son Pepin is believed to have been born around 580.

Chapter 14

Welsh Kings

The ancestors of Cynan Dindaethwy *270,155,778* were omitted from the main chart and included here separately—records from early medieval Wales are notoriously scant, and some sections of the lineage are based on genealogies written in Old Welsh hundreds of years after the death of their subjects. Many connections included here are accepted by historical scholars, but almost all are at least partially contested as possibly being either inaccurate or fictional.

If we accept the more plausible conclusions of documents like Jesus College MS 20 and the Harleian genealogies, this line brings us farther back than any other: Tegid *8,852,464,533,504*, likely born sometime in the 300s, would be in the "Generation 56" chapter, the 53rd great grandfather of the author.

- 540,311,556: **Rhodri Molwynog, King of Gwynedd,** d. abt 754.
- 1,080,623,112: **Idwal Iwrch, King of Gwynedd**

- 2,161,246,224: **Cadwaladr, King of Gwynedd**, d. 682. Died in a plague, later became a major character in Welsh myths.
- 4,322,492,448: **Cadwallon ap Cadfan, King of the Britons**, d. 634. Renowned as an ethnic Briton as a fighter of Anglo-Saxons.
- 8,644,984,896: **Cadfan ap Iago, King of Gwynedd**, abt 569–abt 625.
- 17,289,969,792: **Iago ap Beli, King of Gwynedd**, d. abt 616.
- 34,579,939,584: **Beli ap Rhun, King of Gwynedd**
- 69,159,879,168: **Rhun Hir ap Maelgwn, King of Gwynedd**, d. abt 586.
- 138,319,758,336: **Maelgwn Gwynedd, King of Gwynedd**, d. abt 547. A generous contributor to Welsh Christian churches. May have died in the Plague of Justinian, a pandemic outbreak of bubonic plague unmatched until the Black Death 800 years later.
- 276,639,516,672: **Cadwallon Lawhir, King of Gwynedd**, d. abt 534. His surname translates to "Long Hand."
- 276,639,516,673: **Meddyf**
- 553,279,033,344: **Einion Yrth ap Cunedda, King of Gwynedd**, abt 420–abt 500. His surname is Welsh for "Impetuous." The first ruler of what would then be called Gwynedd.
- 553,279,033,345: **Prawst ferch Deithlyn**
- 553,279,033,346: **Maeldaf**
- 1,106,558,066,688: **Cunedda Wledig**
- 2,213,116,133,376: **Edeyrn**
- 4,426,232,266,752: **Padarn Beisrudd**, believed to have been born in Wales around the turn of the fifth century, under what would have been Roman rule. "Beisrudd"

translates to "Of the Scarlet Robe," a reference to legendary talisman he supposedly wore, which is now listed among the Thirteen Treasures of the Island of Britain.

- 8,852,464,533,504: **Tegid**, may have gone by the Latin name "Tacitus."

Chapter 15

Descent From Antiquity

There are no academically accepted genealogical lines that definitively connect any living people to ancestors any farther back than the Middle Ages, which are considered to have started at some point before the year 500. While there is lots of evidence for the families of the Roman empire, documentation from "Late Antiquity," bridging the fall of Rome in 476 and the rise of the Middle Ages, is sparse and always frustratingly vague.

However, the Abdill tree does include one of the more probable connections, branching backward from Saint Arnulf of Metz *4,324,368,640*, who died in the first half of the 7th century. The (first) disputed link is whether his father was **Arnoald**, who served as bishop of Metz before Arnulf did, and died around 611. There is no surviving documentation definitively linking the two men; however, the most accepted alternative is that Arnoald was instead the father of Doda,

Arnulf's wife. Either way, Arnoald would end up in the ancestry of Charlemagne (and thus in our tree), but the connection in either case is purely speculative.

Arnoald is believed to have been the son of **Ansbertus**, a Frankish noble for whom most documentation was not written until decades (or centuries) after his death. It is believed that he was a Gallo-Roman senator, and the son of **Ferreolus of Rodez**, for whom there is more contemporary documentation than the previous generations. He too was in the Gallo-Roman Senate.

The father of Ferreolus was **Tonantius Ferreolus**, another senator who is believed to have been born before about 450 and lived in Narbonne. Tonantius's father, also named **Tonantius Ferreolus**, was the praetorian prefect of Gaul, the equivalent of a governor of one of Rome's four prefectures. He would have played a major role in resisting the invasion of Attila the Hun. His parentage is relatively undocumented, but his maternal grandfather is believed to have been **Flavius Afranius Syagrius**, who was elected in 382 to the highest elected office in the Roman Empire: consul of Rome. Flavius Afranius Syagrius would be the 57th generation in the tree, bringing the earliest known ancestor back to a birth in the early 300s.

Part III

The Enslaved

It's an unavoidable conclusion that must be drawn when we learn we're descended from 19th century Virginia planters: Our relatives enslaved people, lots of them. We have documented ancestors living in the American South from before Virginia's first slave law in 1656 until after the end of the Civil War more than 200 years later, many of whom made their fortunes by holding generations of men, women and children against their wills, without pay, until they died or were sold off to die elsewhere.

There is no conscionable way to frame it in any other light: Our ancestors stole the lives of dozens of people. Our family prospered by purchasing human beings who had been kidnapped from their homes and brought across an ocean for an unending hell, albeit one that was widely endorsed by their owners' neighbors, politicians and pastors. It was not a tacit agreement that kept our family's slaves at work: It was the knowledge that to resist meant punishment, mutilation or death.

This legacy of cruelty is something we must grapple with on our own—there is no ready answer to a debt that can never be repaid. The identities of untold scores of slaves held by our family have been lost forever, but some have survived, hidden in court documents and government records. If the hundreds of pages of facts and dates in the preceding pages mean anything, it is that to be remembered is a powerful thing. We must not forget them.

The Stone family

Some of the slaves of William Stone *7-80* and his children appear to have spent decades with the family—several were born in Lunenburg County, where the Stone family farm was located in the 1830s, and stayed even after the war, hired as servants and farm workers. We know of many of them because of records kept after the Civil War reflecting official marriages between emancipated slaves. The Civil Rights Act of 1866 extended to former slaves the official right to marry or enter into contracts, and many took the opportunity to officially recognize unofficial relationships that had already been carried on for years, at times separated by great distances as couples were split up and sold off to separate owners.[i]

These records list the "date of commencement of co-habitation"; to better reflect their intent and simplify the descriptions below, that date is given here as their date of "marriage."

Alexander Dawson and Grace Paters

Alexander and Grace were both born abt 1825 in Lunenburg County; they were married 1 Sep 1846. Both were held by William Stone *7-80*.[707]

Millie Walker

Born about 1811, and possibly the mother of Stephen and Philip Walker, both profiled below. Was a servant in the home of Clarissa Stone *7-81* while a slave,[708] and worked there as a cook as of 1870;[709] nothing of her life after that is known. At some point before 1872, she was diagnosed with cancer in her side.[710]

---

[i]It was also favored practice for slaves to have relationships between plantations intentionally: As former slave Moses Gandy explains in his autobiography, "no coloured man wishes to live at the house where his wife lives, for he has to endure the continual misery of seeing her flogged and abused, without daring to say a word in her defence."

Stephen Walker and Frances Williams

Both Frances and Stephen were born in Lunenburg County, Stephen in about 1821 and Frances (also known as "Frankie")[711] in about 1835. They were married 1 Apr 1862; both were held by William Stone.[712] Early records list one daughter witht he name of "Mary"[713] or "Mary Francis"[714] but who may have later gone by the name "Jane." Though she was the only child mentioned in their marriage registration in 1866, in the 1870 census they were living with a total of six children. Evidence suggests they continued to work on the Stone farm after the end of the Civil War, as they are listed in 1870 in a home with Clarissa Stone *7-81* on one side and her sons, Musgrove and John *6-40* on the other.[715]

By 1880, the Walkers were living near John *6-40* and his brother, William E. Stone,[716] though Clarissa *7-81* had died[717] and Musgrove moved away.[718] It's not clear if this is the same farm they were on 10 years prior, but a likely explanation is that it is not: In 1870, Stephen is listed as a "farm laborer"; in 1880, he appears to live farther from the remaining Stones, and is listed only as a "farmer," which may imply running his own farm. His family with Frankie had grown considerably as well:[719] In total:

- **Farris**, b. abt 1857. Worked as a "mill boy."[720] May have been the "Travis Walker" of Virginia who appeared in the 1900 census in Douglas County, Nebraska, working as a porter.[721]
- **Joseph**, b. abt 1860.[722]
- **Jane**, b. abt 1866.[723]
- **Adeline**, b. abt 1868.[724] Also known as "Ada."[725]
- **Mariah**, b. abt 1873,[726] d. 25 Dec 1892.[727]
- **Gertrude**, b. abt 1877.[728]
- **Frank**, b. abt 1879.[729]

There are also two others living there that appear to have been children of Frances and a man named William Winn:[730] Minerva and Jerry. In 1870, they are listed alongside the other children with the last name "Walker," but in the 1880 census, they are listed explicitly as step-children of Stephen and having the last name "Winn." There appear to be a total of five Winn children; all were held by John Stone *6-40* as slaves, but the others are relatively unaccounted for after the war.[731]

- **Minerva Norman**,[732] b. abt 1852. Worked as a cook.[733] Married Casey Wells (b. abt 1852) and had a daughter, Fannie.[734]
- **Amos**, b. abt 1852.[735] Lived on the farm of Clarissa Stone *7-81* after the war and worked as a farm laborer.[736] Married Hellen Sherman 21 Sep 1914.[737]
- **Phares**, b. abt 1855.[738]
- **Joseph**, b. abt 1860.[739]
- **Jerry**, b. abt 1862.[740] Married Lucy Clayton 9 Sep 1886.[741]

The 1870s appear to have been a time of progress for the Walkers: Frances learned to read,[ii] and their daughter Mariah began attending school.[742] After 1880, however, we lose track of the family—because most of the 1890 census was lost, there is a 20-year gap in the records that are most likely to have recorded them, and they drift away.

Lewis Glasville and Maria Boswell

Lewis and Maria were both born in Lunenburg County; Lewis in abt 1833 and Maria abt 1828. They were married

---

[ii]She is listed as unable to read or write in the 1870 census, and only unable to write in 1880.

10 Mar 1857. Both were held by a "William Stone,"[743] likely the son of William A. Stone *7-80*.

Scotland Stokes and Parthena Bragg

Scotland was born in abt 1823; Parthena in 1836. Both were born in Lunenburg County[744] and held by Clara Stone *7-81*.[745] They had nine children; the oldest six[746] appear to also have been enslaved:

- **Cesar**, b. abt 1851.[747]
- **Permelia**, b. abt 1853.[748] Was likely "Pamelia," the "Negroe Girl" mentioned in the will of William Stone *7-80* who was passed to his daughter, Clara Bullard.[749]
- **Richard**,[750] b. abt 1859.[751]
- **Mary Susan**,[752] b. abt 1856.[753]
- **Millie Ann**,[754] b. abt 1858.[755]
- **Harriet Virginia**, b. abt 1862.[756] Went by "Jinnie" later.[757]
- **Robert Dexter**,[758] b. abt 1863.[759][iii] Noted as "sickly" when he was 3;[760] may have died in 1937.[761]
- **Judah**, b. abt 1865.[762]
- **Parthenia**, b. abt 1868.[763]

Parthena does not appear with her husband and children in the 1880 census; she may have died before then, but we have no records indicating either way.

Sarah Bragg

Sarah was born in Lunenburg County in about 1833;[764] her relationship to Parthena Bragg, another Stone family slave profiled above, is unclear. She married Amsted Rollins

---

[iii] A Social Security record for Robert from 1937 gives his birthdate as 2 Nov 1875, but he is listed as 17 years old in the 1880 census.

(b. abt 1804 in Montgomery County), a slave from the plantation of Jacob Zull, on 5 Apr 1858. They had three children:[765]

- **Samuel**, b. abt 1859.
- **Eliza**, b. abt 1862.
- **Willia**, b. abt 1865.

Benjamin Wilson

Benjamin was born abt 1831 in Lunenburg County. He married Lucy Jones (b. abt 1832, Lunenburg County), a slave apparently on loan from Whitehead Coleman, on 25 Dec 1860. They had three children:[766]

- **Vinnie**, b. abt 1861.
- **Jane**, b. abt 1864.
- **Isabella**, b. abt 1866.

Warner

A "Negroe Boy" in the will of William Stone *7-80*, given to Dexter Bullard, the husband of William's daughter Mary.[767]

Judy

A "Negroe Girl" in the will of William Stone *7-80*, given to Dexter Bullard, the husband of William's daughter Mary.[768]

Jim

A "Negroe Boy" in the will of William Stone *7-80*, given to his daughter Clara.[769]

Albert

A "Negroe Boy" in the will of William Stone *7-80*, given to his son John *6-40*.[770]

Vinsey

A "Negroe Woman" in the will of William Stone *7-80*, given to his daughter Mary.[771]

Bettie Shelbourn

Born in about 1770, according to the age (100) given in the 1870 census[772] and in a collection of slave data (95) compiled by the Freedmen's Bureau[iv] several years earlier.[773] Was living with Clara Stone *7-81* in 1870.

Archer Stone

Archer was born in about 1810, and was living with Clara Stone in 1870[774] and with her son William in 1880.[775]

Philip and Gertrude Walker

Philip was born abt 1829 in Lunenburg County; Gertrude[v] was born abt 1846 in Greene County, Va. They were married 15 Mar 1862, when they were enslaved on the farm of Musgrove Stone and had three children:[776]

- **Giles**, b. abt 1863.

[iv]Technically, the Bureau of Refugees, Freedmen, and Abandoned Lands.

[v]Her full name in the register of marriages is given as "Jat True"; Philip is found in Freedmen's Bureau records as living with a "Gertrude" of the same age; the assumption has been made that these are the same people, though her surname has been lost.

- **Angeline**, b. abt 1864.
- **Eliza Jane**, b. abt 1867.

There are nine or 10 people who are listed after the war as being former slaves and working for the Stone family, though this alone isn't evidence that they worked for the Stones when they were slaves as well: For example, the family of Philip and Gertrude Walker described above left the farm of Musgrove Stone after their emancipation to work on a nearby plantation owned by J.P. Whitt:[777] They are listed in Freedmen's Bureau documents as former slaves, and as working for Whitt, but those end up being unrelated facts.

Though we aren't sure about the antebellum status of these families, they are included here in order to at least help researchers in the future who may be looking for them.

Viney Campbell

Viney was born abt 1805. She worked as a servant in the home of Clara Stone *7-81*,[778] and in 1880 was living with the family of William E. Stone.[779]

James Campbell

Born abt 1845; his relation to Viney, if any, is unclear. A laborer who worked for Clara Stone *7-81*.[780]

Samuel and Emma Cheese

Samuel was born abt 1818; his wife Emma in about 1831. They worked on the plantation of John Stone *6-40* and had four children:

- **Catharine**, b. abt 1850.[781]
- **Samuel**, b. abt 1862.[782]
- **Nannie**, b. abt 1863.[783]
- **Ida**, b. abt 1866.[784]

Walla Caton

Born abt 1847; worked on the farm of Clara Stone *7-81*.[785]

Ann Hale

Anne was born abt 1835 and worked on the farm of William Stone, the brother of John Stone *6-40*.[786] There are two boys there with the same last name who appear to be her sons:

- **James**, b. abt 1852.[787]
- **Emanuel**, b. abt 1859.[788]

The Pettus family

Though the slaves of the Stone family are the most extensively documented, we do have some records available for earlier families in the state. Thomas Pettus *10-648*, born in 1712, mentions multiple slaves in his will:[789]

- Marey and her son, Daniel
- Squire
- Sarah
- Rachael (and children)
- Neil
- Sampson, a child
- Warwick, a child
- Phillis, and her two children, Massilve and Sylvia

Thomas's son, David Pettus *9-324*, has records indicating many more:[790]

- Joe
- Sam
- Lyddia
- Bob[vi]
- Ned, purchased for £500
- Charlotte, purchased for 8,000 pounds of tobacco.[791]
- Jane
- Anthony
- Rose (likely inherited from his father) and her daughter, Rachel
- Charlott
- Clarissa
- Lewis
- Isaac
- Pawl
- Lucy
- Betty

There is one slave mentioned in the will of Samuel Pettus *8-162* as well:

- Rachel[792]

The Alsop family

The estate of Benjamin Alsop *9-330* was appraised in early 1833, after his death. Among the inventoried horses, corn and furniture are the names, ages and market values of 35 slaves.[793]

- Guy, 79

[vi]May have been the same person as "Joe." Is missing from a slave inventory that includes a "Joe" but is otherwise present, while "Joe" is not.

- Clue, 70
- Celia, 55
- Gloster, 52
- Bob, 50
- Peter, 45
- Lewis, 37
- Cato, 30
- Grandison, 29
- Beverly, 28
- Sam, 24
- George, 22
- Joe, 20
- Ben, 18
- Caleb, 18
- Joshua, 16
- Richmond, 16
- Sam Miller, 12
- Cornelius, 14
- Delsey, 44 and Betsey, 7 months
- Matilda, 11
- Malvina, 9
- Eliza, 6
- Jenny, 3
- Lester, 37
- Susan, 22 and Francis, 15 months
- Hezekiah, 25
- Rosella, 2
- Emily, 20
- Mary, 23 and Nancy, 9 months
- two others, names illegible

The Lamb family

While there isn't any documentation that has been found of the slave holdings of Richard Lamb *9-326*, a 1773 edition of the *Virginia Gazette* carries an advertisement that he placed, looking for a runaway slave:

* Jack
  The text reads:

FIVE POUNDS REWARD.

Run away last Night, the 4th instant (January) from the Subscriber, a Negro Boy named JACK, about seventeen Years of Age, near five Feet high, and had on, when he went off, a new Suit of green Beaver Coating trimmed with Mohair Basket Buttons, the Jacket and Breeches with white Metal Ones, an old Felt Hat, Yarn Hose, and a Pair of stout imported Shoes. He was born in Antigua, and came in, about fifteen Months ago, to Mr. John Livingston of Norfolk, to which Place it is probable he will make, or endeavour for a Passage to the West Indies, as he is pretty artful, and formerly went by Water. He speaks tolerable plain, is likely, remarkably black, and has a small Scar on his left Cheek. Whoever will bring him to me, near Petersburg, or to Mr. John Greenwood at Norfolk, shall have the above Reward.

RICHARD LAMB.

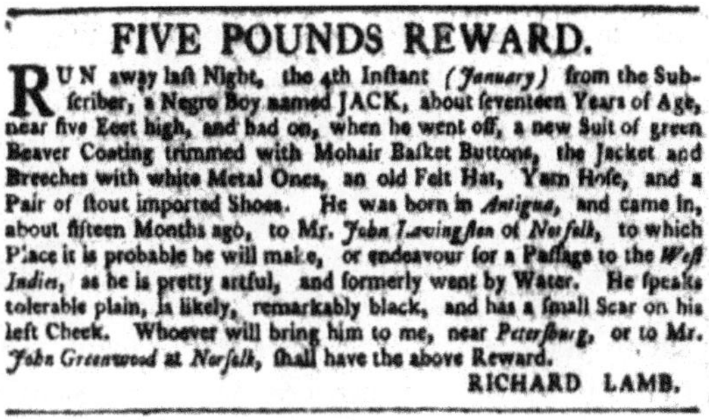

Figure 15.1: A runaway slave advertisement filed by Richard Lamb.[794]

Language

I want to include a brief explanation of the language used to describe slavery in this section, as contemporary readers will notice that it sometimes differs from the conventional terminology, in which we say "slaveowners" were the people who "owned" "slaves." These three terms were the ones that gave me the most grief when writing this, both because they carry such strong connotations and because I am so under-equipped to interpret them.

Language is powerful, and wielding it in the wrong directions has consequences, if not in our current actions, then at least in our interpretation of the past. Challenging the language of American slavery can go in two directions: It could more accurately portray the conditions and relationships of the time, but it could also generate protective euphemisms that paper over the realities of our "peculiar institution," as it were: terms like "houseboy" and "field hand" sound like docile, domestic occupations—"enslaved African captive" has something of a different tone.

The "slave vs. enslaved person" question is one of active scholarly debate, especially in the 21st century. I am neither interested in nor qualified to contribute to the discussion, and both terms have been applied here, but it's not a stretch to see where the argument lies. There are two points that are particularly persuasive for me: Firstly, "enslaved" implies it is a condition that need not be permanent—an "enslaved person" is still a person, though they are in a condition of slavery. A "slave" is a position, a political state. A slave who is freed becomes something else.

I'll readily grant that this is an abstract debate that smacks a bit of of navel-gazing, but it will be interesting to see where the terminology goes over the decades. We're already a long way from "houseboy."

The most important point, for me at least, is that the term "enslaved" implies an active decision to put a person into that state: For someone to be enslaved, *someone had to do the enslaving.* The term "slave" obscures this to a degree: If someone simply "is" a slave, the question of ownership becomes an incidental detail; "owning" a slave becomes as innocent of an act as "owning" a tea kettle: It's not your fault the tea kettle exists, it just happens to be sitting on your stove.

This seems unfair, at least to my amateur interpretation. Enslavement is not a permanent conversion: Once a person was brought to the "New World," it need not have been a foregone conclusion that they would be slaves forever, nor that their children would be slaves, and their children's children, and so on. Slavery was an ongoing process, perpetrated by each successive generation of slave drivers. Our family *could* have excluded themselves from the practice, but didn't. They likewise could have paid their workers—all evidence suggests that they refused to, until the U.S. Army arrived to make them.

So this is why I have spent so much time pondering a single syllable: "owned." I make no claim on having the correct answer, just one that seemed the most just in this circumstance.

Part IV

Appendices

Appendix A

Genetic Testing

The DNA results of two family members were evaluated to help corroborate this branch of the family tree: the author's and Sally Abdill *3-5*, his grandmother. The results were processed by Ancestry.com, which has collected the DNA of millions of people who want to locate unknown but living relatives.

How it works

At its simplest, the AncestryDNA project is just a program that compares the DNA of all its participants to give them a list of their relatives. Based on information extracted from a saliva sample, Ancestry gives you a list of users that are related to you. This alone is fascinating, but the most powerful part takes advantage of Ancestry.com's oldest feature: family trees.

Based on DNA alone, all AncestryDNA tells you is whether someone is related to you, nothing more. You can estimate how closely the relation is based on how similar the samples are (you probably have more of your mother's DNA than your third cousin's), but there isn't any way to determine for sure. However, because many participants in the AncestryDNA program have built their family trees on the website, Ancestry.com uses that data to determine *how* you are mostly likely to be related: Once you are "matched" with another user who is related, the website will compare your family tree to theirs to find where the common ancestor is. The result is a list of people that have traced their family lines back to an intersection somewhere in your tree.

This is powerful information for multiple reasons. Mainly, it is a form of loose validation that your connection to that ancestor is correct: If DNA data says I am related to Person X, and we both have family trees that list John Stone as a great-great-great grandfather, that goes a long way to validating that we are both legitimately connected to John Stone (and that Person X is my fourth cousin).

There are, however, multiple important caveats with this conclusion: For starters, there isn't actually any evidence that either I or Person X are *actually related to John Stone*: John Stone's DNA wasn't tested, so we can't draw any concrete conclusions.[i] What we learn from a match with Person X is:

1. I am related to Person X, and have enough DNA in common to suggest a relationship of fourth cousins.
2. Both I and Person X have included John Stone in our family trees.

So, it's entirely possible that Person X and I are related in an entirely different way, and one (or both) of us is

---

[i]There are two exceptions to this uncertainty: Two ancestors of the author—Sally Abdill *3-5* and Nancy Abdill *2-2*—*did* take the AncestryDNA test, and results reflect that they are related as has been believed.

incorrect about being related to the person we think is our "common" ancestor. This uncertainty grows exponentially with each generation: If someone is your second cousin, that means you share one (or two) of your great-grandparents. You only have eight great-grandparents, so there's relatively little space for mistakes. But what if someone is, say, an eighth cousin? That means you share a pair of 7th great grandparents—you probably have more than 1,000 of those, so the odds are higher that at least one of you misidentified an ancestor that also happens to appear in the other person's tree. Still, the odds are low enough that even a coincidence can give us a little bit of data.

Valuable results

In addition to the author's results, Sally Abdill *3-5* also participated in the AncestryDNA project. This produced much more productive results, in short, because she has more of her ancestors' DNA than the author does—being two generations older, somewhere around four times as much. For this reason, she has far more matches than Richard Abdill *1-1* in this line.

What can we learn?

Despite the uncertainty of the results, it is still a boost to be able to say two distant cousins independently tracked their ancestry back to the same person, coincidence or not. For that reason, the results of Richard Abdill and Sally (Stone) Abdill's known matches are illustrated below. Because some ancestors have multiple matches (you can have lots of first cousins, so you've got even more 7th cousins), each ancestor is marked with an *R* or an *S* for each match registered to either person tested; if an AncestryDNA user was a match connected to both Richard and Sally, they are indicated with a *B*, to avoid double-counting them.

Why, you are likely asking, is this helpful? Basically, the usefulness of the compiled DNA results depends on the increasingly unlikely chance that distant cousins could all independently come to identical conclusions that are not correct: If you don't have any (known) cousins who claim a common ancestor, the connection to that ancestor is based entirely on your research alone.

If you have one match, that means not only did you find a route back to an ancestor, but someone else who *we know is related to you* also found a way back to the same person. Still, as discussed above, it's not impossible that a cousin could coincidentally find the same ancestor. However, what happens if, as in the case of Thomas *10-648* and Amey Pettus *10-649*, there isn't just *one* cousin who discovered that ancestor, but nine cousins? That would mean nine separate people found the exact same ancestor on their own.

There are only three reasonably likely reasons this would happen:

1. We are all **correct about the common ancestor**, and now have genetic corroboration of the relationship. This is the one we are hoping for.

2. There is a group of children that have a **commonly stated *but incorrect* set of parents**. If we are descended from Person X, and a group of AncestryDNA users are descended from the siblings of Person X (say, Person Y and Person Z), then our common ancestor would be the parents of Persons X, Y and Z. We can call the *real* parents Person A and Person B—those are the common ancestors. However, it's possible that there is confusing evidence that suggests different people (say,

Person Q and Person R) are the parents of Persons X, Y and Z—maybe a misunderstood tombstone, or a conflicting census record. If that were the case, then all the cousins would say, "Oh, we're all descended from Person Q and Person R! Look at all these cousins who confirm it," even though all the cousins would have the wrong identity. They would all be correct about the spot in the tree where their lines intersect, but would incorrectly be linked to Persons Q and R instead of Persons A and B.

3. There is a popular ancestor to be descended from, and multiple cousins have **incorrectly found a path to that person**. Some relatives are just more genealogically interesting: Anne West *12-2665* is a good example of this. Finding a connection to Anne West means you've found a connection to European nobility, so the odds are better that amateur genealogists would try to find a route to her, and that it would be simpler to find documentation supporting it. Sally Abdill has five cousins who claim to be linked through Anne and her husband, Henry Fox *12-2664*. It's possible *none* of those cousins is correct, or that we are wrong instead, and those five people are related in some other, unknown way. Because some people are more tempting to put into your tree, the odds are better that incorrectly attributed cousins will "clump" around those relations. There is one way to mitigate this one a little: If all we know is that Sally has 5 cousins who claim to be descended from Anne West, it's possible that some are correct and some aren't, or even that *no one* is correct. However, in many cases below, the cousins attributed to Richard and Sally *have also been matched to each other*. This is a more powerful match: If five people are only matched to, say, Richard, then it's possible that each of the five cousins are related

in five separate, unknown ways. However, if the five cousins are related to Richard, *and related to each other*, that means the most likely explanation is that *all six people share an ancestor*, rather than just individuals paired with Richard.

Basically, the more cousins are matched to an ancestor, the more likely that ancestor has been accurately identified as a relative.

Most entries listed have two ancestors in the match—if we're descended from one ancestor, we're descended from their spouse. There are two exceptions: For William Alsop *11-1320*, we are unsure of the identity of his wife. For Benjamin Spindle *7-82*, it's actually a "half match"—Sally Abdill is descended from Benjamin and his first wife, Maria Wigglesworth *7-83*. The genetic match is descended from Benjamin and his second wife, Sarah Buckner.

Here are the results that have come in so far:

Benjamin Spindle *7-82*	*S*
David Pettus *9-324* and Ann Whitworth *9-325*	*SSSS*
Thomas Pettus *10-648* and Amey Walker *10-649*	*RRBBBSSSS*
Thomas Whitworth *10-650* and Elizabeth Sutherland *10-651*	*BBSSSSSS*
William Alsop *11-1320*	*S*
Thomas Fox *11-1332* and Mary Tunstall *11-1333*	*B*
Henry Fox *12-2664* and Anne West *12-2665*	*SSSSSS*

Appendix B

Will of Thomas Wiglesworth

What follows is a transcription of the last will and testament of Thomas Wiglesworth 8-166 found in a community-maintained internet collection of transcribed legal documents from early-1800s Spotsylvania County. The author has not seen the original document.

I Thomas Wiglesworth of the County of Spotsylvania being weak & low but of sound mind, make this my last will & Testament in manner & form as follows

Viz, 1st I wish all my Just debts to be first paid for which purpose I wish my executors hereafter to be named to sell Negroes sufficient to Pay the same as soon as possible, or any of my Perishable estate that can be spared.

2nd. And after my debts are paid I wish my Children to live together and be supported from the proffits [sic] of my estate untill my youngest shall have received their Education which is to be paid for out of my estate if the profit is not sufficient & no charge made against them for it.

3rd. In the event of any of my Daughters marrying they are to receive their proportion of my Estate & the rest to continue together as long as it may be thought practicable & when other wise shall be the case I wish the ballance [sic] of my estate not given out to those maried [sic] equally divided between my sin[gle] daughters with strict regard to equality, the land whi[ch] I live [on] is to remain a home for all my Children [as] long as they may chose [sic] to remain on it & afterwards to be sol[d] & the proceeds Equally divided between all my seven daughters Mariah C. Mary L Sarah A Philadelphia Frances E Lucy Jane & Lavinia Wiglesworth or their legal representatives & the other Part of my estate to be divided as above described amongst the seven named daughters.

4th & lastly I appoint & constitute my two oldest Daughters Maria C. Wiglesworth & Mary L. Wiglesworth my Executors of this my Last will & Testament of whom I wish the Court to ask no security to execute the above will.

Witness my hand & seal this 4th day of December 182[missing]

Tho. Wiglesworth [Seal]

Teste /s/ John Wiglesworth /s/ Robert Foster /s/ Jas. Wiglesworth

At a Court held for Spotsylvania County the 15th day of January 1829
The last will and testament of Thomas Wiglesworth deceased was proved by the oaths of John Wiglesworth and Robert Foster witnesses thereto and ordered to be recorded and on the motion of Maria C. Wiglesworth one of the executrixes therein named who made oath thereto and entered into and acknowledged a bond in the penalty of $16000

conditioned as the law directs Certificate is granted her for obtaining a probate of said will in due form.

Teste

R. L. Stevenson, C. C.

At a Court held for Spotsylvania County the 2nd day of December 1833

On the motion of Mary L. Wiglesworth one of the executrixes named in the last will and testament of Thomas Wiglesworth deceased who made oath thereto and entered into and acknowledged a bond in the penalty of $16000 conditioned as the law directs Certificate is granted her for obtaining a probate of said will in due form.

Teste

R. L. Stevenson, C. C.

Appendix C

Will of William A. Stone

The following is a transcription of the last will and testament of William Stone (7-80) found in a 1,167-page court file in Montgomery County, Virginia. There are no line breaks in the original; they have been added for clarity.

The last will and testament of William A Stone made This 5th day of November 1858. First I direct that my debts be paid out of my Estate, and if necessary to hire out some of my slaves till the debts can be paid, without selling any property, except stock and crop, so as to leave a sufficiency to keep up my plantation.

Second the property that I have given to my three sons, Wm E. Saml A and Musgrove C Stone, I hereby confirm unto them and their heirs, also the property I have given to my daughter Susan E Wilson, I confirm unto her and her heirs.

3rd I place in the hands of my son-in-law Dexter Bullard

in special trust and confidence for the support and main-tainance of daughter Mary + her children if she should have any, one Negroe boy Warner One Negroe Girl Jude, One horse, One cow, one Bed + furniture. One Bureau, to be used by him in any way he may think proper, for the object above specified.

4th I give to my daughter Clara A Miller, One Negroe boy Jim and One Negroe Girl Pamelia, One horse, one Cow, one bed and furniture + Bureau to her and her heirs forever

5th I give to my son John One Negroe Boy Albert, one horse, One cow, One bed + furniture and four hundred acres of land, commencing a line at my Mill dam: Thence running a line so as to include the tract of land I purchased of my Son William, also my part of the mill on Meadow Creek. The land to be laid off to him by Wm E Stone + Miles A Wilson.

6th I give to my daughter Harriot Two Negroes, One horse 1 cow 1 Bureau, One Bed + furniture, such as my wife may dessignatate [sic] to her + her heirs.

7th I give to my daughter Sophia two Negroes One horse, 1 Cow 1 Bureau One Bed + furniture such as my wife may dessignate.

8th I give to my son Franklin Newton, One Negroe Boy, One horse + saddle, One cow, such as my wife may dessignate.

9th The Balance of my Estate of every description not disposed of, I leave to my wife during her life or widowhood, and at the death of my wife I give (10) To my son Franklin Newton, the tract of land on which I live, after taking off the part given to my son John.

11th After the death of my wife, I will that all of my property not disposed of to be made into eight equal shares, one share I give to my son William, One share to my son

Saml, One share son Musgrove, One share to my daughter Susan, One share to my daughter Clara, One share to my daughter Harriott, One share to my daughter Sophia, One share I wished placed in the hands of my son-in-law Dexter Bullard to be used by him for the same purpose as before stated, and the profits arising from sd trust found after the support + maintainance of my daughter and her children, to be converted into other property, and held under the same trust. At the death of my daughter, I will all the property held as the said trust fund, shall be equally divided among her Children. Should she die and leave no Children, I will that Dexter Bullard be supported out of said trust fund during his life + at his death to return to my Estate + equally divided among my Children + their heirs. In testimony whereof I hereunto set my hand and affix my seal.

Wm A Stone

Codicil to my Will made this 20th day of October 1861

I give to my son Wm E stone the sum of five hundred dollars, to my Daughter Susan E Wilson the sum of five hundred dollars. I give to my son Samuel the amount that I assumed to pay Paul Wilson for him. I give to my son Musgrove the Bond that I hold against him after deducting the amount that I am due him + Saml Stone. I give to my daughter Mary M Bullard One Negroe Woman Vinsey + the sum of six hundred dollars. I give to my daughter Clarissa Ann Miller the sum of nine hundred Dollars Dollars [*sic*] to be paid out of the Bond I hold against Spindle + Miller. I give to my daughter Harriott the sum of nine hundred Dollars. I give to my saughter Sophia Adaline the sum of nine hundred Dollars. I give to my son John fifty acres of land in addition to what I before willed to him. The above sum not provided for shall be raised out of the proffits of my Estate bound to my wife + by hire of Negroes, should the other property that I have + shall directo to be sold prove insufficient.

I direct that all my land except that otherwise directed, to be sold by my executors, either publickly or privately as my executors May think proper. I hereby appoint my son Wm E Stone + my son in law Miles A Wilson + my son Musgrove executors to this my last will and testament. Witness the following signature + seal.

Wm A Stone

Appendix D

John Stone Pension Approval

In early 1898, the Virginia state legislature approved multiple pensions for injured Confederate veterans including John Stone (6-40).

Chap. 743.–An ACT for the relief of John R. Stone.

Approved March 3, 1898.

Whereas John R. Stone, a wounded Confederate soldier of Company G, fourth regiment of Virginia infantry, was a true and gallant soldier during the war; was loyal to Virginia and the Confederate States; and

Whereas he is now suffering from the following disabilities—to wit:

A wound (at Gettysburg) in the side.

A wound (at Wilderness) in right arm below elbow; ball still between bones of same.

A wound (at Winchester); shot through the breast: therefore,

1. Be it enacted by the general assembly of Virginia, That the county court of Pulaski county shall examine into the condition of the above-named John R. Stone, a Confederate soldier, and should it be that he was true and loyal to Virginia through the war, and that he is now afflicted and disabled by his wounds, as above set forth, and incapacitated thereby for manual labor; that he is needy and poor, and should receive aid from Virginia; and if the county court of Pulaski county should send a certificate of the facts to the auditor of public accounts of Virginia, then the auditor of public accounts is directed to place the name of John R. Stone on the pension list, and pay him annually the sum of fifteen dollars, on and after the first day of April, eighteen hundred and ninety-eight.

2. This act shall be in force from its passage.[795]

Appendix E

Henry Our Hero

*"Henry Our Hero" is a typewritten memoir by Henry Stone Jr. (4-10) about his experiences in World War I, written in the 1960s. His daughter Sally Abdill (3-5) has the original copy, which included Henry's World War I Victory Medal casually taped to the back. The text is reprinted here in its entirety; spelling and typographical errors have been reproduced as they were written. Any editorial notes are either in footnotes or framed in text boxes with gray backgrounds and **were not part of the original text**.*[796]

HOH: Henry Our Hero

WHO TRAINED FOR A TRUCK DRIVER TURNED INTO A PACK ANIMAL, NEVER SHOT AT OR SAW AN ENEMY SO CAN'T BE CALLED MUCH OF A HERO.

H.T. STONE

December 1917.

In 1917 I was in Buffalo, N.Y. working for Stone and Webster on the Buffalo Electric Power house, The war hysteria was going good and I got the idea that I should get in. Another fellow and I went to the recruiting office and volunteered to go over and clean the war up for the Democrats. We were told to come back the next morning ready to be sent to Camp.

Our Hero returned to the job, quit, went to rooming house, packed, arranged with Charlie the tailor to ship trunk, and then

Next morning reported for examination, was stripped put in room with 100 other heroes, told to take off glasses and read chart, couldn't, was kicked out so returned to job and went back to work.

Next six months took up collectios for departing ones gave them presents and dinners.

May 1918.
Greetings extended by Mr. Wilson so

Figure E.1: Henry Stone Jr., in a photo dated 1918.[797]

reported to Dr. Showalter in Christiansburg, who without any hesitation said I would do, sent me to the University of

Virginia to train for a Truck Driver about May 24th. On May 20 the Buffalo board extended greetings but had to let them be dissapointed. Six weeks there; then train for Camp Mills om Long Island.

July 1918.
Arrived at Camp Mills dressed in own pants, shoes, and underwear with a Army shirt and broad brimed GI issued hat. Several days of shots etc and then we were issued GI uniforms, shoes and knapsacks. The night before we were to sail a crew of more experienced soldiers showed up and helped us to roll our packs, tied our extra shoes etc on and got us ready to go. A short train ride to Hoboken (I think) and then herded on the SS Melita an English troopship converted from something else. Some of our Southern compadres saw the ferry boats on the way and opined that they looked awful small to take us over the sea. This was, I, believe July 31.

> The *Melita* had been shuttling back and forth across the Atlantic since January.[798] During the most recent return trip to New York, its convoy had been attacked by a German submarine, which sunk one of the other troop ships on July 20.[799]

After losing most of my stomack over the sides of the ship I settled down for an uneventful conveyed trip. We slept in hammocks hung over the dining room tables so close together that one could not fall out. The mess crew started setting the table at 6 a.m. so we were roused out at 5.30. The trip lasted about twelve days and the last night we lost our convoy and came down between Ireland and the English coast alone.

> Pvt. Homer E. Simpson, another Virginian in
> Henry's company wrote, on 6 Aug: "A big day
> in a country boy's life. We passed thru a school
> of whales. Sharks followed the ships. We enjoyed
> watching the porpoise and seeing flying fish jump
> out of the water."[800]

Started this trip with two dollars and thirty cents lost
two dollars in a crap game the first night out and didn't
have any money until the 12th of September when we got
paid for the first time in France.

The trip was uneventful. All were sick until we passed
the Bank and the rought seas. Then some recovered and
some didn't

August 1918 England

Landed in Liverpool after standing on deck for hours with
full packs on. Had a long march to a so called English rest
camp. Arrived after dark dead to the world. Were billeted
in squad tents with wooden floors ready to keel over. Some
fools in a tent nearby wanted to be smart so they started
jigging on the wood floors. We could have killed them.

> 2Lt. Paul W. Mack, writing of his experience, also
> put the "rest" of "rest camp" in quotes, and said,
> "If one is not mad enough to fight Huns when he
> lands in France, a Rest Camp is guaranteed to
> make him fight a buzz saw."[801]

We were put on a train next and taken to a permement
camp not too far from London.[i] On the way I was in a
eight man crowded compartment with my pack between my
knees. This was the first time I had inspected it closely and

---

[i]Likely Camp Woodley.

I was very much surprised and upset to discover that my number 9 1/2 shoes were for the same foot. (In civil life my shoe size was 6 1/2) The company supply sergeant was sitting next to me and promised to remedy this later.

We were here for some few days. How many I can't remember as this was nearly fifty years ago and my memory is notorious for it's lapses. One of the greatest dissapointments of my life was here:[ii]

We were called for details each morning and one bright day I was sent to an English officers mess to help the cook. I was given a cup of tea and a backhanded promise of a good meal after the officers were fed. I worked like a little Trojan all morning and at noon the detail truck picked me up to go back to camp for lunch. I skipped the GI issue of whatever slum was being served for lunch. My mouth was watering with the thoughts of a wonderful meal of steak and the trimmings when I got back to my KP duties. After lining up for afternoon details, I was sent on a ditch digging detail instead. Not even GI slumgullion. C'est le guerre.

We were next sent on our way and arrived in Southhampton[iii] to board a channel ship for Le Harve.

> This was Le Havre, France, one of the largest ports in the country through which an estimated 1.9 million British soldiers passed during the war.[803]

This was I believ late August. Later all soldiers I talked to bellyacked about the British but will never forget one little Englishman who handed me a pack of English cigarettes from his own pocket when we were marching to the camp

---

[ii]Pvt. Simpson's diary notes they stayed only the night of 13 Aug,[802] so it's possible the great disappointment happened elsewhere.

[iii]The English port city is Southampton.

in Liverpool. They tasted wonderful for my funds were low as was my smoking supply.

FINIS JOLLY ENGLAND

August - September 1918.

We left Southhampton or Le Harve on what I took for a regular channel ferry boat[iv] and at our destination were loaded on French narrow guage 40 & 8 cars, forty men and or eight horses.[v] The cars were small and when loaded to the hilt left very little room for expansion. When we tried to sleep it was necessary to put your feet up on the yard bird directly across from you, with your back propped against the side of the box car. During the night some character rammed his foot in my face and cracked one lense of my glasses. This crack stayed with me and I didn't get new glasses until arriving at the A.E.F. University the next Spring.

Finally we arrived in a training area[vi] and started doing squads right and so on. The men from the truck driving school at Charlottsville, in spite of the limited time that had been put in on us at drilling, (which never amounted to more than a coupla hours a day) were better trained than the average men in our battalion. We had been thrown in with a make up bunch, most of whom came from the Southern mountains, with little education or ambitions. Some were from other sections of the Country but the farmer-mountaineers predominated.

[iv] Possibly the "La Margeretta, an old French side wheeler" described by Pvt. Simpson.[804]

[v] The French *Quarante et huit* railcars had already been used to transport troops and goods for 40 years, and were in service through World War II.

[vi] Almost certainly in Tonnerre,[805] in the French region of Bourgogne-Franche-Comté, about 240 miles south of where they landed at Le Havre.

> Henry's unit, the 81st Infantry Division, was or-
> ganized at Camp Jackson in South Carolina with
> recruits from Florida, North Carolina, Alabama,
> Georgia and Tennessee. Curiously, no sources men-
> tion troops from Virginia.[806]

At the start of training quiet a few of us were put in the number one spot in the front ranks. This eventually would have meant we would be made corporals. A privates pay was 30$ per a private 1st class 33, and a corporal 36$ so every time we fellout I would drop back to the number one spot in the rear ranks. This would be PFC which I eventually rated. When a squad made a mistake the Corporal took the bawling out and this wasn't worth three bucks a month.

Rations weren't as plentiful as one would want and one slice of bread was the usual meal issue. The reason was a shortage of trucks to bring in our rations. There was a lot of rain and the streets at tines had about an inch of watery goo all over them. One night while eating my supper, sitting on the curb, I dropped my slice of bread in the mud. Took it back to the mess wagon and got another slice–scraped the goo off the first one and ate both of them.

Smoking was another problem. We were issued one pack of Bull Durham a week. I had been smoking two packs of Luckies a day in Civillian life. This meant saving your stumps for rerolling, also a nice stump that had been discarded made a welcome addition to your own butts.

Occasionally a few extra bags of Bull would be accumu-lated by the supply Sergeant and we eould scramble for it. I didn' have too much luck the first time so found that by stooping down and reaching thru the legs of the others I could grab any bags that hit the ground. This worked very well. Later when cigarettes could be bought Bull Durham was a surplus material and I have gotten it a cartoon at a time.

About September 12 we had our first payday. The over-sized paper francs were something to look at. A francs was then worth about four for a dollar. The gamblers did well and the Vin rouge flowed freely.

After some more drilling we started to explore the French countryside[vii] to the tune of fifty minutes marching and ten minutes rest with 80 to 90 pounds on your back. When the whistle blew for the fall out. Most of us just flopped where we were and didn't move until we started again. We had a big farm boy mamed Jerome Denning from N.C.[viii] that could take a rifle by the barrel end in each hand and raise them to shoulder heights-straight out. He fellout several times and was put on a supply truck. Some of us weaklings never did. The medical officer at Charlottesville looked at my girlish crooked arms and general physical make up and opined; "We've got to make soldiers out of this"

We finially ended up on a quiet front in the Vosges Mountains. This was the last half of September 1918.

Middle of September 1918.

We were made to hike 30 to 40 kilometers a day when moving from location to location. One day about the middle of the afternoon we were stopped and rested up for a coupla hours. Then a forced march was started and we ended up in the Vosge mountains on a quiet sector.

[vii] 14 Sep 1918.[807]

[viii] A North Carolina "Jerome Denning" registered for the draft with the birth date 3 Jul 1893, said he was a "farm laborer" in Sampson County, and could not sign his name on the registration card.[808]

> They stopped in the St. Dié Sector, where they relieved the French 20th Division.[809] The "Vosges Front" was a common first assignment for units newly arrived on the Western Front.[810]

We fell out at a ruined farm about midnight and told not to show any lights as we were in enemy territory. we were so tired and disgusted that about half of us lit up smokes and said to hell with the Bosch.[ix]

About all the activity here was artillery and so far as I know none of the shell did any damage to our men.

> A post was attacked on 9 Oct, to little effect.[812] In addition, a troop train of the 323d may have been strafed on 17 Sep,[813] while the unit was making its way toward the Vosge mountains.

We would be sent up on the mountains for a few days at a time and our rations would be brought up from a portable kitchen a mile or two back.

We would be put on guard duty two to a post.[x] At night looking and listening you would imagine all kind of things. A rat or rabbit or something would make a noise and immediately visions of Huns tenfeet tall would enter your imagination. You would take up a hand grenade, pull the pin, sit shivering and imagining allkinds of things. Then no more unusual noises, put the pin back in and settle back with your imagination. You didn't realize that if a kraut

---

[ix]This was probably 22 Sep, in Étival-Clairefontaine, France, after what Pvt. Simpson reports was a 25-mile hike.[811]

[x]Guards were necessary because the unit was technically on the front lines at this point, sleeping in dugouts and trenches.[814]

had been out there he would have been more scared than you. Still hadn't see a enemy or shot my rifle.[xi]

Mary Lynne had given me a Ingersoll watch with a radium dial, (not an expensive one) and this was the only one in our immediate outfit. It was continually borrowed by who ever happened to be on guard duty.

(handwritten at top of page: Still September 1918)

Shell would come thundering over and had a swishy sound as tho a freight train was rushing thru the air. It was an unnearving sound.

One of the men in my company was named Shelly. He was from North or South Carolina, had no front teeth and couldn't read or write. He had straggly hair, red, and freckles, wore glasses and was built about like Red Middleton. I use to write his letters home for him later on. After the Armistead he learned or was taught enough to write his own. He told me once that you might say neither of his two sisters had any bad habits - between the two of them they didn't dip more than one box of snuff a week.

Shelly was religeous– when he heard a shell coming he would start praying, "O Lord please don't let that shell hit us. etc." The shell would go on it's way and plow into a hill somewhere. Then Shelly would say " The SOB was a dud". Thats real religeon?

23rd Birthday

On September 25th I copped a can of goldfish, picked some small apples and cooked them, separately in my mess kit behind one of the barns. A Frog soldier came along and I gave him 5 francs for a canteen of Vin rouge. I had a feast and started reading some of my 50 letters that had been received that morning. The first mail we had catch up to us;

[xi]There were apparently German trenches nearby, but neither side had made attempts to challenge the other, save for piecemeal patrols.[815]

Also got a package from Mary Lynne which among other things contained a little rubber collapsable wash basin. This was of very little use as we went for days without much washing. The mail deliverer wanted to know why I got all that mail and some got none.

At night there was a distant continous roar that I could never figure out. Years later I realized it must have been truck convoys passing thru the mountains on neighbor hood roads tho I never saw any of the roads.

We had several fairly long train rides, a few moves by trucks, and a number of long hikes covering a hundred or so miles. That was nearly fifty years ago and I can't place the sequence of them very well. One train ride was thru the City of Nevers (Neeves)[xii] and after leaving I said never again for me. We stopped in the railway station and the fellows in my box car pullman scraped up 20 francs and 3 Of us went into the station restuarant and bought a litre of cognac. We saw some M.P.'s coming (The station was off limits) we split up and ran out three different exists and got back to our Pullman but the MP's got the cognac. So Never, Nevers again.

FRANCE Early October 1918.
We went into a training area for the next few weeks which I thing was near Romley[xiii] France as it was from here we loaded our division for the trip into the Meuse-Argonne sector.[xiv] I got a job for a few days in one of the HQ offices doing a little hunt and pick typing. It consisted of typing

---

[xii]It's likely this particular story is misplaced chronologically—there is no evidence the 81st Infantry went that way, which would have been the opposite direction of where they ended up several weeks later.
[xiii]He was likely thinking of Romsey, Hampshire, England,[816] where his unit disembarked from trains on 13 Aug before going to the English rest camp.
[xiv]Likely Rambervillers, about 15 miles west of St. Dié.[817]

up slips-Chronological Records of Events". This finished up and I them was assigned to a make shift Red Cross store where different items were for sale. I swiped a very small shaving brush and I think I have it somewhere now. A good GI didn't steal he simply appropriated. I billeted here and one night the YM man and a coupla officers decided to get a steak from the mess sargeant and cook it. This was done and these big hearted fine specimens ate it without me getting a bite. Some Pals. These North Carolina sissor-bills wer saying that they would be making 25$ a month if they were back home. I had been making sixty or seventy every two week even when back at Duponts Hopewell.[xv]

Our uniforms were pretty well worn and then as now the seat of my pants were out so an officer told me the first time I saw a staff car with two stars on it coming to get out in the middle of the road and lean over with my rear end to the car. I didn't tho.

After some week[xvi] we were loaded on trains with our cook wagons, artillery of the smallersize etc. and started for the front.

> The division's artillery brigade had split off for a different training area when the 81st arrived in France; it didn't rejoin the unit until after the Armistice.[819]

Most of the Heroes spent the francs they had for a last bout, for the time being, with cognac. About November 6 or 7 we started going up and when we fell out for the night, I thought my pack was too heavy so I took my hand spade off my pack and ditched it. Later that evening we

---

[xv] His grandson, Richard *2-2* writes: "50 years later he was still mad about this steak incident."

[xvi] 31 Oct 1918.[818]

were talking to some GI's who had been up and one said the tools for digging were the most valuable part of a mans weapons. Hoh went scrooging around and finally found his spade and tied it back on his pack. He never did use it tho.

> The morning of November 7, the 81st took over the section of the line from Fresnes-en-Woëvre to Ouvrage de Bezonvaux, relieving the 35th Division.
> On 9 Nov, much of the 81st Infantry had staged an attack on nearby German positions; Henry's regiment, the 323d Infantry, had been in reserve.[820]

The night of November 9th we camped in a woods which was close enough to the fighting to hear the steady roar of machine guns. Heavy artillery was also in this section and this added to the din.We finally curely up took off our shoes and tried to get some sleep. During the night a light rain fell. Ifinally got to sleep and dreampt I was back home. This was a wonderful feeling, but I woke up at dawn heard the steady fire of machine guns; some on single shot and some going full blast, reached for my shoes found a slim coating of ice in them and realized the war was still on.

This was the 10th of November 1918 and we started down a hill toward the actual line. On the way we passes some details carring blankets by the 4 corners with killed in them. This wasn't too good a sight to see.

> The 323d Infantry Regiment took up position in Manheulles, relieving the 324th. Some of the gun-fire Henry heard was probably from other units in the 81st Infantry, which was engaged in fighting the entire day.

we got down from the hilly land and found rolling fields.

Away we went in single file at about ten paces between each sodier. Later on a plane flew very low over us with** USA markings and two men in American uniforms. They were low enough to hollow at us. They then flew away and pretty soon the artillery started coming in on us. The plane was a German spotter. We made a beeline for a wooded swampy area and Hoh found a tree to get behind.(Our brave Hero) We stayed here for several hours with an occasional shell splashing in the swamp without apparent damage. Once water and mud was thrown over our crew. We got out of this later in the afternoon.

We followered a muddy trench for a while and I saw a doughboy being carried back on a coupla boards with a bullett in his leg. He was grinning all over his face for this meant the end of the war for him. We heard later that one of our sargeants shot himself in the hand to keep out of it. Our brave North Carolina lawyer-Red Cross man got himself lost on the way to the front and didn't catch up untilit was finished- Our Heroes.

We later got lost and stumbled onto a German dugout that went way down a hill side. It was dark then and we found we were stranded in the middle of No mans land. It was dark and wet and scarry. The Huns were more than likely all around us but they knew the War was getting over and we didn't. All during the night there was a soldier way out in the open screaming for help. It was an errie feeling but nothing we could do.

> Another soldier in Henry's company described the same scene: "How long can a man listen to the sounds of a battle field and not go crazy? Germans kept up a ceaseless machine gun and artillary fire for they were expecting an attack. We had left

> dead and wounded in the swamp when we fell back. Some had been gassed, others were shell shocked. I heard one calling 'Mother.' Above it all the most unearthly and weird noise of it is that of wounded mules. Kept pinching myself to be sure I am awake. This must be a night mare, it couldn't be true."[821]
>
> Richard 2-2 writes again, of his conversations with Henry as a boy: "50 years later this still haunted him."

Around mid-night we were found and guided back to our lines. The morning of the Eleventh came up without any of us knowing it was the finish. About eight thirty a jeep drove past with a Shavetail in it,(This was a ammunition carrier) he said the war will be over at eleven o'clock. This was great news but taken with a grain of salt.

November 11 1918

> An attack on the town of Ville-en-Woëvre was planned for the morning of November 11. The troops of the 323d were to attack at 6:45 a.m., but were delayed until 9:40.[822] Heavy artillery fire prevented making much progress along the line until an hour later, when there were only 20 minutes left in the war.[823] Of an estimated 2,896 men,[824] 17 were killed in the final two days of fighting.[825]

Sure enough at eleven the guns quit. We were scattered across the front and sent in a spread out line to see if any casualties were to be found. None were found but a rabbit was flushed out and the whole line set out after him. The officers raised hell.[xvii] Some of the crew went all the way and had a meeting with the ex-enemy. A good soldier like me never walked when he could sit so I came back.

Arminist Day

We hadn't had any thing to eat for some time. About noon a YMCA man and a Chaplain came up to our company with a pan, (all two men could carry) of bacon. It was of cource cold and the grease was hard over it. No bread but we grabbed a hand full with our paws that hadn't been washed for days and downed it. No bread but it tasted fine.

We heard that two men from our company were killed by snipers. This so far as I know was our only casualties. Not far from us a shell had made a hit in a pup tent of some other outfit and arms and legs were scattered over the barbwire.

> It's possible these casualties were actually from Henry's company: Simpson writes, of the morning of the 11th, "Some of our company were killed as we slept. Spoke to a boy from Manassas, Va., and two minutes later he and nine others were killed by the same shell."[827]

One of the men in our company was a teacher from Chicago a fine, well educated man and he and I were sent back to pick up a coupla boys left to guard some sipplies.We got them and started back to the company.

About dark I saw one of the most beautiful sights I ever saw. Miles and miles of stars exploding on each side of

---

[xvii]Pvt. Simpson, of Company I, puts this rabbit chase (and subsequent "bawling out from Major Willis") as happening 12 Nov, not 11.[826]

Nomans land. It was both sides shooting off very-guns[xviii] and signal flares. As far as the eye could see beautiful lights.

NOVEMBER 12th 1918.

We stayed close to the front for a coupla days and then started the long walk back.I had written a letter to Mary Lynne right after the Armistice, and while marching along five days later I saw a piece of paper on the road looked at it and saw it was the letter I had written telling the home folks I was still around. Evidently the mail orderly just lost it.

Shortly after the arminist we were laying beside a road and I saw an ambulance coming along stopping every now and then.When it got close saw a soldier get out and look all around. It was Jay Childress looking to see if I had come out allright. Jay was one of the few in our training unit that had latched onto a job that we were trained for.

A few days out one of the men told us we had cooties. I laughed at him but took off my shirt and GI sweater to investigate. Sure-nuff ran down about a half dozen the size of Peters[xix] little finger nail.We evidently got them in the German dugout the night before the ~~arminist~~ end of hostilities. I wanted to save one for a souvenir but had to get rid of all of them when we were de-loused.

After several days steady hiking the shoes of some of our men were so badly worn that we were holed up for a coupla days[xx] while new shoes could be brought up and the beasts reshod. The weather had been cold and drizzily. I lay in the hay of an old barn and wrote home giving a menu I wanted when I got there. It was mostly cake, preserves

---

[xviii] "Very pistols," named for inventor Lt. Edward Very, are the common single-shot flare guns used even now.

[xix] Likely Peter Abdill, Henry's grandson.

[xx] Likely in Sommedieue, Grand Est, France.[828]

etc for we were starved for sweets. When I finally got home and the menu was served the longing had evaporated.

In the army I learned that only three things were absolutely necessary in this life:
EAT * SLEEP** AND SMOKES*.

One of the rest periods we got now and then,on a long hike that covered days of marching; either on the way to the front or coming back I don't just remember which we were billeted in a littletown for a few days and most of the crew had a slight dose of vin rouge. The GI that was supposed to go on guard duty was E Pluribus Unum and the sarge pulled me into a detail for this purpose. I was manfully walking my beat when the officer of the day came along. I smartly came to present arms and kept walking towards him. He said that in all his army experience this was the first time he had ever seen this done.Suppose he was a 90 day wonder too[xxi]

On the trip back from the front we passed two of the Big Bertha's. They were the large cannons mounted on rail cars.[xxii]

> Even by the shortest route, it's about 140 miles from that part of the Western Front to Côte-d'Or. A soldier in the unit reported they'd marched 181 miles in three weeks.[830]

[xxi] "90-day wonder" was a pejorative term for graduates of three-month military training camps for commissioning new officers in the rapidly growing U.S. Army during the war.[829] It became a more popular term after the permanent Officer Candidate Schools were set up leading up to World War II.

[xxii] Technically, "Big Bertha" was a German howitzer model that weighed 94,000 pounds—but was not mounted on rail cars. The German *Langer Max* cannon was on rails; only eight were produced, so a sighting would have been rare.

Finally after endless 50 & 10's of marching we arrived in Grancy-Sur- Ource, Cote d-Orr, and M.Paul Simone Fleury.

Late November 1918.

We finally arrived in the barn yard of the French farm on which M. Paul Simon-Fleury was the guiding star. It was located in a little village called Grancy-Sur-Ource. As we moved to the barn that was to be our home for the next few month, a couple of the natives were setting up a still on the biggest manure pile in the yard. The was to make our Cognac for the time being.

When I was in school I was in a French play and learned a phrase that went about like this– "Je ne rentra pas a la caserne devant ce solr. Joresta ice avec vous tour la jour." This was supposed to mean "I will not return to the camp before this evening, I will remain with you all the day". To this I added–"Apre le guerre vous venie a la Amerique avec mois." which was supposed to mean,"After the war you go to America with me."

There was a little Wop in our company named Frank Gasparro from the West somewhere-Denver I believe. He would go up to one of the Frogs and spout a mouthful of Italian at them. Then I would come along and make my speach and through a coupla "OUI,Oui" in. The natives told me "we understand you better than the other one." The Mountain Boys would stand around with their mouths open to think that any one could talk and be answered by the natives. They of course didn't know any more what I was saying than I knew the French they were handing me.

Later we all got so we could make our self understood and got along very well.My Buddy a fellow named Shumate, (Ernest H.) from the territory around Richmond, Virginia and I were kinder adopted by Messr Simon-Fleury and his family. We would sit around at night in his combination kitchen, dining and living room and either talk, write letters or read, he had one light bulb hanging from a cord in the middle of the room and a big fireplace used for heat. cooking etc. Later on when it got cold at nights the two of us were settled in a bed room away from their quarters in this old big rambling stone house. This was really the life of Riley. Big four poster bed with feather mattress and big feather comforter, just before we would get ready to go to bed a big copper cannister would be filled with hot coals and one of the girls would go put it under the comforter so when we got in bed it would be nice and warm. We were well chaparoned so don't get ideas.The whole family would gather outside the house for our goodnights.

The Simone-Fleury consisted of Messr. and Madame, Mlle Geneive about sixteen or seventeen, Jeanne about thirteen or fourteen and two or three young boys. We were given a meal now and thena nd on pay day when we tried to give them some money they were indignant. If Simon is still alive (which he wont be)he would be still wearing GI shoes. Under the barn room our company was assigned was a cellar. Every time there was a shoes issue eight or nine pairs of new shoes would go down the trap door.

About once a week was bake day and I have never tasted as good bread as we got here. There was a big brick oven in the barn lot.It was shapes like a beehive with brick bottom and oval shaped half circle sides. Fagots were put in this and burnt until all the brick were piping hot, then the bread was put on wooden paddles and shoved in. Eventually it was baked thru and when you sat down at the table and a round big loaf was passed from hand to hand. You took your pocket knife cut a slice, passed it on got a piece of cheese and a glass of vin-ordinaire and that really was eating.

Some of the boys taught Simone a word or two of American. We would line up for evening flag lowering and when the Company was at attention and the bugle was playing, Mr Simone-Fleury was repeating in a loud voice- "American soldiers O.K. officers sonuverbitch", over and over. Don't know what the officers thought.

Our Top Sargeant was named Burkett and the Company Clerk was Johnnie Oldenbuttle. They wer from the Carolinas. Both were good men. Johnnie was well educated but had a slight limp.They wanted to make him a sergeant but he couldn't hold the clerks job and get the higher rating. I had been hanging around the headquarters and one day the Top kick said if I got a bottle of cognac he would let me stay there for a while.I borrowed the franks and got the bottle. This meant no drills stc and was worth the price of admission. This allowed John to get the rank and still do the work. I was a figurehead.

Applications came in for a Christmas leave at one of Frances noted resorts.Most of the Mountain boys said to hell with it you'll be put on a labor detail if you volunteer to go. Old Henry didn't think so and as I was in the orderly room I picked my spot on the list and put my name about third on the list.Used a little psychology, as I figured the officer that picked the names at headquarters would go down two or three names to check the ones to go. This worked and I used the same tactics later either near the top or bottom of the lists and got an appointment in one week to the AEF University at Beaunne and The University of Grenoble.

My leave came thru for 7 days at Aix Les Baines starting December 18th 1918. This would have meant we would be back at Camp on the 25. Due to lack of transportation we actually had both Christmas and New Years there and got our trip back after January 1.

This trip was wonderful we were two in a room at a fine

hotel, with beds and real sheets for the first time in ages. No formations, two meals a day and an ex-gambling Casino for enertainments put on by the Red Cross. Had a trip up an inclined rail road to the skeing area in the French Alps nearby. This was my one and only experience with skeis. I put a pair on went about ten feet went ass over appetite; took off skeis for good.

We had a Christmas dinner with gleaming white table cloths a bottle of champagne for each four men and all the trimmings. Then a celebration at the Casino Christmas night.

I knew that the army paid for this but I always had a warm spot in my heart for the Red Cross.There were a lot of tales about the Red Cross selling sweaters knitted for the boys and that malarky but a doboy always was like a construction worker–never happy unless he had something to belly-acke about. The YM , Jewish Welfare and K of C always treated the boy fine without any favorites. The only one I ever squaked about was the Salvation Army.They had a reputation for their coffee and donuts. Just before we were shipped back from Brest I was put on a detail to set up a tent and thing s for a show to be put on that night. After working all day we were told to come back that night to see the show. When got there that night we were put to one side until the work-batallions were admitted. When the SOS men were inside there was no room for us and we didn't even get a donut. So poopoo to the S.A.

The weather was nice and some evenings we would sit on the front veranda which was elevated from the street.This was a mountainous country. The ladies of the night would come strolling by. A soldier would say combien. The lady would say twenty francs. The haggling would start and each price set would be lowered. Finally some soldier would say how about two sous (4 cents) then the fair ones would be insulted and leave. This was nearing the time for a return to the States and the boys knew that a VD would mean a special camp and no home trip so their morals were very high indeed. One of the saddest things I saw in the Army was at Brest just before we returned home. One of the nicest boys in our company marched down our company street in full pack going back to a VD camp instead of home.

Finally the vacation was over and we were back in Grancey and the same old grind for the next two or three months. In the next month or so moral began to get pretty low.There seemed to be no hope of an early return to the states and there seemed to be very little sense in the whole thing.I saw some of the fellows pass out from the new cognac, get the shakes and turn green in the face. Some of them turned to Madam Pomme-de-terre for relaxation. It was rumored that for 5 francs you would get a mess of french fried potatoes, a litre of wine and other services. The huspand being oresent at all operations peeling potatoes. This I do not know from actual experience just from hearsay.

I was busy all this time in the orderly room but decided I better get out before my moral slipped. One week a list came in for applications to the AEF University at Beaune .I put in for this using the third or fourth name from the start of list.

The next week a list came in for the University of Grenoble, You wer supposed to have two years of college, fifty dollars cash and other qualifying items. I had none but figured a year at W&L and a truck drivers course at the University of Virginia would qualify me.The boys that went to the French school didn't care if they never got home. You were giving living allowances lived with French families and had no army restrictions.

Spring of 1919.

On the application for the University of Grenoble I used the third or fourth line from the bottom technique.

In a week or two orders came in for me to report to The American University at Beaune. The morning these orders came in I had been playing a kick ball game in the yard and the football caught me on the side of the head knocking off my glasses and shattering the lense that had been cracked on my first night in France. I therefore started my foreign education blind as a bat as my vision is nil without glasses. I was in this condition for about a month as when we got to Beaune the optical officer was on vacation and there was no one else in the hospital who could take care of glasses.

Finally the Doctor examined my eyes and I got new glasses. I went in he put a coupla lenses in the frame ,asked how they were, I said OK put a coupla more in they looked better, so he said OK. It took about ten minutes and they were evidently satisfactory as the next time I had them changed was by Dr.E.S.Gifford in Philadelphia in 1944. Just twenty-five years.

I heard later that two or three days after I left for Beaune and the AEF University an appointment came in for me to attend the University of Grenoble. Understand the Brass raised a big stink about me getting both appointments. Just shows what psychology properly applied will do.

The barracks at the University were not completed when we got in the territory and we were temoorally housed in tents 10 or 15 miles out of Beaune. When we were ready to move into permament quarters a detail was asked for. The ones on thid details would get to ride into Beaune instead of hiking.Old yardbird Henry thought this sounded good so he volunteered not knowing the detail was Honeydipping. (Clening out latrines) After this no more volunteering.

We were housed in fair barracks and I signed up for a business administration course as this seemed the easiest Classes were held in hanger type buildings. Each so called student was assigned a class number. This was supposed to be put on a little card about 2 inches square and dropped in a box at the class-room entrance. We soon were taking turns going to class and dropping the other fellows numbers in. I read about forty of Zane Greys novels and considered by general knowledge broadened by the stay at this temple of Learning.

Spring 1919.
Spent a veryquiet few months here waiting for orders to return to the states. That was one of the stipulated point made that we would be returned to our regular outfits when they wer returnrd to the States.

Shortly after we arrived volunteers wer asked from Infantry outfits to mount a formal guard unit. Members of this were excused from all other details. I reported wasn't used for some reason probably because I didn't know enough about drilling. As I had volunteered figured that my intentions had been good and therefore morally I was excused from all other details. This worked and I was only called on a coupla times. When asked why I wasn't out policing up I always said that I had volunteered for Formal Guard Mount Duty. I didn't tell the officer that I had been turned down as he didn't ask.So no details.

We were allowed daily passes into town but my recollections of the City are very vague. It was maybe three quarters of a mile into town and we made life miserable for the officers both going and coming, We would space ourselves just far enough apart so that an officer passing would just get thru saluting one group when another would come along. Finally they got so they would come to salute and walk the whole lengh at salute with a sickly grin on their faces.

Made som very good friends here one afellow named Harry Samuels a Jewish boy from Brooklyn gave me his new shirt when time came for us to leave for the embarking site and I was short a shirt. I called him some years later when I was going thru New York for the Company, he invited me to visit him but I didn't have the time and at thepresent time have never encountered any of these old playmates.

We caught up with the outfit at Brest finally loaded on the Walter A Luckenback and came back to the Promised Land. I remembered the trip over and chose my bunk accordingly. The bunks were three tiered folding iron cots and I chose the one on top so sea sick boys wouldn't bother me.

We had a msooth trip back to Newport News in about six days I believe. Off the coast of France we ran into a school of flying fish. Some sight. Also one night just as the sun was goingdown we passed a full rigged sailing ship in the distance. this was a really beautifil sight as the sea was smooth as glass.

Arrived Newport News about June 19th 1919 and aftera boat trip up the James River arrived at City Point, Virginia, and Camp Lee, Hopewell from which point I had left for Buffalo about four years before.

On June 25, 1919 I was given 99.55$ a discharge and a ticket to Christiansburg, Virginia. So ended the Military portion of the SAGA of HOH.

Notes

[1] Claire, Richard, Lauren and Katie Abdill, Dec. 2016; digital image held by the author. Photograph taken by Richard Abdill *2-2*.

[2] "United States World War I Draft Registration Cards, 1917–1918," images, Ancestry.com (http://interactive.ancestry.com/6482/005153702_00477?bm=true : accessed 11 Mar 2017), card for Henry Thomas Stone Jr., Local Draft Board, Montgomery County, Va.

[3] "United States World War II Draft Registration Cards, 1942," images, Ancestry.com (http://interactive.ancestry.com/1002/2wwii_2383026-0275 : accessed 11 Mar 2017), card for Henry Thomas Stone Jr.

[4] "United States World War I Draft Registration Cards, 1917–1918," card for Henry Thomas Stone Jr.

[5] Social Security Administration, "United States Social Security Death Index," database, Ancestry.com (http://search.ancestry.com/cgi-bin/sse.dll?indiv=1&dbid=3693&h=60291905 : accessed 8 Jul 2016), entry for Henry Stone, SS no. 164-09-4407. This provides the month, but not the day: Henry's death date is given as 6 Dec 1972 in a funeral program provided by Sally Abdill *3-5*.

[6] "Henry Our Hero," see Appendix E.

[7] U.S. Census Office, *Twelfth Census of the United States, Census Reports Volume I – Population Part I* (Washington: United States Census Office, 1901), 399, "Table 5, Population of States and Territories by Minor Civil Divisions: 1890 and 1900."

[8] F. Douglas Wharam, Jr., "Only a Matter of Time: Christiansburg Institute and Desegregation in Southwestern Virginia: 1959–1960," p. 4; online report (http://www2.vcdh.virginia.edu/civilrightstv/essays/wharam.pdf : accessed 9 July 2016), May 2005; Television News of the Civil Rights Era 1950–1970, Virginia Center for Digital History, University of Virginia.

[9] National Register of Historic Places, "Old Christiansburg Industrial Institute, Montgomery County, Virginia"; online image of nomination form, 6 Apr 1979, Virginia Department of Historic Resources (http://www.dhr.virginia.gov/registers/Counties/Montgomery/154-5004_OldChristiansburgIndustrialInstitute_1979_Final_Nomination.pdf : accessed 9 July 2016). National Register #79003056 issued later.

[10]Erin M. Lord, et al., *Edgar A. Long, Principal of Christiansburg Institute: A Life Devoted to Education* (Blacksburg, Va.: Virginia Tech, 2011), 2.

[11]"Virginia, Death Records, 1912-2014," Ancestry.com (http://interactive.ancestry.com/9278/43006_162028006072_0219-00071? : accessed 13 Mar 2017). Death certificate for Agnes Wade Ellett, state file number 29039, 12 Dec 1953.

[12]"Christiansburg [local news]," *Richmond Times-Dispatch*, 9 Mar 1913, page 6; digital image (http://www.richmond.com/archive/).

[13]Washington and Lee University, *The Calyx* (Lexington, Va., 1915), p. 110.

[14]Sally Abdill *3-5*, in a conversation with the author.

[15]*The Calyx*, 234.

[16]Ibid., 134.

[17]Ibid., 175.

[18]"Christiansburg [local news]," *Richmond Times-Dispatch*, 12 Sep 1915, page 3; digital image, Richmond Times-Dispatch (http://www.richmond.com/archive/).

[19]"Henry Our Hero," see Appendix E.

[20]"United States World War I Draft Registration Cards, 1917–1918," card for Henry Thomas Stone Jr.

[21]"The Niagara River Station," *Engineering Record, Building Record and Sanitary Engineer* volume 75 (January–March 1917), p. 19; digital images by Google (https://books.google.com/books?id=aaIgAQAAMAAJ : accessed 9 July 2016).

[22]Esther and Sally Stone, 1929, Gulf of Mexico. Image courtesy Sally Abdill *3-5*. Photographer unknown.

[23]"Henry Our Hero," see Appendix E.

[24]Paul Stanley Bond, et al., *The R.O.T.C Manual: A Text Book for the Reserve Officers Training Corps, Volume 4* (Baltimore: The Johns Hopkins Press, 1921), p. 100.

[25]"Henry Our Hero"; see Appendix E.

[26]1930 U.S. census, Los Angeles County, California, population sched-

ule, Assembly District 58, p. 77 (stamped), dwelling 32, family 49; Henry, Esther, and Sally Ann Stone; image, Ancestry.com (`http://interactive.ancestry.com/6224/4532472_00688?bm=true` : accessed 1 Jul 2016).

[27] Social Security Administration, "United States Social Security Applications and Claims Index, 1936-2007," database, Ancestry.com (`http://search.ancestry.com/cgi-bin/sse.dll?indiv=1&dbid=60901&h=16212884` : accessed 9 Jul 2016), entry for Esther Amanda Stone, SS no. 136-54-5011.

[28] Social Security Administration, "United States Social Security Death Index," database, Ancestry.com (`http://search.ancestry.com/cgi-bin/sse.dll?indiv=1&dbid=3693&h=60285483` : accessed 9 Jul 2016), entry for Esther Amanda Stone, SS no. 136-54-5011.

[29] Charles E. Williams, *Along the Allegheny River: The Southern Watershed* (Charleston: Arcadia Publishing, 2006), p. 57.

[30] 1910 U.S. census, Westmoreland County, Pennsylvania, population schedule, Seward borough, dwelling 24, family 24; Elliott, Kate V., and Ester [*sic*] A. Rager, others; image, Ancestry.com (`http://interactive.ancestry.com/7884/4450137_00950?bm=true` : accessed 13 Mar 2017).

[31] U.S. Department of the Interior, "Topographic and Geologic Survey, Pennsylvania, New Florence Quadrangle," 1922 edition; online image, *U.S. Geological Survey National Geologic Map Database* (`http://ngmdb.usgs.gov/img4/ht_icons/Browse/PA/PA_New%20Florence_171770_1922_62500.jpg` : accessed 9 July 2016).

[32] "United States World War I Draft Registration Cards, 1917–1918," images, Ancestry.com (`http://interactive.ancestry.com/6482/005272231_03643?pid=10776442` : accessed 11 Mar 2017), card for James Thomas Gatehouse, Local Draft Board, Fayette Co..

[33] End of date range approximated by: "Cumberland Marriage Licenses," *Pittsburgh Gazette Times*, 22 Sep 1916, digital image, *Newspapers.com* (`https://www.newspapers.com/image/85876696` : accessed 10 July 2016), p. 9–10.

[34] Thomas Rager Gatehouse, Application for World War II Compensation, "Pennsylvania, Veteran Compensation Application Files, WWII, 1950-1959," *Ancestry.com* (`http://interactive.ancestry.com/3147/41226_2321306652_0576-02139` : accessed 9 July 2016).

[35] "United States World War I Draft Registration Cards, 1917–1918," images, Ancestry.com, card for James Thomas Gatehouse.

[36] 1920 U.S. census, Centre County, Pennsylvania, population schedule, Philipsburg Borough, p. D1-578 (stamped), dwelling 515, family 533; Thos. W., James J., Ester [*sic*] A., and Thos. R. Gatehouse; image, Ancestry.com (http://interactive.ancestry.com/6061/4384790_00151?bm=true : accessed 9 Jul 2016).

[37] 1930 U.S. census, Cambria County, Pennsylvania, population schedule, Cresson Borough, p. 25 (written), dwelling 68, family 78; James and Sue R. Gatehouse; image, Ancestry.com (http://interactive.ancestry.com/6224/4639683_00067?bm=true : accessed 28 Jan 2017).

[38] 1930 U.S. census, Los Angeles County, California, pop. sch., p. 77 (stamped), dwell. 32, fam. 49; Henry, Esther, and Sally Ann Stone.

[39] 1930 U.S. census, Cambria County, Pennsylvania, pop. sch., dwell. 68, fam. 78; James and Sue R. Gatehouse.

[40] Ibid.

[41] 1930 U.S. census, Los Angeles County, California, pop. sch., p. 77 (stamped), dwell. 32, fam. 49; Henry, Esther, and Sally Ann Stone.

[42] "United States Social Security Death Index," Ancestry.com, entry for Henry Stone, SS no. 164-09-4407.

[43] "United States Social Security Death Index," entry for Esther Amanda Stone, SS no. 136-54-5011.

[44] Image courtesy Peter Abdill. Digitized in 2006 from slides and negatives kept by Sally *3-5* and Richard Abdill *3-4*.

[45] Ibid.

[46] William Walker Pettus IV, *Thomas Petyous of Norwich, England and His Pettus Descendants in England and Virginia, Volume I* (Baltimore: Otter Bay Books, 2011), 109 and 121.

[47] *Virginia, Incorporated Places and Minor Civil Divisions Datasets: Subcounty Resident Population Estimates: April 1, 2010 to July 1, 2015*, image of document (United States Census Bureau, 2015), (http://www.census.gov/data/datasets/2015/demo/popest/total-cities-and-towns.html : accessed 28 Jan 2017).

[48] U.S. Census Bureau, "Census Reports Volume I, Population Part I," *Twelfth Census of the United States, 1900*, p. 399.

[49] *Historic Christiansburg Walking Tour* (`http://montgomerymuseum.org/learn/historic-christiansburg-walking-tour/christiansburg-high-school` : accessed 9 July 2016), "Christiansburg High School."

[50] "Miss Wardlaw Dies; Starved Herself," *The New York Times*, 12 Aug 1910, HTML edition, archived (`http://query.nytimes.com/gst/abstract.html?res=9903E1DA1E39E333A25751C1A96E9C946196D6CF` : accessed 9 July 2016).

[51] *Find A Grave*, database with images (`http://www.findagrave.com/cgi-bin/fg.cgi?page=gr&GRid=9529736` : accessed 9 July 2016), memorial 9529736; Virginia Oceana Wardlaw; Sunset Cemetery; gravestone added by Philip Church.

[52] "Sunset Cemetery Master Plan," Town of Christiansburg, online document (`http://www.christiansburg.org/DocumentCenter/View/5074` : accessed 15 Mar 2017).

[53] *The Black Sisters* (`http://montgomerymuseum.org/the-black-sisters` : accessed 9 July 2016), "Chapter X: The Black Sisters, Veiled In Gloom."

[54] Virginia Chancery Court records, Library of Virginia. Digital images (`http://www.lva.virginia.gov/chancery/`). Spotsylvania County, case "Chester Bullard vs Exec of William A. Stone etc.," 1870.

[55] "Memorial to Henry Fox, Gentleman, of 'Huntington', King William County, Virginia," *Tyler's Quarterly Historical and Genealogical Magazine*, 872.

[56] 1860 U.S. census, Montgomery County, Virginia, population schedule, dwelling 495, family 467; William A., Clara A., John R., Harriet L., Sophia A., Franklin W, Margaret, and Mary L. Stone; image, Ancestry.com (`http://interactive.ancestry.com/7667/4298858_00126?bm=true` : accessed 14 Aug 2016); citing FHL microfilm 805,363.

[57] "Virginia, Deaths and Burials Index, 1853–1917," Ancestry.com (`http://search.ancestry.com/cgi-bin/sse.dll?indiv=1&dbid=2558&h=502432` : accessed 20 Aug 2016). Entry for William A Stone, died 13 Nov 1861 in Montgomery County.

[58] 1850 U.S. census, Lunenburg County, Virginia, population schedule, dwelling 654, family 654; Wm. A., Clarissa A., Musgreve, Mary, Clara, John, Harriett, and Adaline Stone; image, Ancestry.com (`http:`

//interactive.ancestry.com/8054/4206380_00093?bm=true : accessed
19 Mar 2017).

[59]Ibid.

[60]"Virginia, Compiled Marriages, 1740-1850," Ancestry.com (http://
search.ancestry.com/cgi-bin/sse.dll?indiv=1&dbid=3723&h=147598
: accessed 20 Aug 2016). Entry for William A. Stone and Clarisa [*sic*]
A. Pettus, married 14 Aug 1822.

[61]"Virginia, Deaths and Burials Index, 1853-1917," Ancestry.com
(http://search.ancestry.com/cgi-bin/sse.dll?indiv=1&dbid=2558&
h=366847 : accessed 21 Aug 2016). Entry for Clara A Stone, died
24 Dec 1878.

[62]Landon C. Bell, *The Old Free State* (Richmond, Va.: The
William Byrd Press, 1927), 333. Digital images via Ancestry.com
(http://search.ancestry.com/search/db.aspx?dbid=30029 : accessed
11 Mar 2017).

[63]"John Stone," obituary, *Times Dispatch*, Richmond, Va.,
2 Mar 1907; digital image, *Newspapers.com* (https://www.newspapers.
com/image/215196613/ : accessed 28 Jan 2017).

[64]*Daily State Journal*, Alexandria, Va., 4 Nov 1873, page 1; digital image, *Newspapers.com* (https://www.newspapers.com/image/80613953/
: accessed 12 Sep 2016).

[65]Compiled service record, James M. Wade, 1Lt., Co. G, 4th VA
Infantry; Carded Records, Volunteer Organizations, Civil War; Record
Group 94: Records of the Adjutant General's Office, 1780s–1917; Na-
tional Archives, Washington, D.C.

[66]*The Millennial Harbinger: A Monthly Publication devoted to Primitive Christianity, Vol. III* (Bethany, Va.: published by Alexander
Campbell, 1839), p. 74–75. Digital images via Google (https://books.
google.com/books?id=9pkoAAAAYAAJ : accessed 19 Mar 2017).

[67]Jeannette Tillotson Acklen, et al., compiler, *Tennessee Records:
Bible Records and Marriage Bonds* (Heritage Books, 2007), 183. Digital images via Google (https://books.google.com/books?id=Wnl6p_
e-51gC : accessed 11 Mar 2017).

[68]*Find A Grave*, database with images (https://www.findagrave.
com/cgi-bin/fg.cgi?page=gr&GRid=30655865 : accessed 15 Mar 2017),
memorial 30655865; William E. Stone; Sunset Cemetery, Christiansburg,
Va.; gravestone added by Brenda Dudley Eanes.

[69] "Virginia, Deaths and Burials Index, 1853–1917," Ancestry.com (http://search.ancestry.com/cgi-bin/sse.dll?indiv=1&dbid=2558& h=695855 : accessed 20 Aug 2016). Entry for William Elliott Stone, died 24 Feb 1885.

[70] R.A. Brock, *Virginia and Virginians: Eminent Virginians, Montgomery County*, reprint (Signal Mountain, Tenn.: Mountain Press), 30.

[71] Compiled service record, William E. Stone, Pvt., Co. F, 4th VA Infantry; Carded Records, Volunteer Organizations, Civil War; Record Group 94: Records of the Adjutant General's Office, 1780s–1917; National Archives, Washington, D.C.

[72] "14th Virginia Regiment History," 14th Virginia Regimental Cavalry, web page (http://www.14thvirginiacavalry.org/regiment_history.htm : accessed 28 Jan 2017).

[73] Compiled service record, William E. Stone, Pvt., Co. G, 14th VA Cavalry; Carded Records, Volunteer Organizations, Civil War; Record Group 94: Records of the Adjutant General's Office, 1780s–1917; National Archives, Washington, D.C.

[74] Brock, *Eminent Virginians, Montgomery County*, 30.

[75] *Find A Grave*, database with images (https://www.findagrave.com/cgi-bin/fg.cgi?page=gr&GRid=30406127 : accessed 20 Aug 2016), memorial 30406127; Susan E. Wilson; Sunset Cemetery, Christiansburg, Va.; gravestone added by Brenda Dudley Eanes.

[76] Ibid.

[77] "Virginia, Deaths and Burials Index, 1853–1917," Ancestry.com (http://search.ancestry.com/cgi-bin/sse.dll?indiv=1&dbid=2558& h=439485 : accessed 20 Aug 2016). Entry for Susan Elizabeth Wilson, died 23 Jan 1877.

[78] "Virginia, Compiled Marriages, 1740-1850," Ancestry.com (http://search.ancestry.com/cgi-bin/sse.dll?indiv=1&dbid=3723& h=1109432 : accessed 20 Aug 2016). Entry for Miles A. Wilson and Susan Elizabeth Stone, married 19 Oct 1846.

[79] Linda Killen, *The Whartons' Town: New River Depot, 1870–1940* (Radford University, 1993), p. 12. Transcription via Radford University (http://monk.radford.edu/cdm/ref/collection/NRVAAP/id/353 : accessed 19 Mar 2017).

[80] 1900 U.S. census, Auburn County [*sic*], Virginia, population sched-

ule, Radford City, p. 203 (stamped), dwelling 100, family 107; Musgrove and Mary I. Stone; image, Ancestry.com (`http://interactive.ancestry.com/7602/004117943_00410?bm=true` : accessed 28 Jan 2017).

[81] "The District Fair-Grounds Secured – Death of Dr. Stone," *Richmond Dispatch*, 3 Jul 1901, page 3; digital image, *Newspapers.com* (`https://www.newspapers.com/image/92967971/` : accessed 28 Jan 2017).

[82] 1850 U.S. census, Lunenburg County, Virginia, pop. sch., dwell. 654, fam. 654; Wm. A., Clarissa A., Musgreve, Mary, Clara, John, Harriett, and Adaline Stone.

[83] "Wisconsin, Deaths, 1820-1907," file index, Ancestry.com (`http://search.ancestry.com/cgi-bin/sse.dll?indiv=1&dbid=4984&h=48038` : accessed 20 Aug 2016). Entry for Mary S Bullard, died 24 May 1895.

[84] Will of William A. Stone; see Appendix C.

[85] "Virginia, Select Marriages, 1785–1940," Ancestry.com (`http://search.ancestry.com/cgi-bin/sse.dll?indiv=1&dbid=60214&h=3291244` : accessed 20 Aug 2016). Entry for Dexter Bullard and Mary Mcf. Stone, married 5 May 1858.

[86] "Virginia, Select Marriages, 1785–1940," Ancestry.com (`http://search.ancestry.com/cgi-bin/sse.dll?indiv=1&dbid=60214&h=1851645` : accessed 14 Aug 2016). Entry for Jno. R. Stone marriage to Virginia M. Spindle, 21 Dec 1865.

[87] "Alabama, Texas and Virginia, Confederate Pensions, 1884-1958," Ancestry.com (`http://interactive.ancestry.com/1677/31867_B034420-00760` : accessed 14 Aug 2016). Application by Ida. V. Stone for the Confederate Soldier's pension for John Richard Stone, state file number 100571, 7 Jun 1934.

[88] "Virginia, Select Marriages, 1785–1940," Ancestry.com (`http://search.ancestry.com/cgi-bin/sse.dll?indiv=1&dbid=60214&h=5124829` : accessed 13 Mar 2017). Entry for Hattie L. Stone marriage to P.B. Sale, 15 Dec 1875.

[89] Ibid.

[90] 1900 U.S. census, Montgomery County, Virginia, population schedule, Auburn Township, dwelling 125, family 128; Philip B. and Hattie L. Sale, others; image, Ancestry.com (`http://interactive.ancestry.com/7602/004117888_00422?bm=true` : accessed 13 Mar 2017); citing FHL microfilm 1,241,718.

[91] "Virginia, Select Marriages, 1785–1940," Ancestry.com. Entry for Hattie L. Stone marriage to P.B. Sale, 15 Dec 1875.

[92] Virginia Chancery Court records, Library of Virginia. Digital images (`http://www.lva.virginia.gov/chancery/`). Montgomery County, case "ADMR OF Robert M Craig ETC vs. EXR OF William A Stone ETC," 1897, p. 139.

[93] "Virginia, Deaths and Burials Index, 1853-1917," Ancestry.com (`http://search.ancestry.com/cgi-bin/sse.dll?indiv=1&dbid=2558&h=366847` : accessed 21 Aug 2016). Entry for Addie Williams, died 5 Jun 1869.

[94] Ibid.

[95] Virginia Chancery Court records, Library of Virginia. Digital images (`http://www.lva.virginia.gov/chancery/`). Montgomery County, case "John N Williams FOR ETC vs. EXR OF William A Stone ETC," 1881.

[96] 1870 U.S. census, Montgomery County, Virginia, mortality schedule, Auburn Township, p. 1 (written); Adeline and Elisha Williams; image, Ancestry.com (`http://interactive.ancestry.com/8756/VAT1132_10-0277` : accessed 13 Mar 2017).

[97] Ibid.

[98] Will of William A. Stone; see Appendix C.

[99] 1860 U.S. census, Montgomery Co., Va., pop. sch., dwell. 495, fam. 467; William A., Clara A., John R., Harriet L., Sophia A., Franklin W, Margaret, and Mary L. Stone.

[100] *Catalog of the Officers and Students of Kentucky University for the Session of 1868–1869* (Louisville, Ky.: John P. Morton and Company, 1869), p. 19.

[101] 1870 U.S. census, Montgomery County, Virginia, pop. sch., Auburn Township, dwell. 309, fam. 324; Clara A, Harriett L., and Frank M. Stone.

[102] Virginia Chancery Court records, Library of Virginia. Digital images (`http://www.lva.virginia.gov/chancery/`). Montgomery County, case "John N Williams FOR ETC vs. EXR OF William A Stone ETC," 1881.

[103] Will of William A. Stone, see Appendix C.

[104] 1850 U.S. census, Lunenburg County, Virginia, pop. sch., dwell.

654, fam. 654; Wm. A., Clarissa A., Musgreve, Mary, Clara, John, Harriett, and Adaline Stone.

[105] Ibid.

[106] "Virginia, Select Marriages, 1785–1940," Ancestry.com (http://search.ancestry.com/cgi-bin/sse.dll?indiv=1&dbid= 60214&h=3283106 : accessed 21 Aug 2016). Entry for Clarissa A. Stone and Robert Miller, married 5 May 1858.

[107] Virginia Chancery Court records, Library of Virginia. Digital images (http://www.lva.virginia.gov/chancery/). Montgomery County, case "John N Williams FOR ETC vs. EXR OF William A Stone ETC," 1881.

[108] Will of William A. Stone; see Appendix C.

[109] Ibid.

[110] Virginia Chancery Court records, Library of Virginia. Digital images (http://www.lva.virginia.gov/chancery/). Montgomery County, case "ADMR OF Robert M Craig ETC vs. EXR OF William A Stone ETC," 1897, p. 148–149.

[111] Virginia Chancery Court records, Library of Virginia. Digital images (http://www.lva.virginia.gov/chancery/). Montgomery County, case "William E Stone vs. Samuel A. Stone," 1875.

[112] "Personal" column, *Clinch Valley News*, Tazewell, Va., 16 Feb 1900, page 4; digital image, *Newspapers.com* (https://www.newspapers.com/ image/79857734/ : accessed 11 Mar 2017).

[113] 1830 U.S. census, Lunenburg County, Virginia, p. 25 (written); William A Stone; image, Ancestry.com (http://interactive.ancestry. com/8058/4411345_00055?bm=true : accessed 10 Sep 2016).

[114] 1840 U.S. census, Lunenburg County, Virginia, p. 17 (written); William A Stone; image, Ancestry.com (http://interactive.ancestry. com/8057/4409478_00657?bm=true : accessed 28 Jan 2017).

[115] 1850 U.S. census, Montgomery County, Virginia, slave schedule; William A Stone; image, Ancestry.com (http://interactive.ancestry. com/8055/VAM432_990-0072 : accessed 18 Mar 2017).

[116] 1850 U.S. census, Lunenburg County, Virginia, pop. sch., dwell. 654, fam. 654; Wm. A., Clarissa A., Musgreve, Mary, Clara, John, Harriett, and Adaline Stone.

[117] 1860 U.S. census, Montgomery County, Virginia, agricultural sched-

ule, p. 396–397 (stamped); Wm. A. Stone; image, Ancestry.com (http://interactive.ancestry.com/1276/T1132_2-00541 : accessed 28 Jan 2017).

[118] 1850 U.S. census, Lunenburg County, Virginia, pop. sch., dwell. 654, fam. 654; Wm. A., Clarissa A., Musgreve, Mary, Clara, John, Harriett, and Adaline Stone.

[119] 1860 U.S. census, Montgomery Co., Va., pop. sch., dwell. 495, fam. 467; William A., Clara A., John R., Harriet L., Sophia A., Franklin W, Margaret, and Mary L. Stone.

[120] 1860 U.S. census, Montgomery Co., Va., slave schedule, p. 9 (written), dwell. 654, fam. 654; William A Stone.

[121] Virginia Chancery Court records, Library of Virginia. Digital images (http://www.lva.virginia.gov/chancery/). Montgomery County, case "ADMR OF Robert M Craig ETC vs. EXR OF William A Stone ETC," 1897, p. 1136.

[122] Pettus, 478.

[123] *The Old Free State*, 416.

[124] Whitworth Family History Association, *Whitworth and Related Lines, Volume I* (Utica, Ky.: McDowell Publication, 2001), 105.

[125] *Marriages of Lunenburg County, Virginia, 1746-1853*, image of document, Ancestry.com (http://interactive.ancestry.com/49051/ FLHG_MarrLunenburgCntyVA-0129 : accessed 28 Oct 2016), page 117. Entry for Isaac Stone marriage to Rebecca Whitworth, 1793.

[126] *The Old Free State*, 421.

[127] Ibid., 435.

[128] Virginia Stone. Image courtesy Sally Abdill. Note: If the unknown creator of this portrait died after 1946, it could theoretically still be under copyright. If someone owns the rights to this picture, they are welcome to get in touch—I have many questions.

[129] "Virginia, Select Marriages, 1785–1940," Ancestry.com (http://search.ancestry.com/cgi-bin/sse.dll?indiv=1&dbid= 60214&h=1851645 : accessed 14 Aug 2016). Entry for Jno. R. Stone marriage to Virginia M. Spindle, 21 Dec 1865.

[130] 1850 U.S. census, Lunenburg County, Virginia, pop. sch., dwell.

654, fam. 654; Wm. A., Clarissa A., Musgreve, Mary, Clara, John, Harriett, and Adaline Stone.

[131] *Find A Grave*, database with images (https://www.findagrave. com/cgi-bin/fg.cgi?page=gr&GRid=30378833 : accessed 14 Aug 2016), memorial 30378833; Virginia Spindle; Sunset Cemetery, Christiansburg, Va.; gravestone added by Brenda Dudley Eanes.

[132] Ibid.

[133] "Virginia, Death Records, 1912-2014," Ancestry.com (http: //interactive.ancestry.com/9278/43006_172028008152_0158-00283 : accessed 13 Mar 2017). Death certificate for Mamie Stone Alexander, state file number 14816, 29 Jun 1958.

[134] Virginia Chancery Court records, Library of Virginia. Digital images (http://www.lva.virginia.gov/chancery/). Montgomery County, case "ADMR OF Robert M Craig ETC vs. EXR OF William A Stone ETC," 1897, p. 147–149.

[135] Compiled service record, John R. Stone, Pvt., 4th Virginia Inf.; Carded Records, Volunteer Organizations, Civil War; Record Group 94: Records of the Adjutant General's Office, 1780s–1917; National Archives, Washington, D.C.

[136] *Richmond Dispatch*, 19 Jan 1859, page 1; digital image, *Newspapers.com* (https://www.newspapers.com/image/79753882/ : accessed 11 Mar 2017).

[137] "U.S., Appointments of U. S. Postmasters, 1832-1971," database with images, Ancestry.com (http://interactive.ancestry.com/1932/ 30439_065518-00494 : accessed 14 Mar 2017). Entry for William E. Stone.

[138] "U.S., Appointments of U. S. Postmasters, 1832-1971," database with images, Ancestry.com (http://interactive.ancestry.com/1932/ 30439_065518-00496 : accessed 14 Mar 2017). Entries for William E. Stone and John R. Stone.

[139] "U.S., Appointments of U. S. Postmasters, 1832-1971," database with images, Ancestry.com (http://interactive.ancestry.com/1932/ 30439_065518-00498 : accessed 14 Mar 2017). Entry for John R. Stone.

[140] Compiled service record, John R. Stone.

[141] Ibid.

142 James I. Robertson Jr., *The Stonewall Brigade* (Baton Rouge: Louisiana State University Press, 1977), p. 12.

143 Compiled service record, John R. Stone.

144 Ibid.

145 Ibid.

146 Clement Anselm Evans ed., *Confederate Military History: A Library of Confederate States History, Vol. 3* (Atlanta: Confederate Publishing Company, 1899), p. 673.

147 Larry Tagg, *The Generals of Gettysburg* (Baton Rouge: Da Capo Press, 2003), page 280.

148 James I. Robertson, *4th Virginia Infantry* (Lynchburg, Va.: H.E. Howard, 1982), pgs. 26–28.

149 Louis-Philippe-Albert d'Orleans, *The Battle of Gettysburg: From The History of the Civil War in America* (Philadelphia: Porter & Coates, 1886), p. 305.

150 Compiled service record, John R. Stone.

151 Ibid.

152 "The Wilderness: Facts and Resources," web page, Civil War Trust, `http://www.civilwar.org/battlefields/the-wilderness.html?tab=facts` : accessed 14 Mar 2017.

153 *Acts and Joint Resolutions passed by the General Assembly of the State of Virginia During the Session of 1897–1898* (Richmond: J.H. O'Bannon, 1898), p. 778. Digital images via Google (`https://books.google.com/books/about/Acts_and_Joint_Resolutions_Passed_by_the.html?id=3znctwAACAAJ` : accessed 19 Mar 2017).

154 "Object record, catalog number WD 137," American Civil War Museum (`http://moconfederacy.pastperfectonline.com/webobject/C40E968B-48D5-4FD3-A18E-582796334361` : accessed 15 Mar 2017).

155 Gordon C. Rhea, *The Battles for Spotsylvania Court House and the Road to Yellow Tavern* (Baton Rouge: Louisiana State University Press, 1997), 6.

156 Ibid., 235.

157 Ibid.

[158] Ibid., 418.

[159] *The Stonewall Brigade*, 12.

[160] Clement Anselm Evans ed., *Confederate Military History: A Library of Confederate States History, Vol. 3* (Atlanta: Confederate Publishing Company, 1899), p. 673.

[161] "6415 8th St NW," web page, Redfin (https://www.redfin.com/DC/Washington/6415-8th-St-NW-20012/home/10053159 : accessed 14 Mar 2017).

[162] "Maps of Fort Stevens, District of Columbia (1864)," web page, Civil War Trust, http://www.civilwar.org/battlefields/fort-stevens.html : accessed 14 Mar 2017.

[163] Letter from Dr. J.W. Farmer, 6 May 1879, pension application for John Stone, "Confederate pension rolls, veterans and widows" collection, digital images, Library of Virginia.

[164] Compiled service record, John R. Stone.

[165] "Organization of the Army of Northern Virginia, commanded by General Robert E. Lee, November 30, 1864," *The Miscellaneous Documents of the House of Representatives for the First Session of the Fifty-Third Congress* (Washington, D.C: Government Printing Office, 1863), p. 1247.

[166] Compiled service record, John R. Stone.

[167] Compiled service record, M.C. Stone, Pvt., 25th Virginia Cav.; Carded Records, Volunteer Organizations, Civil War; Record Group 94: Records of the Adjutant General's Office, 1780s–1917; National Archives, Washington, D.C.

[168] Dobbie E. Lambert, *25th Virginia Cavalry* (Lynchburg, Va.: H.E. Howard, 1994), 91.

[169] Ibid., 137.

[170] Ibid., 98.

[171] Compiled service record, Thomas W. Spindle, Pvt., 4 VA Inf., Co. G; Record Group 94: Records of the Adjutant General's Office, 1780s–1917; National Archives, Washington, D.C.

[172] Compiled service record, Thomas W. Spindle, 2Lt., 25 VA Cav., Co. E; Record Group 94: Records of the Adjutant General's Office, 1780s–1917; National Archives, Washington, D.C.

[173]Will of William A. Stone; see Appendix C.

[174]1870 U.S. census, Montgomery County, Virginia, population schedule, Auburn Township, p. 49 (written), dwelling 312, family 327; John R., Maria V., Henry T. and John A. Stone; image, Ancestry.com (http://interactive.ancestry.com/7163/4268795_00122?bm=true : accessed 19 Jul 2016); citing FHL microfilm 553,163.

[175]Ibid.

[176]Virginia Chancery Court records, Library of Virginia. Digital images (http://www.lva.virginia.gov/chancery/). Montgomery County, case "ADMR OF Robert M Craig ETC vs. EXR OF William A Stone ETC," 1897, p. 757 and 1153.

[177]Letter from Dr. J.W. Farmer, 6 May 1879, pension application for John Stone, "Confederate pension rolls, veterans and widows" collection, digital images, Library of Virginia.

[178]State of Virginia, "Application of Soldier, Sailor or Marine for a Pension," John R. Stone, Pulaski County, 4 Apr 1898. *Confederate Disability Applications and Receipts*, collections, digital images, Library of Virginia.

[179]*Find A Grave*, memorial 30378833; Virginia Spindle; gravestone added by Brenda Dudley Eanes.

[180]"Virginia, Deaths and Burials Index, 1853-1917," Ancestry.com (http://search.ancestry.com/cgi-bin/sse.dll?indiv=1&dbid=2558&h=544877 : accessed 14 Aug 2016). Entry for M.V. Stone (M.V. Spindle), died 26 May 1884.

[181]*Find A Grave*, database with images (https://www.findagrave.com/cgi-bin/fg.cgi?page=gr&GRid=30636246 : accessed 19 Jul 2016), memorial 30636246; Henry Thomas Stone; Sunset Cemetery, Christiansburg, Va.; gravestone added by Neil B.

[182]"Virginia, Death and Burials Index, 1853–1917," Ancestry.com (http://search.ancestry.com/cgi-bin/sse.dll?indiv=1&dbid=2558&h=366810 : accessed 24 Aug 2016). Entry for John Allen Stone, died June 1877 age 8.

[183]1880 U.S. census, Montgomery County, Virginia, population schedule, 55th Enumeration Dist., p. 11 (written), dwelling 92, family 92; Jno. R., M. V., Thos. H., Mary, and Ella Stone; image, Ancestry.com (http://interactive.ancestry.com/6742/4244676-00742/42816279 : accessed 19 Jul 2016); citing FHL microfilm 1,255,378.

[184] "Virginia, Death Records, 1912-2014," Ancestry.com. Death certificate for Mamie Stone Alexander.

[185] Ibid.

[186] *Find A Grave*, database with images (https://www.findagrave.com/cgi-bin/fg.cgi?page=gr&GRid=26708281 : accessed 14 Mar 2017), memorial 26708281; Charles Lyde Alexander; Maplewood Cemetery, Tazewell County, Va.; gravestone added by Virginia Gal.

[187] "Virginia, Select Marriages, 1785–1940," Ancestry.com (http://search.ancestry.com/cgi-bin/sse.dll?indiv=1&dbid=60214&h=3152801 : accessed 14 Mar 2017). Entry for Mamie C. Stone marriage to Charles L. Alexander, 21 Feb 1900.

[188] "Virginia, Death Records, 1912-2014," Ancestry.com. Death certificate for Mamie Stone Alexander.

[189] 1930 U.S. census, Tazewell County, Virginia, population schedule, Clear Fork District, p. 98 (stamped), dwelling 89, family 91; Charles L and Mamie C Alexander; image, Ancestry.com (http://interactive.ancestry.com/6224/4547860_00769?bm=true : accessed 14 Mar 2017); citing FHL microfilm 2,342,196.

[190] "Virginia, Death Records, 1912-2014," Ancestry.com (http://mv.ancestry.com/viewer/d129dff9-5e8c-42b7-9e58-d93fe5179ff9/84096417/44499488744?_phsrc=mpv1654&usePUBJs=true : accessed 24 Aug 2016). Death certificate for Virginia E. Stone, state file number 70 022624, 8 Sep 1970.

[191] Ibid.

[192] "Personal" column, *Clinch Valley News*, Tazewell, Va., 16 Feb 1900, page 4.

[193] "Virginia, Death Records, 1912-2014." Death certificate for Virginia E. Stone, state file number 70 022624, 8 Sep 1970.

[194] 1880 U.S. census, Montgomery Co., Va., pop. sch., dwell. 92, fam. 92; Jno. R., M. V., Thos. H., Mary, and Ella Stone.

[195] *Find A Grave*, database with images (https://www.findagrave.com/cgi-bin/fg.cgi?page=gr&GRid=81440939 : accessed 24 Aug 2016), memorial 81440939; Ida V Gillespie Stone; Sunrise Burial Park, Fairlawn, Pulaski County, Va.; gravestone added by SWVA Genealogy Searcher.

[196] "A Guide to the Records of Southwestern State Hospital, 1887-

1948," Library of Virginia, online index of collection (http://ead.
lib.virginia.edu/vivaxtf/view?docId=lva/vi03032.xml : accessed
14 Mar 2017).

197 "Brevities," *Roanoke Times*, 11 Jun 1892, page 2; digital image,
Newspapers.com (https://www.newspapers.com/image/77800600/ : accessed 11 Mar 2017).

198 "Confederate Pension Rolls, Veterans and Widows," Ancestry.com
(http://interactive.ancestry.com/1677/31867_B034420-00760 : accessed 14 Aug 2016). Application by Ida. V. Stone for the Confederate Soldier's pension for John Richard Stone, state file number 100571,
7 Jun 1934.

199 "Virginia, Death Records, 1912-2014," Ancestry.com (http:
//interactive.ancestry.com/9278/43006_172028004422_0188-00014 :
accessed 14 Mar 2017). Death certificate for Ida Gillespie Stone, state
file number 28382, 27 Dec 1948.

200 "Brevities," *Roanoke Times*, 11 Jun 1892.

201 "Alabama, Texas and Virginia, Confederate Pensions, 1884-1958,"
digital collection, Library of Virginia. Application by Ida. V. Stone
for the Confederate Soldier's pension for John Richard Stone, state file
number 100571, 7 Jun 1934.

202 "Chewed Poison Oak," *The Times*, Richmond, Va., 5 Sep 1901,
page 4; digital image, *Newspapers.com* (https://www.newspapers.com/
image/81015725/ : accessed 11 Mar 2017).

203 "Alabama, Texas and Virginia, Confederate Pensions, 1884-1958,"
Ancestry.com. Application by Ida. V. Stone for the Confederate
Soldier's pension for John Richard Stone, state file number 100571,
7 Jun 1934.

204 Untitled social column, *Roanoke Times Dispatch*, 29 Jan 1906,
page 6; digital image, *Newspapers.com* (https://www.newspapers.com/
image/146244428/ : accessed 11 Mar 2017).

205 "Alabama, Texas and Virginia, Confederate Pensions, 1884-1958,"
Ancestry.com. Application by Ida. V. Stone for the Confederate
Soldier's pension for John Richard Stone, state file number 100571,
7 Jun 1934.

206 *Find A Grave*, memorial 81440939; Ida V Gillespie Stone; gravestone
added by SWVA Genealogy Searcher.

[207] *Find A Grave*, database with images (https://www.findagrave.com/cgi-bin/fg.cgi?page=gr&GRid=80460527 : accessed 24 Aug 2016), memorial 80460527; Clara Stone Conklin; Sunrise Burial Park, Fairlawn, Pulaski County, Va.; gravestone added by SWVA Genealogy Searcher.

[208] "John Stone," *Richmond Times Dispatch*, 2 Mar 1907, page 2; digital image, *Newspapers.com* (https://www.newspapers.com/image/215196613/ : accessed 11 Mar 2017).

[209] "The District Fair-Grounds Secured – Death of Dr. Stone," *Richmond Dispatch*, 3 Jul 1901, page 3.

[210] "Mrs. Mary Stone," *The Times*, Richmond, Va., 17 Dec. 1902, page 2; digital image, *Newspapers.com* (https://www.newspapers.com/image/80977716/ : accessed 11 Mar 2017).

[211] *Find A Grave*, database with images (https://www.findagrave.com/cgi-bin/fg.cgi?page=gr&GRid=105366854 : accessed 10 Sep 2016), memorial 105366854; Dr John W. Stone; West View Cemetery, Radford, Va.

[212] "Brevities," *Roanoke Times*, 11 Jun 1892.

[213] "John Stone," *Richmond Times Dispatch*, 2 Mar 1907, page 2; digital image, *Newspapers.com* (https://www.newspapers.com/image/215196613/ : accessed 11 Mar 2017).

[214] *Find A Grave*, memorial 30636246; Henry Thomas Stone; gravestone added by Neil B.

[215] 1880 U.S. census, Montgomery Co., Va., pop. sch., dwell. 92, fam. 92; Jno. R., M. V., Thos. H., Mary, and Ella Stone.

[216] "Virginia, Death and Burials Index, 1853–1917," Ancestry.com (http://search.ancestry.com/cgi-bin/sse.dll?indiv=1&dbid=2558&h=366810 : accessed 24 Aug 2016). Entry for John Allen Stone, died June 1877 age 8.

[217] 1910 U.S. census, Montgomery County, Virginia, population schedule, Christiansburg District, p. 150 (stamped), dwelling 63, family 63; Henry T., Mary L. and Henry T. Stone Jr.; image, Ancestry.com (http://interactive.ancestry.com/7884/4454829_00304?bm=true : accessed 18 Jul 2016); citing FHL microfilm 1,375,649.

[218] "Virginia, Death Records, 1912-2014," Ancestry.com (http://interactive.ancestry.com/9278/43006_172028004422_0214-00130 :

accessed 21 Jul 2016). Death certificate for Mary Lynn Stone, state file number 4505, 24 Feb 1955.

[219] 1870 U.S. census, Montgomery County, Virginia, population schedule, Christiansburg Town, p. 7 (written), dwelling 35, family 39; James M., Margaret C., and Mary Wade, and Catharine and Nannie Brown; image, Ancestry.com (http://interactive.ancestry.com/7163/4268795_00252?bm=true : accessed 14 Mar 2017); citing FHL microfilm 553,163.

[220] "State news," *Daily State Journal*, Alexandria, Va., 4 Nov 1873, page 1; digital image, *Newspapers.com* (https://www.newspapers.com/image/?spot=6609623 : accessed 10 Mar 2017).

[221] 1880 U.S. census, Montgomery County, Virginia, population schedule, Forty 1st District, p. 365 (stamped), dwelling 952, family 952; Margaret C., Charles I., Fannie L., McClanahan, Agnes Mc, Mary L., and Robert E. Wade; image, Ancestry.com (http://interactive.ancestry.com/6742/4244676-00548/13806945 : accessed 15 Aug 2016); citing FHL microfilm 1,255,378.

[222] Henry T., Charles I., and John Allen Stone, spring 1918. Photo privately held by Sally Abdill.

[223] "Virginia, Select Marriages, 1785–1940," Ancestry.com (http://search.ancestry.com/cgi-bin/sse.dll?indiv=1&dbid=60214&h=4869074 : accessed 19 Jul 2016). Entry for Henry T. Stone marriage to Mary Lynn Wade, 29 Nov 1894.

[224] 1900 U.S. census, Montgomery County, Virginia, population schedule, Christiansburg District, p. 130 (stamped), dwelling 315, family 333; Henry T., Mary L., and Henry T. Stone; image, Ancestry.com (http://interactive.ancestry.com/7602/004117888_00563?bm=true : accessed 8 Jul 2016); citing FHL microfilm 1,241,718.

[225] Virginia Chancery Court records, Library of Virginia. Digital images (http://www.lva.virginia.gov/chancery/). Montgomery County, case "Spindle Harless & Stone vs. Thaddeus H Morgan," 1895.

[226] 1910 U.S. census, Montgomery County, Virginia, population schedule, Christiansburg District, p. 150 (stamped), dwelling 63, family 63; Henry T., Mary L. and Henry T. Stone Jr.; image, Ancestry.com (http://interactive.ancestry.com/7884/4454829_00304?bm=true : accessed 18 Jul 2016); citing FHL microfilm 1,375,649.

[227] Listed as working at the dry goods store in this document: 1930 U.S. census, Montgomery Co., Va., pop. sch., dwell. 38, fam. 39; Henry

T., Mary L., Frances H., and John A. Stone. But no longer employed in this one, 10 years later: 1940 U.S. census, Montgomery Co., Va., pop. sch., hhold 413; Henry T. and Mary L. Stone.

[228]Phone conversation between Sally Abdill *3-5* and the author, 27 Feb 2017.

[229]1910 U.S. census, Montgomery County, Va., pop sch., dwell. 63, fam. 63; Henry T., Mary L. and Henry T. Stone Jr.

[230]Ibid.

[231]"United States World War I Draft Registration Cards, 1917–1918," images, Ancestry.com (http://interactive.ancestry.com/6482/005153702_00474?bm=true : accessed 11 Mar 2017), card for Chas. Ingles W. Stone, Local Draft Board, Montgomery County, Va..

[232]"Virginians Are Not Included in List of Rescued," *Richmond Times-Dispatch*, 14 Nov 1928, page 1–2; digital image, Richmond Times-Dispatch (http://www.richmond.com/archive/).

[233]1910 U.S. census, Montgomery County, Va., pop sch., dwell. 63, fam. 63; Henry T., Mary L. and Henry T. Stone Jr.

[234]*Find A Grave*, database with images (https://www.findagrave.com/cgi-bin/fg.cgi?page=gr&GRid=104474547 : accessed 10 Sep 2016), memorial 104474547; Margaret Alan Stone; Sunset Cemetery, Christiansburg, Va.; gravestone added by Angi Weast King.

[235]Ibid.

[236]1910 U.S. census, Montgomery County, Va., pop sch., dwell. 63, fam. 63; Henry T., Mary L. and Henry T. Stone Jr.

[237]"Virginia, Death Records, 1912-2014," Ancestry.com (http://interactive.ancestry.com/9278/43004_162028001249_0133-00084 : accessed 29 Aug 2016). Death certificate for Agnes McClanahan Stephens, state file number 18980, 6 Aug 1924.

[238]"Virginia, Select Marriages, 1785–1940," Ancestry.com (http://search.ancestry.com/cgi-bin/sse.dll?indiv=1&dbid=60214&h=105148 : accessed 29 Aug 2016). Entry for Agnes Mcclanahan Stone to John Henry Stephens, 29 Nov 1894; citing FHL microfilm 2,038,462.

[239]"Virginia, Death Records, 1912-2014." Death certificate for Agnes McClanahan Stephens.

[240] 1910 U.S. census, Montgomery County, Va., pop sch., dwell. 63, fam. 63; Henry T., Mary L. and Henry T. Stone Jr.

[241] "Virginia, Death Records, 1912-2014," Ancestry.com (http://interactive.ancestry.com/9278/43006_162028001249_0378-00285 : accessed 29 Aug 2016). Death certificate for Frances Stone Roedel, state file number 72 013284, 26 Apr 1972.

[242] "Virginia, Select Marriages, 1785–1940," Ancestry.com (http://search.ancestry.com/cgi-bin/sse.dll?indiv=1&dbid=60214&h=2762975 : accessed 29 Aug 2016). Entry for Frances Hartwell Stone to John Gibson Davis, 6 May 1927; citing FHL microfilm 2,048,462.

[243] "Virginia, Marriage Records, 1936-2014," Ancestry.com (http://interactive.ancestry.com/9279/43067_162028006052_0667-00299 : accessed 29 Aug 2016). Virginia marriage certificate for John H. Roedel and Frances Stone Davis, state file number 23960, 1 Jul 1939.

[244] 1910 U.S. census, Montgomery County, Va., pop sch., dwell. 63, fam. 63; Henry T., Mary L. and Henry T. Stone Jr.

[245] "Virginia, Death Records, 1912-2014," Ancestry.com (http://interactive.ancestry.com/9278/43006_172028008877_0273-00159 : accessed 29 Aug 2016). Death certificate for John A Stone, state file number 77 025157, 6 Sep 1977.

[246] Ibid.

[247] Conversation between the author and Sally Stone *3-5*.

[248] "Virginia, Death Records, 1912-2014," Ancestry.com (http://interactive.ancestry.com/9278/43006_182029001786_0078-00106/2502979 : accessed 19 Jul 2016). Death certificate for Henry Thomas Stone, state file number 21677, 9 Sep 1940.

[249] Ibid.

[250] "Virginia, Death Records, 1912-2014," Ancestry.com. Death certificate for Mary Lynn Stone, state file number 4505, 24 Feb 1955.

[251] Ibid.

[252] *Find A Grave*, database with images (https://www.findagrave.com/cgi-bin/fg.cgi?page=gr&GRid=30378819 : accessed 14 Aug 2016), memorial 30378819; Mary Lynn Wade Stone; Sunset Cemetery, Christiansburg, Va.; gravestone added by Byron Dickerson.

[253] Frances Stone, c. 1930. Photo privately held by Sally Abdill.

[254] Mary Stone, 1918. Photo privately held by Sally Abdill.

[255] Pettus, 31.

[256] G.D. Burtchaell, compiler, *The Knights of England, vol. II* (London: Sherrat and Hughes, 1906), 151. Digital images via Archive.org (https://archive.org/stream/knightsofengland02shawuoft : accessed 28 Jan 2017).

[257] Pettus, 6.

[258] Ibid., 5.

[259] Ibid., 7.

[260] Ibid., 11

[261] Pocahontas Hutchinson Stacy and Alice Bömer Rudd, *The Pettus Family* (Washington: Self-published, 1957), 1.

[262] Pettus, 17.

[263] "England, Select Marriages, 1538–1973," Ancestry.com (http://search.ancestry.com/cgi-bin/sse.dll?indiv=1&dbid=9852&h=14327251 : accessed 29 Aug 2016). Entry for John Pettus to Beatrice Duckett, 1 Feb 1542; citing FHL microfilm 993,654.

[264] Pettus, 25.

[265] Ibid., 27.

[266] Image was obtained from Pettus p. 31. According to British law, even the very old manuscripts in the collection of the British Library are still technically under copyright until at least 2039; even the library, however, does not seem particularly bothered by this, saying on their website, "for anonymous unpublished material created many centuries ago and in the public domain in most other countries, the Library believes this material to be very unlikely to offend anyone."

[267] "England, Select Marriages, 1538–1973," Ancestry.com (http://search.ancestry.com/cgi-bin/sse.dll?indiv=1&dbid=9852&h=8012090 : accessed 31 Aug 2016). Entry for Thomas Pettus to Christian Dethick, 29 Oct 1548; citing FHL microfilm 993,654.

[268] *Find A Grave*, database with images (https://www.findagrave.com/cgi-bin/fg.cgi?page=gr&GRid=123855295 : accessed 31 Aug 2016),

memorial 123855295; Rose Crowe Dethick; entry added by Todd White-
sides.

[269] Pettus, 29.

[270] Francis Blomefield, *An Essay Towards A Topographical History of
the County of Norfolk: Volume 5* (London: W. Miller, 1806), 46–49.

[271] Pettus, 31.

[272] Ibid., 33.

[273] Ibid., 41.

[274] University of London, "PETTUS, John (1550–1614)," The History of Parliament, web page (http://www.historyofparliamentonline.
org/volume/1558-1603/member/pettus-john-1550-1614 : accessed
31 Aug 2016).

[275] Burtchaell, *The Knights of England, vol. II*, 142.

[276] "England, Select Births and Christenings, 1538-1975," An-
cestry.com (http://search.ancestry.com/cgi-bin/sse.dll?indiv=1&
dbid=9841&h=36400864 : accessed 31 Aug 2016). Entry for Isabell Pettus, baptized 28 Jun 1551 in Saint Simon and Saint Jude, Norwich,
Norfolk, England; referencing FHL microfilm 993,654.

[277] Pettus, 33.

[278] "England, Select Births and Christenings, 1538-1975," An-
cestry.com (http://search.ancestry.com/cgi-bin/sse.dll?indiv=1&
dbid=9841&h=126714321 : accessed 31 Aug 2016). Entry for Elizabeth
Pettus, baptized 28 Jun 1554 in Saint Simon and Saint Jude, Norwich,
Norfolk, England; referencing FHL microfilm 993,654.

[279] "England, Select Marriages, 1538–1973," Ancestry.com
(http://search.ancestry.com/cgi-bin/sse.dll?indiv=1&dbid=
9852&h=38350739 : accessed 31 Aug 2016). Entry for Elizabeth Pettus
marriage to Augustin Whall on 29 Aug 1573; referencing FHL microfilm
993,654.

[280] "U.S. and International Marriage Records, 1560-1900," An-
cestry.com (http://search.ancestry.com/cgi-bin/sse.dll?indiv=1&
dbid=7836&h=950910 : accessed 31 Aug 2016). Entry for William Pettus
marriage to Elizabeth Rolfe, undated.

[281] Pettus, 33.

[282] Ibid., 62.

[283] Pettus, volume II, 1361.

[284] Ibid.

[285] "U.S. and International Marriage Records, 1560-1900," Ancestry.com (http://search.ancestry.com/cgi-bin/sse.dll?indiv=1&dbid=7836&h=950845 : accessed 31 Aug 2016). Entry for Cecily Pettus marriage to Humphery Camden, married 1581.

[286] Pettus, 33.

[287] Ibid.

[288] "U.S. and International Marriage Records, 1560-1900," Ancestry.com (http://search.ancestry.com/cgi-bin/sse.dll?indiv=1&dbid=7836&h=950901 : accessed 31 Aug 2016). Entry for Thomas Pettus marriage to Cecily King, married 1574.

[289] Pettus, 58.

[290] Ibid.

[291] "England, Select Marriages, 1538–1973," Ancestry.com (http://search.ancestry.com/cgi-bin/sse.dll?indiv=1&dbid=9852&h=13997369 : accessed 31 Aug 2016). Entry for Willm Pettus marriage to Mary Gleane, married 21 Dec 1607; citing FHL microfilm 993,675.

[292] "England, Select Births and Christenings, 1538-1975," Ancestry.com (http://search.ancestry.com/cgi-bin/sse.dll?indiv=1&dbid=9841&h=650279 : accessed 31 Aug 2016). Entry for Edward Pettus, baptized 17 Dec 1585; citing FHL microfilm 993,654.

[293] "England, Select Births and Christenings, 1538-1975," Ancestry.com (http://search.ancestry.com/cgi-bin/sse.dll?indiv=1&dbid=9841&h=139136753 : accessed 31 Aug 2016). Entry for Henry Pettus, baptized 5 Oct 1586; citing FHL microfilm 993,654.

[294] "England, Select Births and Christenings, 1538-1975," Ancestry.com (http://search.ancestry.com/cgi-bin/sse.dll?indiv=1&dbid=9841&h=52176091 : accessed 31 Aug 2016). Entry for George Pettus, baptized 1 Dec 1591; citing FHL microfilm 993,654.

[295] "England, Select Births and Christenings, 1538-1975," Ancestry.com (http://search.ancestry.com/cgi-bin/sse.dll?indiv=1&dbid=9841&h=172464353 : accessed 31 Aug 2016). Entry for Francis Pettus, baptized 24 Mar 1592; citing FHL microfilm 993,654.

[296] "England, Select Births and Christenings, 1538-1975," Ancestry.com (http://search.ancestry.com/cgi-bin/sse.dll?indiv=1& dbid=9841&h=165073949 : accessed 31 Aug 2016). Entry for Mary Pettus, baptized 19 Apr 1594; citing FHL microfilm 993,654.

[297] "England, Select Births and Christenings, 1538-1975," Ancestry.com (http://search.ancestry.com/cgi-bin/sse.dll?indiv=1& dbid=9841&h=126180025 : accessed 31 Aug 2016). Entry for Thomas Pettus, baptized 8 Aug 1596; citing FHL microfilm 993,654.

[298] "England, Select Births and Christenings, 1538-1975," Ancestry.com (http://search.ancestry.com/cgi-bin/sse.dll?indiv=1& dbid=9841&h=126179860 : accessed 31 Aug 2016). Entry for Thomas Pettus, baptized 19 Feb 1598; citing FHL microfilm 993,654.

[299] Pettus, 121.

[300] H.R. McIlwaine ed., *Minutes of the Council and General court of colonial Virginia, 1622-1632, 1670-1676* (Richmond: Virginia State Library, 1924), 6.

[301] "England, Select Births and Christenings, 1538-1975," Ancestry.com (http://search.ancestry.com/cgi-bin/sse.dll?indiv=1& dbid=9841&h=191880777 : accessed 31 Aug 2016). Entry for Christian Pettus, baptized 26 Jul 1601; citing FHL microfilm 993,654.

[302] "England, Select Births and Christenings, 1538-1975," Ancestry.com (http://search.ancestry.com/cgi-bin/sse.dll?indiv=1& dbid=9841&h=126722393 : accessed 31 Aug 2016). Entry for Robart Pettus, baptized Feb 1607; citing FHL microfilm 993,654.

[303] Image was obtained from Pettus p. 61. See note attached to his father's signature regarding copyright.

[304] McIlwaine, *Minutes of the Council and General court of colonial Virginia, 1622-1632, 1670-1676*, 6.

[305] Pettus, 109.

[306] Ibid.

[307] Dr. Linwood "Little Bear" Custalow and Angela L. Daniel, "Silver Star", *The True Story of Pocahontas: The Other Side of History* (Golden, Co.: Fulcrum Publishing, 2007), 43.

[308] *The True Story of Pocahontas*, 51.

[309] "Our Patawomeck Ancestors," *Patawomeck Tides*, 15 Sep 2009,

page   2;   digital   image   (https://home.nps.gov/jame/learn/
historyculture/upload/Patawomeck-Tides-2009.pdf   :   accessed
31 Aug 2016).

[310]Pettus, vol. II, 1353–1356

[311]"Palm   Coast   author   solves   160-year   'Pocahontas'   mystery,"
Palm Coast Observer, web page (http://www.palmcoastobserver.com/
article/palm-coast-author-solves-160-year-pocahontas-mystery :
accessed 28 Jan 2017).

[312]Pettus, 119.

[313]Kelso, *Kingsmill Plantations, 1619–1800*, 6–7.

[314]"U.S. and International Marriage Records, 1560-1900," An-
cestry.com (http://search.ancestry.com/cgi-bin/sse.dll?indiv=1&
dbid=7836&h=950863 : accessed 31 Aug 2016). Entry for John Pettus
marriage to Anne Overton, married 1703.

[315]Pettus, 311.

[316]Ibid., 310.

[317]"U.S. and International Marriage Records, 1560-1900," An-
cestry.com (http://search.ancestry.com/cgi-bin/sse.dll?indiv=1&
dbid=7836&h=950840 : accessed 1 Sep 2016). Entry for Anne Overton
Pettus marriage to Joseph Eggleston, undated.

[318]"U.S. and International Marriage Records, 1560-1900," An-
cestry.com (http://search.ancestry.com/cgi-bin/sse.dll?indiv=1&
dbid=7836&h=950906 : accessed 1 Sep 2016). Entry for Thomas Pettus marriage to Amey Walker, 1735.

[319]Pettus, 362.

[320]Acklen, 182.

[321]Pettus, 374.

[322]Ibid., 365.

[323]Ibid., 366.

[324]*The Old Free State*, 69.

[325]Ibid., 70.

[326]"Pettus, Freeman," web page, Texas State Historical Associa-

tion (https://tshaonline.org/handbook/online/articles/fpe49 : accessed 14 Mar 2017).

[327] "Pettus, William Albert," web page, Texas State Historical Association (https://tshaonline.org/handbook/online/articles/fpe52 : accessed 14 Mar 2017).

[328] "Old Three Hundred," web page, Texas State Historical Association (https://tshaonline.org/handbook/online/articles/umo01 : accessed 14 Mar 2017).

[329] Pettus, 373.

[330] George H.S. King, "Memorial to Henry Fox, Gentleman, of 'Huntington', King William County, Virginia," *Tyler's Quarterly Historical and Genealogical Magazine*, 870.

[331] Pettus, 373.

[332] *Whitworth and Related Lines, Volume I*, 97.

[333] Pettus p. 483 states this was on 1 Nov 1776 and signed by Gov. Patrick Henry, but another (allegedly) transcribed record from Lunenburg County courts puts this date at 12 Sep 1776: *Historical Collections of the Joseph Habersham Chapter, Daughters of the American Revolution, Volume II* (Atlanta: Blosser Printing Co., 1902), p. 73.

[334] Pettus, 373.

[335] *Whitworth and Related Lines, Volume I*, 93.

[336] Ibid., p. 18.

[337] Ibid.

[338] Ibid.

[339] Ibid.

[340] Ibid.

[341] Ibid.

[342] Ibid.

[343] "Virginia, Compiled Marriages, 1740-1850," Ancestry.com (http://search.ancestry.com/cgi-bin/sse.dll?indiv=1&dbid=3723&h=23496 : accessed 5 Sep 2016). Entry for DAVID Sr. Pettus marriage to Elenor Willson, 25 Sep 1802.

[344] Pettus, 487

[345] National Society of the Daughters of the American Revolution, *Lineage Book, volume LXIV, 1907* (Washington, D.C.: self-published, 1923) 291. Digital images via Ancestry.com (`http://interactive.ancestry.com/61157/46155_b290201-00296` : accessed 11 Mar 2017).

[346] Acklen, 183.

[347] Ibid.

[348] 1830 U.S. census, Lunenburg County, Virginia, p. 21 (written); Samuel Pettus; image, Ancestry.com (`http://interactive.ancestry.com/8058/4411345_00047?bm=true` : accessed 10 Sep 2016).

[349] 1840 U.S. census, Lunenburg County, Virginia, p. 17 (written); Samuel Pettus; image, Ancestry.com (`http://interactive.ancestry.com/8057/4409478_00647?bm=true` : accessed 10 Sep 2016).

[350] Acklen, 183.

[351] Ibid.

[352] Ibid.

[353] Pettus, 601.

[354] "Virginia, Deaths and Burials Index, 1853-1917," Ancestry.com (`http://search.ancestry.com/cgi-bin/sse.dll?indiv=1&dbid=2558&h=366847` : accessed 21 Aug 2016). Entry for Clara A Stone, died 24 Dec 1878.

[355] Acklen, 183.

[356] Pettus, 601.

[357] 1860 U.S. census, Mecklenburg County, Virginia, population schedule, The 22nd Regt [Regiment], dwelling 458, family 457; Mustrove [*sic*], Susan, Flourney, Arlona and Sophia Pettus; image, Ancestry.com (`http://interactive.ancestry.com/7667/4297391_00219?bm=true` : accessed 14 Mar 2017).

[358] Acklen, 183.

[359] Ibid.

[360] *Find A Grave*, database with images (`https://www.findagrave.com/cgi-bin/fg.cgi?page=gr&GRid=15981016` : accessed 5 Sep 2016), memorial 15981016; John Richard Pettus; Morton Cemetery, Richmond, Texas; gravestone added by Nancy Ann Mull Buchanan.

[361] Acklen, 183.

[362] 1850 U.S. census, Lunenburg County, Virginia, population schedule, dwelling 676, family 676; Saml. and Sophia Pettus; image, Ancestry.com (`http://interactive.ancestry.com/8054/4206380_00095?bm=true` : accessed 13 Mar 2017).

[363] George Sherwood, editor, *The Pedigree Register, Volume III* (London: self-published, 1916), 188.

[364] Ibid.

[365] Pettus, 25.

[366] Ibid.

[367] G. A. Carthew, *The Hundred of Launditch and Deanery of Brisley, Volume III* (Norwich, England: Miller and Leavins, 1879), 132.

[368] *The Pedigree Register, Volume III*, 189.

[369] Ibid., 190.

[370] Ibid., 189.

[371] Ibid., 189.

[372] "England, Select Deaths and Burials, 1538-1991," Familysearch.org (`https://familysearch.org/ark:/61903/1:1:JDHF-R6J` : accessed 11 Mar 2017). Entry for Simon Dethike, 1 Mar 1542.

[373] *The Pedigree Register, Volume III*, 188.

[374] "U.S. and International Marriage Records, 1560-1900," Ancestry.com (`http://search.ancestry.com/cgi-bin/sse.dll?indiv=1&dbid=7836&h=1320873` : accessed 28 Oct 2016). Entry for John Whitworth marriage to Mary Claiborne, 1684.

[375] "U.S. and International Marriage Records, 1560-1900," Ancestry.com (`http://search.ancestry.com/cgi-bin/sse.dll?indiv=1&dbid=7836&h=1320875` : accessed 28 Oct 2016). Entry for Thomas Whitworth marriage to Mary Wintson [*sic*], 1725.

[376] "U.S. and International Marriage Records, 1560-1900," entry for John Whitworth marriage to Mary Claiborne, 1684.

[377] "U.S. and International Marriage Records, 1560-1900," entry for Thomas Whitworth marriage to Mary Wintson, 1725.

[378] *Whitworth and Related Lines, Volume I*, 92.

[379] Ibid.

[380] Ibid.

[381] Ibid.

[382] Ibid.

[383] Ibid.

[384] "Family Data Collection - Births," Ancestry.com (http://search.ancestry.com/cgi-bin/sse.dll?indiv=1&dbid=5769&h=4863351 : accessed 28 Oct 2016). Entry for Thomas Whitworth, born 26 Jun 1726.

[385] "U.S. and International Marriage Records, 1560-1900," Ancestry.com (http://search.ancestry.com/cgi-bin/sse.dll?indiv=1&dbid=7836&h=1320865 : accessed 28 Oct 2016). Entry for Thomas Whitworth marriage to Elizabeth Southerland, 1745.

[386] The year of Thomas's birth has appeared in multiple sources; the date, however, appears only in the "Family Data Collection," a database based on records from genetic studies that did not have particularly high standards of proof for genealogical data such as birth dates.

[387] Landon C. Bell, "Lunenburg County Virginia Wills 1746-1825," transcription via Rootsweb (http://ftp.rootsweb.ancestry.com/pub/usgenweb/va/lunenburg/wills/1746-1825-b.txt : accessed 28 Oct 2016). Entry for Thomas Whitworth, will written 6 Jun 1797.

[388] Acklen, 182–184.

[389] *Whitworth and Related Lines, Volume I*, 93.

[390] Bell, "Lunenburg County Virginia Wills 1746-1825," entry for Thomas Whitworth, will written 6 Jun 1797.

[391] Acklen, 182–184.

[392] King, "Memorial to Henry Fox," 870.

[393] Bell, "Lunenburg County Virginia Wills 1746-1825," entry for Thomas Whitworth, will written 6 Jun 1797.

[394] Acklen, 182–184.

[395] Pettus, 373.

[396] Bell, "Lunenburg County Virginia Wills 1746-1825," entry for Thomas Whitworth, will written 6 Jun 1797.

[397] Acklen, 182–184.

[398] *Whitworth and Related Lines, Volume I*, 93.

[399] Bell, "Lunenburg County Virginia Wills 1746-1825," entry for Thomas Whitworth, will written 6 Jun 1797.

[400] Ibid.

[401] Acklen, 182–184.

[402] "U.S. and International Marriage Records, 1560-1900," Ancestry.com (http://search.ancestry.com/cgi-bin/sse.dll?indiv=1& dbid=7836&h=1320839 : accessed 28 Oct 2016). Entry for Edward Couch marriage to Mary Whitworth, undated.

[403] *Whitworth and Related Lines, Volume I*, 93.

[404] Ibid.

[405] "U.S. and International Marriage Records, 1560-1900," Ancestry.com (http://search.ancestry.com/cgi-bin/sse.dll?indiv=1& dbid=7836&h=1320839 : accessed 28 Oct 2016). Entry for Edward Couch marriage to Mary Whitworth, undated.

[406] *Whitworth and Related Lines, Volume I*, 93.

[407] Ibid.

[408] Ibid., 99.

[409] Ibid.

[410] Bell, "Lunenburg County Virginia Wills 1746–1825," entry for Thomas Whitworth, will written 6 Jun 1797.

[411] Ibid.

[412] Acklen, 182.

[413] *Whitworth and Related Lines, Volume I*, 101.

[414] Bell, "Lunenburg County Virginia Wills 1746–1825," entry for Thomas Whitworth, will written 6 Jun 1797.

[415] Acklen, 182.

[416] *Whitworth and Related Lines, Volume I*, 93.

[417] Bell, "Lunenburg County Virginia Wills 1746–1825," entry for Thomas Whitworth, will written 6 Jun 1797.

[418] Bell, "Lunenburg County Virginia Wills 1746–1825," entry for Thomas Whitworth, will written 6 Jun 1797.

[419] Acklen, 182.

[420] *Whitworth and Related Lines, Volume I*, 94.

[421] Ibid., 102.

[422] Acklen, 182.

[423] *Whitworth and Related Lines, Volume I*, 103.

[424] Bell, "Lunenburg County Virginia Wills 1746–1825," entry for Thomas Whitworth, will written 6 Jun 1797.

[425] Acklen, 182.

[426] *Whitworth and Related Lines, Volume I*, 103.

[427] Ibid.

[428] "North Carolina, Marriage Records, 1741-2011," image of document, Ancestry.com (http://interactive.ancestry.com/60548/42091_334948-00073 : accessed 28 Oct 2016), page 132. Entry for Southerland Whitworth marriage to Marey Hood, 3 Jan 1792.

[429] *Whitworth and Related Lines, Volume I*, 94.

[430] Bell, "Lunenburg County Virginia Wills 1746–1825," entry for Thomas Whitworth, will written 6 Jun 1797.

[431] Acklen, 182.

[432] Ibid., 105.

[433] *Find A Grave*, database with images (https://www.findagrave.com/cgi-bin/fg.cgi?page=gr&GRid=28307052 : accessed 28 Oct 2016), memorial 28307052; Rebecca Elizabeth Whitworth Stone; Hart Cemetery, Chester County, Tenn.; gravestone added by Donna Hampton.

[434] *Whitworth and Related Lines, Volume I*, 94.

[435] Ibid., 105.

[436] *Marriages of Lunenburg County, Virginia, 1746-1853*, 117. Entry for Isaac Stone marriage to Rebecca Whitworth, 1793.

[437] *Whitworth and Related Lines, Volume I*, 105.

[438] Frances Beale Smith Hodges, *The Genealogy of the Beale Family, 1399–1956* (Ann Arbor, Mich.: Edwards Brothers, 1956), 194. (https://hdl.handle.net/2027/wu.89062850532 : accessed 14 Mar 2017.)

[439] "U.S. and Canada, Passenger and Immigration Lists Index, 1500s–1900s," Ancestry.com (http://search.ancestry.com/cgi-bin/

sse.dll?indiv=1&dbid=7486&h=4147039 : accessed 28 Jan 2017). Entry for Richard Lamb, arriving 1749 in Virginia; source publication code 3675.1.

[440] "For Liverpool," *Rind's Virginia Gazette*, 5 Jan 1769, page 3; digital image, *Newspapers.com* (https://www.newspapers.com/image/40480227 : accessed 28 Jan 2017).

[441] "For Liverpool," *Rind's Virginia Gazette*, 12 Jan 1769, page 4; digital image, *Newspapers.com* (https://www.newspapers.com/image/40481978 : accessed 28 Jan 2017).

[442] "To be Sold, or Rented for a Term of Years, and entered upon the 1st of March," *Rind's Virginia Gazette*, 12 Mar 1772, page 4; digital image, *Newspapers.com* (https://www.newspapers.com/image/40481355 : accessed 28 Jan 2017).

[443] "For Liverpool," *Rind's Virginia Gazette*, 5 Jan 1769, page 3.

[444] "Five Pounds Reward," *Rind's Virginia Gazette*, 14 Jan 1773, page 3; digital image, *Newspapers.com* (https://www.newspapers.com/image/40481532 : accessed 28 Jan 2017).

[445] Beale, 194.

[446] *Jefferson Papers*, "Founders Online," National Historical Publications and Records Commission (http://founders.archives.gov/documents/Jefferson/01-04-02-0024 : accessed 5 Nov 2016); letter to Thomas Jefferson from Horatio Gates, 9 October 1780.

[447] *Jefferson Papers*, "Founders Online," National Historical Publications and Records Commission (http://founders.archives.gov/documents/Jefferson/01-04-02-0044 : accessed 5 Nov 2016); Commission to Richard? Lamb, 15 October 1780.

[448] *Jefferson Papers*, "Founders Online," National Historical Publications and Records Commission (http://founders.archives.gov/documents/Jefferson/01-04-02-0055 : accessed 5 Nov 2016); letter to Thomas Jefferson from Horatio Gates, 20 October 1780.

[449] "Revolutionary War Pensions," Fold3 (https://www.fold3.com/image/11036229 : accessed 4 Nov 2016). Letter from Stephen Biggs to Green County Court, Kentucky, 16 Nov 1835.

[450] "U.S. and International Marriage Records, 1560-1900," Ancestry.com (http://search.ancestry.com/cgi-bin/sse.dll?indiv=1&

dbid=7836&h=713152 : accessed 5 Nov 2016). Entry for Clarissa Borwell [*sic*] Lamb marriage to William Whitehead, 1790.

[451] Ibid.

[452] Beale, 194.

[453] National Society of the Daughters of the American Revolution, *Lineage Book, volume LXV, 1907,* image of document (Washington, D.C.: self-published, 1923), (http://interactive.ancestry.com/61157/46155_b290201-00296 : accessed 19 Mar 2017), p. 271.

[454] Beale, 194.

[455] *Find A Grave,* database with images (https://www.findagrave.com/cgi-bin/fg.cgi?page=gr&GRid=94334294 : accessed 5 Nov 2016), memorial 94334294; William Boswell Lamb; Cedar Grove Cemetery, Norfolk City, Va.; gravestone added by SWF.

[456] *Find A Grave,* database with images (https://www.findagrave.com/cgi-bin/fg.cgi?page=gr&GRid=94334446 : accessed 5 Nov 2016), memorial 94334446; Margaret Stuart Kerr Lamb; Cedar Grove Cemetery, Norfolk City, Va.; gravestone added by SWF.

[457] Beale, 194.

[458] "Virginia, Marriages, 1740-1850," Ancestry.com (http://search.ancestry.com/cgi-bin/sse.dll?indiv=1&dbid=5685&h=716 : accessed 5 Nov 2016). Entry for Mary E. Lamb to John Moody Robertson, 1 Mar 1792.

[459] Beale, 194.

[460] 1850 U.S. census, Charlotte County, Virginia, population schedule, Charlotte division, dwelling 28, family 28; John and Clarissa H. Booth; image, Ancestry.com (http://interactive.ancestry.com/8054/4191530-00010/14949796 : accessed 5 Nov 2016).

[461] "Lunenburg County, Virginia, Marriage Bonds Index, 1763-1839," Ancestry.com (http://search.ancestry.com/cgi-bin/sse.dll?indiv=1&dbid=5685&h=716 : accessed 5 Nov 2016). Entry for Clarissa H. Lamb to John Booth, 19 Jun 1826; Samuel Pettus, surety.

[462] 1850 U.S. census, Charlotte County, Virginia, population schedule, Charlotte division, dwelling 28, family 28; John and Clarissa H. Booth; image, Ancestry.com (http://interactive.ancestry.com/8054/4191530-00010/14949796 : accessed 5 Nov 2016).

[463] Beale, 194.

[464] "Virginia, Compiled Marriages, 1740-1850," Ancestry.com (http://search.ancestry.com/cgi-bin/sse.dll?indiv=1&dbid=3723& h=1082140 : accessed 14 Mar 2017). Entry for Harriet Lamb to John Day, 23 Jul 1804.

[465] Beale, 194.

[466] Ibid.

[467] "Virginia, Marriages, 1660-1800," Ancestry.com (http://search. ancestry.com/cgi-bin/sse.dll?indiv=1&dbid=3002&h=40394 : accessed 5 Nov 2016). Entry for Margaret P Lamb to Richard Whitehead, 13 Jan 1800.

[468] Beale, 193.

[469] Compiled service record, Richard Lamb, Lt., Baldwin's Regiment Artificers; Record Group 94: Records of the Adjutant General's Office, 1780s–1917; National Archives, Washington, D.C.

[470] "Letters from Maj. Gen. Nathaniel Greene, 1776–85," Fold3 (https://www.fold3.com/image/418443?xid=1945 : accessed 4 Nov 2016). Papers of the Continental Congress, compiled 1774–1789. Citing roll number 175. Page 102.

[471] "Letters from Maj. Gen. Nathaniel Greene, 1776–85," 105.

[472] 1860 U.S. census, Spotsylvania County, Virginia, mortality schedule, St. Georges Parish, p. 4 (written); Elizabeth Spindle and Harriet Leavell; image, Ancestry.com (http://interactive.ancestry.com/ 8756/VAT1132_5-0329 : accessed 4 Dec 2016).

[473] 1830 U.S. census, Spotsylvania County, Virginia, Eastern District, William Spindle; image, Ancestry.com (http://interactive.ancestry. com/8058/4411345_00200?bm=true : accessed 15 Mar 2017).

[474] Virginia Chancery Court records, Library of Virginia. Digital images (http://www.lva.virginia.gov/chancery/). Spotsylvania County, case "Gdn. of John A. Spindle, etc. vs Harriet A. Spindle, etc.," 1838.

[475] 1850 U.S. census, Stafford County, Virginia, population schedule, Eastern District, dwelling 754, family 754; Jefferson, Maria A., Charles W. and John Spindle; image, Ancestry.com (http://interactive. ancestry.com/8054/4206468_00100?bm=true : accessed 4 Dec 2016).

[476] Alsup, Vol. I, 307.

[477] 1880 U.S. census, Fauquier County, Virginia, population schedule, Rappahannock, p. 214 (stamped), dwelling 6, family 6; Charles, Nannie, Sallie J. and Maria Spindle; image, Ancestry.com (http://interactive. ancestry.com/6742/4244616-00198/18758755 : accessed 4 Dec 2016).

[478] Alsup, Vol. III, 309.

[479] "Virginia, Deaths and Burials Index, 1853-1917," Ancestry.com (http://search.ancestry.com/cgi-bin/sse.dll?indiv=1&dbid=2558& h=20223 : accessed 4 Dec 2016). Entry for William W Spindle, died Apr 1868.

[480] Alsup, Vol. I, 305.

[481] *Find A Grave*, database with images (https://www.findagrave. com/cgi-bin/fg.cgi?page=gr&GRid=102508333 : accessed 4 Dec 2016), memorial 102508333; Harriet A. Leavell; Snow Hill Plantation Cemetery, Spotsylvania County, VA; gravestone added by Leslyn Lang.

[482] 1860 U.S. census, Spotsylvania County, Virginia, mortality schedule, St. Georges Parish, p. 4 (written); Elizabeth Spindle and Harriet Leavell; image, Ancestry.com (http://interactive.ancestry.com/ 8756/VAT1132_5-0329 : accessed 4 Dec 2016).

[483] "Virginia, Compiled Marriages, 1740-1850," Ancestry.com (http://search.ancestry.com/cgi-bin/sse.dll?indiv=1&dbid=3723& h=1027317 : accessed 4 Dec 2016). Entry for Harriett A. Spindle and Edmund S. Leavell, married 7 Sep 1837.

[484] *Find A Grave*, memorial 102508333, Harriet A. Leavell; gravestone added by Leslyn Lang.

[485] 1860 U.S. census, Spotsylvania County, Virginia, mortality schedule, St. Georges Parish, p. 6 (written); Benjamin Spindle; image, Ancestry.com (http://interactive.ancestry.com/8756/VAT1132_5-0331 : accessed 10 Nov 2016).

[486] Middle initial based on entry in hospital records referenced later.

[487] Alsup, Vol. I, 309.

[488] 1850 U.S. census, Spotsylvania County, Virginia, population schedule, Eastern District, p. 412 (stamped), dwelling 631, family 631; James and Frances Quesenberry, and Mary S. Spindle; image, Ancestry.com (http://interactive.ancestry.com/8054/4206467_00343?bm= true : accessed 28 Nov 2016).

[489] "Virginia, Compiled Marriages, 1740-1850," Ancestry.com

(http://search.ancestry.com/cgi-bin/sse.dll?indiv=1&dbid=3723&
h=1058392 : accessed 4 Dec 2016). Entry for Frances A. Spindle and
James M. Quisenberry, married 9 Jun 1840.

[490] *Virginia: Rebirth of the Old Dominion, Vol. III* (Chicago: Lewis
Publishing Co., 1929), 247. Digital images via Archive.org (https://
archive.org/stream/virginiarebirtho03bruc : accessed 11 Mar 2017).

[491] 1860 U.S. census, Spotsylvania County, Virginia, mortality schedule, St. Georges Parish, p. 6 (written); Benjamin Spindle; image, An-
cestry.com (http://interactive.ancestry.com/8756/VAT1132_5-0331 :
accessed 10 Nov 2016).

[492] *Find A Grave*, database with images (https://www.findagrave.
com/cgi-bin/fg.cgi?page=gr&GRid=30378749 : accessed 15 Nov 2016),
memorial 30378749; William Henry Spindle; Sunset Cemetery, Christiansburg, Va.; gravestone added by Brenda Dudley Eanes.

[493] *Find A Grave*, database with images (https://www.findagrave.
com/cgi-bin/fg.cgi?page=gr&GRid=30378749 : accessed 15 Nov 2016),
memorial 30378749; William Henry Spindle; Sunset Cemetery, Christiansburg, Va.; gravestone added by Brenda Dudley Eanes.

[494] Compiled service record, William H. Spindle, Pvt., Co. B, 30th VA
Infantry; Carded Records, Volunteer Organizations, Civil War; Record
Group 94: Records of the Adjutant General's Office, 1780s–1917; Na-
tional Archives, Washington, D.C.

[495] Compiled service record, William H. Spindle, Sgt., Co. E, 9th VA
Cavalry; Carded Records, Volunteer Organizations, Civil War; Record
Group 94: Records of the Adjutant General's Office, 1780s–1917; Na-
tional Archives, Washington, D.C.

[496] 1850 U.S. census, Spotsylvania County, Virginia, population schedule, Eastern District, dwelling 301, family 301; Benj, Ellen, Wm H. and
Tho. W. Spindle; image, Ancestry.com (http://interactive.ancestry.
com/8054/4206467_00304?bm=true : accessed 24 Nov 2016).

[497] "Capt. T.W. Spindle Dies at Roanoke," *Bluefield Daily
Telegraph*, 14 Feb 1905; digital image, Ancestry.com (http:
//mv.ancestry.com/viewer/38e19d66-633a-4aed-a5d7-42731e3b0167/
84096417/44499494174?_phsrc=eiR2439 : accessed 24 Nov 2016).

[498] "Virginia, Select Marriages, 1785–1940," Ancestry.com
(http://search.ancestry.com/cgi-bin/sse.dll?indiv=1&dbid=

60214&h=3483659 : accessed 24 Nov 2016). Entry for Thos. W. Spindle marriage to Lavinia C. Shelburn, 25 Jan 1870.

[499]Compiled service record, Thomas W. Spindle, Pvt., 4 VA Inf., Co. G; Record Group 94: Records of the Adjutant General's Office, 1780s–1917; National Archives, Washington, D.C.

[500]Compiled service record, Thomas W. Spindle, 2Lt., 25 VA Cav., Co. E; Record Group 94: Records of the Adjutant General's Office, 1780s–1917; National Archives, Washington, D.C.

[501]"M.E. Shelburne (obit)," *Washington Post*, 11 Sep 1903; digital image, Ancestry.com (http://mv.ancestry.com/viewer/77aa0b51-3fef-4da5-be03-02ce80ff0008/84096417/44499494197?_phsrc=eiR2447&usePUBJs=true : accessed 25 Nov 2016).

[502]*Find A Grave*, database with images (https://www.findagrave.com/cgi-bin/fg.cgi?page=gr&GRid=30378497 : accessed 28 Jan 2017), memorial 30378497; Mary E. Spindle Shelburne; Sunset Cemetery, Christiansburg, Va.; gravestone added by Angi Weast King.

[503]Ibid.

[504]*Find A Grave*, memorial 30378833; Virginia Spindle; gravestone added by Brenda Dudley Eanes.

[505]1850 U.S. census, Spotsylvania County, Virginia, population schedule, Eastern District, p. 412 (stamped), dwelling 631, family 631; James and Frances Quesenberry, and Mary S. Spindle; image, Ancestry.com (http://interactive.ancestry.com/8054/4206467_00343?bm=true : accessed 28 Nov 2016).

[506]1850 U.S. census, Spotsylvania County, Virginia, population schedule, Eastern District, dwelling 301, family 301; Benj, Ellen, Wm H. and Tho. W. Spindle; image, Ancestry.com (http://interactive.ancestry.com/8054/4206467_00304?bm=true : accessed 24 Nov 2016).

[507]1860 U.S. census, Spotsylvania County, Virginia, population schedule, St. Georges Parish, p. 78 (written), dwelling 617, family 612; Ellen E. Spindle; image, Ancestry.com (http://interactive.ancestry.com/7667/4298875_00369?bm=true : accessed 3 Dec 2016).

[508]S.A. Cunningham ed., *Confederate Veteran, Volume X* (Nashville, 1902), p. 456.

[509]"Murder at the Second Market," *Out of the Box: Notes from the Archives at the Library of Virginia*, website

(http://www.virginiamemory.com/blogs/out_of_the_box/2011/
03/02/murder-at-the-second-market/ : accessed 14 Mar 2017).

[510] "Virginia, Death Records, 1912-2014," Ancestry.com (http:
//interactive.ancestry.com/9278/43006_162028001249_0261-00069 :
accessed 28 Nov 2016). Death certificate for Ella Spindle, state file
number 15267, 6 Jul 1948.

[511] *Virginia: Rebirth of the Old Dominion, Vol. III*, 248.

[512] "Virginia, Select Marriages, 1785-1940," Ancestry.com
(http://search.ancestry.com/cgi-bin/sse.dll?indiv=1&dbid=
60214&h=5999318 : accessed 10 Nov 2016). Entry for Benjamin Spindle
to Sarah Buckner, 16 Nov 1853, referencing FHL film 34039.

[513] 1860 U.S. census, Spotsylvania County, Virginia, mortality schedule, St. Georges Parish, p. 6 (written); Benjamin Spindle; image, An-
cestry.com (http://interactive.ancestry.com/8756/VAT1132_5-0331 :
accessed 10 Nov 2016).

[514] 1860 U.S. census, Spotsylvania County, Virginia, population schedule, St. Georges Parish, p. 106–107 (written), dwelling 828, family 816;
Sarah, Wm. H., Mary E., Maria V., Richard and Ella T. Spindle; image, Ancestry.com (http://interactive.ancestry.com/7667/4298875_
00398?bm=true : accessed 14 Aug 2016); citing FHL microfilm 805,380.

[515] *Virginia: Rebirth of the Old Dominion, Vol. III*, 248.

[516] *Find A Grave*, database with images (http://www.findagrave.
com/cgi-bin/fg.cgi?page=gr&GRid=30378698 : accessed 14 Mar 2017,
memorial 30378698; Richard Buckner Spindle; Sunset Cemetery, Christiansburg, Montgomery County, Va.; entry added by Brenda Dudley
Eanes.

[517] 1860 U.S. census, Spotsylvania Co., Va., pop. sch., dwell. 828, fam.
816; Sarah, Wm. H., Mary E., Maria V., Richard and Ella T. Spindle.

[518] "Virginia, Death Records, 1912-2014," Ancestry.com (http:
//interactive.ancestry.com/9278/43004_172028008877_0091-00097 :
accessed 14 Mar 2017). Death certificate for Richard Buckner Spindle,
state file number 21109, 26 Sep 1928.

[519] "Virginia, Death Records, 1912-2014." Death certificate for Ella
Spindle, state file number 15267, 6 Jul 1948.

[520] Virginia Chancery Court records, Library of Virginia. Digital images

(http://www.lva.virginia.gov/chancery/). Spotsylvania County, case "Lavinia W. Wigglesworth vs. Gdn. of John Wigglesworth, etc.," 1841.

[521] 1860 U.S. census, Spotsylvania County, Virginia, mortality schedule, St. Georges Parish, p. 6 (written); Benjamin Spindle; image, Ancestry.com (http://interactive.ancestry.com/8756/VAT1132_5-0331 : accessed 10 Nov 2016).

[522] "Virginia, Deaths and Burials Index, 1853-1917," Ancestry.com (http://search.ancestry.com/cgi-bin/sse.dll?indiv=1&dbid=2558&h=527685 : accessed 28 Nov 2016). Entry for Benjamin Spindle, died 24 Jan 1860.

[523] 1860 U.S. census, Spotsylvania County, Virginia, slave schedule, p. 71 (written), dwelling 654, family 654; Sarah Spindle; image, Ancestry.com (http://interactive.ancestry.com/7668/VAM653_1397-0158 : accessed 20 Aug 2016).

[524] 1860 U.S. census, Spotsylvania Co., Va., pop. sch., dwell. 828, fam. 816; Sarah, Wm. H., Mary E., Maria V., Richard and Ella T. Spindle.

[525] 1860 U.S. census, Montgomery County, Virginia, population schedule, dwelling 730, family 680; Robert A., Clara A. and Roberta Miller, and Thomas W. Spindle; image, Ancestry.com (http://interactive.ancestry.com/7667/4298858_00157?bm=true : accessed 28 Nov 2016); citing FHL microfilm 805,363.

[526] Compiled service record, Thomas W. Spindle.

[527] "Spotsylvania Court House," web page, Civil War Trust (http://www.civilwar.org/battlefields/spotsylvania-court-house.html : accessed 14 Mar 2017).

[528] Cora Brien and Clarence R. Geier, "Third Time's the Charm: Historical Archaeology and the Sarah Spindle House on the Battlefield of Spotsylvania Court House," *Fredericksburg History and Biography, Vol. IV* (Fredericksburg, Va.: Central Virginia Battlefields Trust, 2005), p. 49.

[529] Gordon C. Rhea, *The Battles for Spotsylvania Court House and the Road to Yellow Tavern* (Baton Rouge: Louisiana State University Press, 1997), 62.

[530] 1860 U.S. census, Spotsylvania County, Virginia, mortality schedule, St. Georges Parish, p. 6 (written); Benjamin Spindle; image, Ancestry.com (http://interactive.ancestry.com/8756/VAT1132_5-0331 : accessed 10 Nov 2016).

(http://www.lva.virginia.gov/chancery/). Spotsylvania County, case "Charles Metcalfe v. Benjamin Alsop etc.," 1790.

[571] "Revolutionary War Pensions," Ancestry.com. Benjamin Alsop pension application, 1832.

[572] "Record of Pay and Service of Officers and Men of Virginia, New York, and Georgia, 1775–1856," Fold3 (https://www.fold3.com/image/286702678?xid=1945 : accessed 28 Jan 2017). Entry for Benjamin Alsop, p. 78.

[573] "Revolutionary War Rolls, Virginia, 6th Regiment (1776–78)," Fold3 (https://www.fold3.com/image/9565120/?terms=benjamin%20alsop&xid=1945 : accessed 28 Jan 2017). Entry for Benjamin Alsop, p. 36.

[574] "Revolutionary War Pensions," Ancestry.com. Benjamin Alsop pension application, 1832, p. 32.

[575] Alsup, Vol. I, 145.

[576] Ibid.

[577] Ibid., 151.

[578] "Revolutionary War Pensions," Ancestry.com. Benjamin Alsop pension application, 1832, p. 2.

[579] Alsup, Vol. I, 147.

[580] Ibid., 145

[581] "Virginia, Select Marriages, 1785-1940," Ancestry.com (http://search.ancestry.com/cgi-bin/sse.dll?indiv=1&dbid=60214&h=4147824 : accessed 14 Mar 2017). Entry for Stapleton Crutchfield marriage to Sarah Ann Alsop, 13 Jun 1833.

[582] *Find A Grave*, database with images (http://www.findagrave.com/cgi-bin/fg.cgi?page=gr&GRid=102509000 : accessed 14 Mar 2017, memorial 102509000; Sally Ann Alsop Crutchfield; Snow Hill Plantation Cemetery, Spotsylvania County, Va.; entry added by Leslyn Lang.

[583] 1860 U.S. census, Spotsylvania County, Virginia, mortality schedule, St. Georges Parish, p. 6 (written); Stapleton Crutchfield; image, Ancestry.com (http://interactive.ancestry.com/8756/VAT1132_5-0331 : accessed 14 Mar 2017).

[584] Alsup, Vol. II, Chapter XVI.

[585] "Revolutionary War Pensions," Ancestry.com. Benjamin Alsop pension application, 1832, p. 2, 32.

[586] Alsup, Vol. 1, 147.

[587] "Revolutionary War Rolls, 1775-1783," record for Virginia 6th Regiment 1776–78, Fold3 (`https://www.fold3.com/image/9565120/?terms=benjamin%20alsop&xid=1945` : accessed 14 Mar 2017).

[588] "Records of Pay and Service of Officers and Men of Virginia, New York, and Georgia, 1775 - 1856," Fold3 (`https://www.fold3.com/image/286702678` : accessed 14 Mar 2017).

[589] Crozier, 62.

[590] Ibid., 33.

[591] Ibid., 257.

[592] Ibid.

[593] Ibid.

[594] Ibid.

[595] King, "Memorial to Henry Fox, Gentleman, of 'Huntington', King William County, Virginia," 58.

[596] King, 204.

[597] Emily Griffith Roberts, *Ancestral Study of Four Families* (Terrell, TX: self-published, 1939), 445. Digital images via Google (`https://books.google.com/books?id=s2lPAAAAMAAJ` : accessed 11 Mar 2017).

[598] "U.S. and Canada, Passenger and Immigration Lists Index, 1500s–1900s," Ancestry.com (`http://search.ancestry.com/cgi-bin/sse.dll?_phsrc=eiR3358&_phstart=successSource&usePUBJs=true&indiv=1&db=pili354&gss=angs-d&new=1&rank=1&msT=1&gsln=wiglesworth&gsln_x=0&MSAV=1&uidh=956&pcat=40&fh=1&h=4121349&recoff=4&ml_rpos=2` : accessed 11 Mar 2017). Entry for John Wiglesworth, arriving 1738 in Virginia; source publication code 3299.40.

[599] King, "Memorial to Henry Fox," 55.

[600] Crozier, 49.

[601] Ibid., 317, 321, 349, 358.

[602] Virginia Chancery Court records, Library of Virginia. Digital images

(http://www.lva.virginia.gov/chancery/). Spotsylvania County, case "Lavinia Wigglesworth vs Gdn. of John Wigglesworth, etc.," 1839.

[603] Virginia Chancery Court records, Library of Virginia. Digital images (http://www.lva.virginia.gov/chancery/). Shenandoah County, case "Admr. of Thomas Fox, et als vs. Thomas Frazier," 1835.

[604] Ibid.

[605] King, 756.

[606] Ibid.

[607] Ibid.

[608] "Virginia, Compiled Marriages, 1740-1850," Ancestry.com (http://search.ancestry.com/cgi-bin/sse.dll?indiv=1&dbid=3723& h=1019462 : accessed 22 Jan 2017). Entry for Clabourne [*sic*] Wiglesworth to Lavinia Ward Farish, 26 Oct 1818.

[609] Virginia Chancery Court records, Library of Virginia. Digital images (http://www.lva.virginia.gov/chancery/). Shenandoah County, case "Admr. of Thomas Fox, et als vs. Thomas Frazier," 1835.

[610] Virginia Chancery Court records, Library of Virginia. Digital images (http://www.lva.virginia.gov/chancery/). Spotsylvania County, case "Lavinia Wigglesworth vs Gdn. of John Wigglesworth, etc.," 1839.

[611] King, 756.

[612] Virginia Chancery Court records, Library of Virginia. Digital images (http://www.lva.virginia.gov/chancery/). Shenandoah County, case "Admr. of Thomas Fox, et als vs. Thomas Frazier," 1835.

[613] Virginia Chancery Court records, Library of Virginia. Digital images (http://www.lva.virginia.gov/chancery/). Spotsylvania County, case "Lavinia Wigglesworth vs Gdn. of John Wigglesworth, etc.," 1839.

[614] Virginia Chancery Court records, Library of Virginia. Digital images (http://www.lva.virginia.gov/chancery/). Shenandoah County, case "Admr. of Thomas Fox, et als vs. Thomas Frazier," 1835.

[615] Ibid.

[616] Virginia. Spotsylvania County Chancery Court records, Library of Virginia. Digital images (http://www.lva.virginia.gov/chancery/). Case "Lavinia W. Wigglesworth vs. Gdn. of John Wigglesworth, etc.," 1839; index number 1839-004.

[617] King, 756.

[618] Ibid., 715.

[619] Ibid., 718.

[620] Ibid.

[621] Joseph E. Steadman Sr. and Shirley Faucette, *Ancestry of the Fox family of Richland and Lexington Counties, South Carolina* (Batesburg, SC: self-published, 1972), 21.

[622] Ibid., 17

[623] King, 718.

[624] Ibid., 719.

[625] Ibid., 721.

[626] Ibid., 721.

[627] Joseph M. Fox III and David E. Fox, "Y-DNA Testing of a Paper Trail: The Fox Surname Project," *Journal of Genetic Genealogy,* 2.

[628] Steadman, 74.

[629] Ibid.

[630] King, 721.

[631] Steadman, 24.

[632] Ibid., 21.

[633] Ibid., 43.

[634] King, 737.

[635] Steadman, 27.

[636] Ibid.

[637] King, 743.

[638] Ibid., 748.

[639] Ibid., 747.

[640] Virginia Chancery Court records, Library of Virginia. Digital images (http://www.lva.virginia.gov/chancery/). Shenandoah County, case "Admr. of Thomas Fox, et als vs. Thomas Frazier," 1835.

[641]King, 747.

[642]Virginia Chancery Court records, Library of Virginia. Digital images (http://www.lva.virginia.gov/chancery/). Shenandoah County, case "Admr. of Thomas Fox, et als vs. Thomas Frazier," 1835.

[643]King, 747.

[644]Virginia Chancery Court records, Library of Virginia. Digital images (http://www.lva.virginia.gov/chancery/). Shenandoah County, case "Admr. of Thomas Fox, et als vs. Thomas Frazier," 1835.

[645]Ibid.

[646]King, 747.

[647]Ibid., 757.

[648]Ibid., 747.

[649]Virginia Chancery Court records, Library of Virginia. Digital images (http://www.lva.virginia.gov/chancery/). Shenandoah County, case "Admr. of Thomas Fox, et als vs. Thomas Frazier," 1835.

[650]Ibid.

[651]Ibid.

[652]King, 762.

[653]Ibid., 763.

[654]Ibid., 747.

[655]Steadman, 27.

[656]King, 743.

[657]Ibid.

[658]Ibid., 744.

[659]Ibid.

[660]Ibid.

[661]Ibid., 745.

[662]Ibid.

[663]Ibid.

[664]Public domain; image via Wikimedia Commons user Evadb (https:

//commons.wikimedia.org/wiki/File:GarterInsigniaBurkes.JPG : accessed 15 Mar 2017).

[665]Public domain; image via Wikimedia Commons user Howcheng (https://commons.wikimedia.org/wiki/File:George_Percy.jpg : accessed 15 Mar 2017).

[666]Robert Alonzo Brock, *Virginia and Virginians: Eminent Virginians, Vol. I* (Richmond: H.H. Hardesty, 1888), 15.

[667]Public domain; image via Wikimedia Commons user PKM (https://commons.wikimedia.org/wiki/File:Steven_van_der_Meulen_Catherine_Carey_Lady_Knollys.jpg : accessed 15 Mar 2017).

[668]Created by Ollie Martin; used under the terms of the Creative Commons Attribution-Share Alike 3.0 Unported license. (https://en.wikipedia.org/wiki/File:Arms_of_the_Carey_family_of_Chilton_Foliat.png : accessed 4 Feb 2017.)

[669]Created by Wikimedia Commons user Jimmy44; used under the terms of the Creative Commons 3.0 Unported license. (https://commons.wikimedia.org/wiki/File:Blason_Michael_de_la_Pole_(selon_Gelre).svg : accessed 4 Feb 2017.)

[670]Created by Wikimedia Commons user Lobsterthermidor; used under the terms of the Creative Commons Attribution-Share Alike 3.0 Unported license. (https://en.wikipedia.org/wiki/File:MowbrayArms.png : accessed 4 Feb 2017.)

[671]Jane E. Sayers, "The English Royal Chancery: Structure and Productions," *Diplomatique royale du Moyen Age XIIIe-XIVe siècles* (http://elec.enc.sorbonne.fr/cid/cid1991/art_03 : accessed 15 Mar 2017.)

[672]Public domain; image via Wikimedia Commons user Andrew Dalby (https://en.wikipedia.org/wiki/File:Thomas_Holland_1430.jpg : accessed 15 Mar 2017).

[673]Public domain; image via Wikimedia Commons user Andrew Dalby (https://commons.wikimedia.org/wiki/File:Warwick_1430.jpg : accessed 15 Mar 2017).

[674]Howard de Walden, *Some Feudal Lords and Their Seals*, p. xxvii. https://archive.org/details/somefeudallordst00howauoft

[675]*An Inventory of the Historical Monuments in London, Volume 1, Westminster Abbey*, p. 185. Digitized by British History Online

(http://www.british-history.ac.uk/rchme/london/vol1/plate-185 : accessed 4 Feb 2017.)

[676] Created by Wikimedia Commons user Brianann MacAmhlaidh; used under the terms of the Creative Commons Attribution-Share Alike 3.0 Unported license. (https://en.wikipedia.org/wiki/File:William_de_Braose,_coat_of_arms,_Falkirk_Roll.svg : accessed 4 Feb 2017.)

[677] Created by Wikimedia Commons user AlexD commonswiki; used under the terms of the Creative Commons Attribution-Share Alike 3.0 Unported license. (https://commons.wikimedia.org/wiki/File:CoA_Gilbert_de_Clare.svg : accessed 4 Feb 2017.)

[678] Created by Wikimedia Commons user Brianann MacAmhlaidh; used under the terms of the Creative Commons Attribution-Share Alike 3.0 Unported license. (https://en.wikipedia.org/wiki/File:Coat_of_arms_of_Roger_de_Lacy,_Constable_of_Chester.svg : accessed 4 Feb 2017.)

[679] Image public domain, courtesy of Wikimedia Commons user Ireas (https://commons.wikimedia.org/wiki/File:Ermordung_Philipps_von_Schwaben.jpg : accessed 4 Feb 2017.)

[680] Image from *Principes Hollandiae et Zelandiae, domini Frisiae*, by Michiel Vosmeer, courtesy Wikimedia Commons user Odejea https://commons.wikimedia.org/wiki/File:Florent_IV_de_Hollande.png : accessed 4 Feb 2017).

[681] From *Founders' and benefectors' [sic] book of Tewkesbury Abbey*, image courtesy of Wikimedia Commons (https://en.wikipedia.org/wiki/File:William2ndEarl_OfGloucester_PresentsGreatCharter_ToTewkesburyAbbey.JPG : accessed 5 Feb 2017).

[682] Image from *Album du cortége des Comtes de Flandre*, by Edmond De Busscher and Félix De Vigne, courtesy Wikimedia Commons user Acoma https://en.wikipedia.org/wiki/File:Baldwin_V,_Count_of_Hainaut.jpg : accessed 4 Feb 2017).

[683] Created by Wikimedia Commons user Odejea; used under the terms of the Creative Commons Attribution-Share Alike 3.0 Unported license. (https://en.wikipedia.org/wiki/File:Armoiries_Bourbon_Dampierre.svg : accessed 4 Feb 2017.)

[684] From *A Descriptive Catalogue of the Antiquities in the Museum of the Royal Irish Academy, Vol. I*, by W.R. Wilde, p. 310; image courtesy

of Wikimedia Commons user FinnWikiNo (`https://en.wikipedia.org/wiki/File:Dermot_Mac_Murrough.JPG` : accessed 5 Feb 2017.)

[685] Created by Wikimedia Commons user Ssire; used under the terms of the Creative Commons Attribution-Share Alike 3.0 Unported license. (`https://commons.wikimedia.org/wiki/File:Blason_ville_fr_Ch%C3%A2tellerault_(Vienne).svg` : accessed 4 Feb 2017.)

[686] Public domain; image via Wikimedia Commons user Agricolae (`https://commons.wikimedia.org/wiki/File:Raymondsign.jpg` : accessed 5 Feb 2017).

[687] Public domain; image via Wikimedia Commons user Agricolae (`https://commons.wikimedia.org/wiki/File:Urracasign.jpg` : accessed 5 Feb 2017).

[688] Public domain; image via Wikimedia Commons user Georg-hessen (`https://en.wikipedia.org/wiki/File:Signum-ramon-berenguer-III-barcelona.jpg` : accessed 5 Feb 2017).

[689] Public domain; image via Wikimedia Commons users David Levy and Odejea (`https://commons.wikimedia.org/wiki/File:BNF,_Mss_fr_68,_folio_399.jpg` : accessed 5 Feb 2017).

[690] Public domain; image via Wikimedia Commons users Mhmrodrigues and Alonso de Mendoza (`https://commons.wikimedia.org/wiki/File:Godfrid1.jpg` : accessed 5 Feb 2017).

[691] Public domain; image via Wikimedia Commons user Lobsterthermidor (`https://en.wikipedia.org/wiki/File:RobertFitzHamon_BodleianMS_TopGloucD2.JPG` : accessed 5 Feb 2017).

[692] Public domain; image via Wikimedia Commons user Willtron (`https://en.wikipedia.org/wiki/File:Signun_Regis_Remiro_II_d%27Arag%C3%B3n.svg` : accessed 6 Feb 2017).

[693] Public domain; image via Wikimedia Commons user Agricolae (`https://en.wikipedia.org/wiki/File:AlfonsoVIsign.jpg` : accessed 6 Feb 2017).

[694] Public domain; image via Wikimedia Commons user Georg-hessen (`https://commons.wikimedia.org/wiki/File:Signum-ramon-berenguer-II-barcelona.jpg` : accessed 6 Feb 2017).

[695] C. Warren Hollister, *Henry I* (New Haven, Conn.: Yale University Press, 2008), 75.

[696] Public domain; image via Wikimedia Commons user Escarlati

(https://commons.wikimedia.org/wiki/File:Ego_Ruderico.jpg : accessed 6 Feb 2017).

[697]Public domain; image via Wikimedia Commons (https://commons.wikimedia.org/wiki/File:Herzog_Magnus_von_Sachsen.jpg : accessed 6 Feb 2017).

[698]Public domain; image via Wikimedia Commons user Georg-hessen (https://en.wikipedia.org/wiki/File:Signum-ramon-berenguer-I-barcelona.jpg : accessed 14 Feb 2017).

[699]Public domain; image via Wikimedia Commons user Bingocicica447 (https://en.wikipedia.org/wiki/File:Portrait_of_Oddone_di_Savoia.PNG : accessed 14 Feb 2017).

[700]Public domain. Drawing by Johann Agricola c. 1562; image via Wikimedia Commons user "Druyts.t" (https://commons.wikimedia.org/wiki/File:BernhardIISachsen_(cropped).jpg : accessed 14 Feb 2017).

[701]Public domain; image via Wikimedia Commons user Pylaemenes (https://commons.wikimedia.org/wiki/File:Emperor_Henry_III,_charter_of_1049.jpg : accessed 14 Mar 2017).

[702]Public domain; image via Wikimedia Commons user Szczepan1990 (https://commons.wikimedia.org/wiki/File:Coat_of_arms_of_Norway.svg : accessed 15 Mar 2017).

[703]Public domain; image via Wikimedia Commons user Dcoetzee (https://commons.wikimedia.org/wiki/File:New_Minster_Charter_966_detail_Edgar.jpg : accessed 15 Mar 2017).

[704]Public domain; image via Wikimedia Commons user Otets (https://commons.wikimedia.org/wiki/File:Siegfried_I_of_Luxembourg.jpg : accessed 15 Mar 2017).

[705]Public domain; image via Wikimedia Commons user Mhmrodrigues (https://commons.wikimedia.org/wiki/File:Baldwin_II_the_Bald.jpg : accessed 14 Mar 2017).

[706]Public domain; image via Wikimedia Commons user Acoma (https://commons.wikimedia.org/wiki/File:Dalimilova_kronika_vrazda_Ludmily.jpg : accessed 15 Mar 2017).

[707]"Cohabitation Registers," database with images, Library of Virginia, p. 2.

[708]"Virginia, Freedmen's Bureau Field Office Records, 1865-1872,"

NOTES

database with images, *FamilySearch.org* (https://familysearch.org/
search/collection/1596147 : accessed 17 Mar 2017), p. 204.

[709] 1870 U.S. census, Montgomery Co., Va., pop. sch., dwell. 309, fam.
324; Clara A, Harriett L., and Frank M. Stone.

[710] "Virginia, Freedmen's Bureau Field Office Records, 1865-1872," p.
204.

[711] 1880 U.S. census, Montgomery County, Virginia, population schedule, 55th Enumeration Dis., p. 11 (written), dwelling 145, family 148; Stephen, Frankey, Jane, Ada, Mariah, Gertrude, and
Frank Walker; image, Ancestry.com (http://interactive.ancestry.
com/6742/4244676-00742/18982716 : accessed 25 Jan 2017).

[712] "Cohabitation Registers," p. 11.

[713] Ibid.

[714] "Virginia, Freedmen's Bureau Field Office Records, 1865-1872," p.
204.

[715] 1870 U.S. census, Montgomery County, Virginia, population schedule, Auburn Township, p. 49 (written), dwelling 310, family 325;
Stephen Francis, Minerva, Farris, Joseph, Jerry, Jane, and Adeline Walker; image, Ancestry.com (http://interactive.ancestry.com/
7163/4268795_00122?bm=true : accessed 25 Jan 2017).

[716] 1880 U.S. census, Montgomery Co., Va., pop. sch., dwell. 145, fam.
148; Stephen, Frankey, Jane, Ada, Mariah, Gertrude, and Frank Walker.

[717] "Virginia, Deaths and Burials Index, 1853-1917," Ancestry.com
(http://search.ancestry.com/cgi-bin/sse.dll?indiv=1&dbid=2558&
h=366847 : accessed 21 Aug 2016). Entry for Clara A Stone, died
24 Dec 1878.

[718] 1880 U.S. census, Pulaski County, Virginia, population schedule,
Newbern District, p. 18 (written), dwelling 145, family 148; Musgrove
Stone; image, Ancestry.com (http://interactive.ancestry.com/6742/
4244683-00361/13983556 : accessed 25 Jan 2017).

[719] 1880 U.S. census, Montgomery Co., Va., pop. sch., dwell. 145, fam.
148; Stephen, Frankey, Jane, Ada, Mariah, Gertrude, and Frank Walker.

[720] 1870 U.S. census, Montgomery Co., Va., pop. sch., dwell. 310, fam.
325; Stephen Francis, Minerva, Farris, Joseph, Jerry, Jane, and Adeline
Walker.

[721] 1900 U.S. census, Douglas County, Nebraska, population schedule, Second Precinct, dwelling 12, family 17; Stephen, Frankey, Jane, Ada, Mariah, Gertrude, and Frank Walker; image, Ancestry.com (`http://interactive.ancestry.com/6742/4244676-00742/18982716` : accessed 25 Jan 2017).

[722] 1870 U.S. census, Montgomery Co., Va., pop. sch., dwell. 310, fam. 325; Stephen Francis, Minerva, Farris, Joseph, Jerry, Jane, and Adeline Walker.

[723] Ibid.

[724] Ibid.

[725] 1880 U.S. census, Montgomery Co., Va., pop. sch., dwell. 145, fam. 148; Stephen, Frankey, Jane, Ada, Mariah, Gertrude, and Frank Walker.

[726] Ibid.

[727] "Virginia, Death and Burials Index, 1853–1917," Ancestry.com (`http://search.ancestry.com/cgi-bin/sse.dll?indiv=1&dbid=2558&h=422956` : accessed 25 Jan 2017). Entry for Mariah Walker, died 25 Dec 1892 age 22.

[728] 1880 U.S. census, Montgomery Co., Va., pop. sch., dwell. 145, fam. 148; Stephen, Frankey, Jane, Ada, Mariah, Gertrude, and Frank Walker.

[729] Ibid.

[730] "Virginia, Select Marriages, 1785–1940," Ancestry.com (`http://search.ancestry.com/cgi-bin/sse.dll?viewrecord=1&r=an&db=FS1VirginiaMarriages&indiv=try&h=4595410` : accessed 25 Jan 2017). Entry for Jerry Winn marriage to Lucy Clayton, 9 Sep 1886.

[731] "Virginia, Freedmen's Bureau Field Office Records, 1865-1872," p. 204.

[732] Ibid.

[733] 1870 U.S. census, Montgomery Co., Va., pop. sch., dwell. 310, fam. 325; Stephen Francis, Minerva, Farris, Joseph, Jerry, Jane, and Adeline Walker.

[734] 1880 U.S. census, Montgomery Co., Va., pop. sch., dwell. 145, fam. 148; Stephen, Frankey, Jane, Ada, Mariah, Gertrude, and Frank Walker.

[735] "Virginia, Freedmen's Bureau Field Office Records, 1865-1872," p. 204.

[736]1870 U.S. census, Montgomery Co., Va., pop. sch., dwell. 309, fam. 324; Clara A, Harriett L., and Frank M. Stone.

[737]"Virginia,   Select   Marriages,   1785–1940,"   Ancestry.com (`http://search.ancestry.com/cgi-bin/sse.dll?indiv=1&dbid= 60214&h=4598609` : accessed 28 Jan 2017).   Entry for Amos Winn marriage to Hellen Sherman, 21 Sep 1914.

[738]"Virginia, Freedmen's Bureau Field Office Records, 1865-1872," p. 204.

[739]Ibid.

[740]1870 U.S. census, Montgomery Co., Va., pop. sch., dwell. 310, fam. 325; Stephen Francis, Minerva, Farris, Joseph, Jerry, Jane, and Adeline Walker.

[741]"Virginia,   Select   Marriages,   1785–1940,"   Ancestry.com (`http://search.ancestry.com/cgi-bin/sse.dll?viewrecord=1& r=an&db=FS1VirginiaMarriages&indiv=try&h=4595410`   :   accessed 25 Jan 2017).   Entry for Jerry Winn marriage to Lucy Clayton, 9 Sep 1886.

[742]1880 U.S. census, Montgomery Co., Va., pop. sch., dwell. 145, fam. 148; Stephen, Frankey, Jane, Ada, Mariah, Gertrude, and Frank Walker.

[743]"Cohabitation Registers," p. 8.

[744]Ibid., p. 3.

[745]"Virginia, Freedmen's Bureau Field Office Records, 1865-1872," p. 198.

[746]Ibid.

[747]"Cohabitation Registers," p. 3.

[748]Ibid.

[749]Will of William A. Stone; see Appendix C.

[750]"Cohabitation Registers," p. 3.

[751]1880 U.S. census, Montgomery County, Virginia, population schedule, 55th Enumeration District, dwelling 107, family 107; Scott, Permelia, Susan, Anna, Richard, Jinnie, Dexter, Nannie, and Parthenia Stokes; image, Ancestry.com (`http://interactive.ancestry.com/ 6742/4244676-00744/18982803` : accessed 26 Jan 2017).

752 "Virginia, Freedmen's Bureau Field Office Records, 1865-1872," p. 198.

753 1880 U.S. census, Montgomery Co., Va., pop. sch., dwell.107, fam. 107; Scott, Permelia, Susan, Anna, Richard, Jinnie, Dexter, Nannie, and Parthenia Stokes.

754 "Virginia, Freedmen's Bureau Field Office Records, 1865-1872," p. 198.

755 1880 U.S. census, Montgomery Co., Va., pop. sch., dwell.107, fam. 107; Scott, Permelia, Susan, Anna, Richard, Jinnie, Dexter, Nannie, and Parthenia Stokes.

756 "Cohabitation Registers," p. 3.

757 1880 U.S. census, Montgomery Co., Va., pop. sch., dwell.107, fam. 107; Scott, Permelia, Susan, Anna, Richard, Jinnie, Dexter, Nannie, and Parthenia Stokes.

758 "Cohabitation Registers," p. 3.

759 1880 U.S. census, Montgomery Co., Va., pop. sch., dwell.107, fam. 107; Scott, Permelia, Susan, Anna, Richard, Jinnie, Dexter, Nannie, and Parthenia Stokes.

760 "Virginia, Freedmen's Bureau Field Office Records, 1865-1872," p. 198.

761 Social Security Administration, "United States Social Security Applications and Claims Index, 1936-2007," database, Ancestry.com (http://search.ancestry.com/cgi-bin/sse.dll?viewrecord=1&r=an&db=Numident&indiv=try&h=11851763 : accessed 26 Jan 2017), entry for Robert Dexter Stokes, SS no. 704-162-954.

762 "Virginia, Freedmen's Bureau Field Office Records, 1865-1872," p. 198.

763 1880 U.S. census, Montgomery Co., Va., pop. sch., dwell.107, fam. 107; Scott, Permelia, Susan, Anna, Richard, Jinnie, Dexter, Nannie, and Parthenia Stokes.

764 "Cohabitation Registers," p. 8.

765 Ibid., p. 11.

766 Ibid., p. 13.

767 Will of William A. Stone. See Appendix C.

[768] Ibid.

[769] Ibid.

[770] Ibid.

[771] Ibid.

[772] 1870 U.S. census, Montgomery Co., Va., pop. sch., dwell. 309, fam. 324; Clara A, Harriett L., and Frank M. Stone.

[773] "Virginia, Freedmen's Bureau Field Office Records, 1865-1872," p. 196.

[774] 1870 U.S. census, Montgomery Co., Va., pop. sch., dwell. 309, fam. 324; Clara A, Harriett L., and Frank M. Stone.

[775] 1880 U.S. census, Montgomery County, Virginia, population schedule, 55th Enumeration District, dwelling 94, family 94; William E. Stone, Archer Stone; image, Ancestry.com (http://interactive.ancestry.com/6742/4244676-00743/18982819? : accessed 26 Jan 2017).

[776] "Cohabitation Registers," p. 13.

[777] "Virginia, Freedmen's Bureau Field Office Records, 1865-1872," p. 206.

[778] Ibid., p. 158.

[779] 1880 U.S. census, Montgomery Co., Va., pop. sch., dwell. 94, fam. 94; William E. Stone, Archer Stone; image, Ancestry.com (http://interactive.ancestry.com/6742/4244676-00743/18982819? : accessed 26 Jan 2017).

[780] "Virginia, Freedmen's Bureau Field Office Records, 1865-1872," p. 158.

[781] Ibid., p. 160.

[782] Ibid., p. 158.

[783] Ibid., p. 160.

[784] Ibid.

[785] Ibid., p. 162.

[786] Ibid., p. 171.

[787] Ibid.

[788] Ibid.

[789] Pettus, 485

[790] Ibid., 485–486.

[791] Pettus, 483.

[792] Ibid., 600

[793] Alsup, Vol. II, Chapter XVI.

[794] "Five Pounds Reward," *Virginia Gazette*, 14 Jan 1773,; digital image, *Newspapers.com* (http://www.newspapers.com/image/40481534/ : accessed 27 Jan 2017).

[795] *Acts and Joint Resolutions passed by the General Assembly of the State of Virginia During the Session of 1897–1898* (Richmond: J.H. O'Bannon, 1898), p. 778.

[796] Copy courtesy Richard Abdill *2-2.*

[797] Henry Stone Jr., 1918. Photo privately held by Sally Abdill *3-5.*

[798] Tyler Bugg, "Melita Museum - Did You Know?" *Melita New Era* (http://www.melitanewera.ca/community/local-community/melita-museum-did-you-know-1.2033781 : accessed 18 Mar 2017).

[799] Tad Fitch and Michael Poirier, *Into the Danger Zone: Sea Crossings of the First World War* (Stroud, U.K.: The History Press, 2015).

[800] Homer E. Simpson, *Over There and Back: The Diary of Homer E. Simpson as Kept During the Great War*, presented by Google (https://www.google.com/culturalinstitute/beta/u/0/exhibit/QRAX8hg8 : accessed 18 Mar 2017).

[801] "WWI Officer Experience Reports," database with images, *Fold3* (https://www.fold3.com/image/250/271899406 : accessed 19 Mar 2017).

[802] Simpson, *Over There and Back.*

[803] "Période contemporaine (1914–1988)," Le Havre Archives Municipales (http://archives.lehavre.fr/delia-CMS/archives/site/article_id-23904/sstopic_id-/topic_id-758/topic_parent_id-757/periode-contemporaine-1914-1988.html : accessed 18 Mar 2017).

[804] Simpson, *Over There and Back.*

[805] *81st Division, Summary of Operations in the World War* (Washington: U.S. Government Printing Office, 1944), 4.

[806] Ibid., 1.

[807] *81st Division, Summary of Operations in the World War*, 4.

[808] "World War I Draft Registration Cards," images, Fold3.com (`https://www.fold3.com/image/551916451/` : accessed 18 Mar 2017), card for Jerome Denning, Local Draft Board, Sampson County, NC. United States, Selective Service System.

[809] *81st Division, Summary of Operations in the World War*, 5.

[810] "American Operations on the Vosges Front," `https://www.abmc.gov/sites/default/files/publications/Section7.pdf`, 420.

[811] Simpson, *Over There and Back.*

[812] "American Operations on the Vosges Front," 424.

[813] Ibid.

[814] Ibid.

[815] Simpson, *Over There and Back.*

[816] Proctor M. Fisk, *History of the Three Hundred Fiftieth Regiment of U. S. Infantry, Eighty-Eighth Division, American Expeditionary Forces* (Cedar Rapids, Iowa: The Laurance Press Company, 1919), 117.

[817] *81st Division, Summary of Operations in the World War*, 5.

[818] Ibid., 5.

[819] Ibid., 4.

[820] Ibid., 12.

[821] Simpson, *Over There and Back*

[822] *81st Division, Summary of Operations in the World War*, 19.

[823] Ibid.

[824] Ibid., 24.

[825] Ibid., 22.

[826] Simpson, *Over There and Back.*

[827] Ibid.

[828] Ibid.

[829] Donald M. Kington, "The Plattsburg Movement and its Legacy,"

Relevance, Volume 6, Issue 4 (http://www.worldwar1.com/tgws/rel011. htm : accessed 18 Mar 2017).

[830]Simpson, *Over There and Back.*

Bibliography

Books and documents

81st Division, Summary of Operations in the World War, from the American Battle Monuments Commission. Washington: United States Government Printing Office, 1944.

Acts and Joint Resolutions Passed by the General Assembly of the State of Virginia During the Session of 1897–1898. Richmond: J.H. O'Bannon, 1898.

Anonymous, "14th Virginia Regiment History," http://www.14thvirginiacavalry.org/regiment_history.htm : 2016.

Anonymous, "American Operations on the Vosges Front." American Battle Monuments Commission, https://www.abmc.gov/sites/default/files/publications/Section7.pdf : 2017.

Anonymous, "The Black Sisters," Montgomery Museum, http://montgomerymuseum.org/the-black-sisters : 2016.

Anonymous, "Murder at the Second Market," *Out of the Box: Notes from the Archives at the Library of Virginia*, www.virginiamemory.com/blogs/out_of_the_box : 2017.

Anonymous, "Revolutionary War Pension Records and Patterns of American Mobility, 1780–1830," U.S. National Archives, https://www.archives.gov/publications/prologue/1984/fall/pension-mobility.html : 2017.

Anonymous, "Spindle House wayside marker," *Stone Sentinels*, http://stonesentinels.com/spotsylvania/

battle-spotsylvania-auto-tour/laurel-hill-trail/
spindle-house/ : 2016.

Civil War Battlefields, Civil War Trust, http://www.civilwar.
org/battlefields/ : 2017.

Yearbook, *The Calyx*. Lexington, Va.: Washington & Lee University, 1915.

Yearbook, *Catalog of the Officers and Students of Kentucky University for the Session of 1868–1869*. Louisville, Ky.: John P. Morton and Company, 1869.

"Christiansburg High School," *Historic Christiansburg Walking Tour*, http://montgomerymuseum.org/
learn/historic-christiansburg-walking-tour/
christiansburg-high-school : 2016.

"Chronologies par périodes historiques," Le Havre Archives Municipales, http://archives.lehavre.
fr/delia-CMS/archives/site/article_id-/
sstopic_id-/topic_id-758/topic_parent_id-757/
chronologies-par-periodes-historiques.html : 2017.

"A Guide to the Records of Southwestern State Hospital, 1887–1948," Library of Virginia, http://ead.lib.virginia.edu/
vivaxtf/view?docId=lva/vi03032.xml : 2017.

The Handbook of Texas Online. Texas State Historical Association, https://tshaonline.org/handbook : 2017.

The History of Parliament. University of London,
http://www.historyofparliamentonline.org/volume/
1558-1603/member/pettus-john-1550-1614 : 2016.

An Inventory of the Historical Monuments in London, Volume I. London: Royal Commission on the Historical Monuments of England, 1924. Digitized plates, http://www.
british-history.ac.uk/rchme/london/vol1 : 2017.

The Millennial Harbinger: A Monthly Publication devoted to Primitive Christianity, Vol. III. Bethany, Va.: Alexander Campbell, 1839.

The Miscellaneous Documents of the House of Representatives for the First Session of the Fifty-Third Congress. Washington: Government Printing Office, 1863.

"The Niagara River Station," *Engineering Record, Building Record and Sanitary Engineer* volume 75 (January–March 1917).

"Sunset Cemetery Master Plan," Town of Christiansburg, `http://www.christiansburg.org/DocumentCenter/View/5074` : 2017.

Twelfth Census of the United States, Census Reports Volume I – Population Part I. Washington: United States Census Office, 1901.

Virginia: Rebirth of the Old Dominion, Volume III. Chicago: The Lewis Publishing Company, 1929.

Whitworth and Related Lines, Volume I. Utica, Ky.: McDowell Publications, 2001.

Acklen, Jeannette Tillotson, compiler, *Tennessee Records: Bible Records and Marriage Bonds.* Berwyn Heights, Md.: Heritage Books, 2007.

Alsup, Jerry David, *Alsop's Tables, Volume I.* Self-published, 2014.

——, *Alsop's Tables, Volume II.* Walnut, Miss.: The Alsup Press, 1994. Kindle edition.

——, *Alsop's Tables, Volume III, Part I.* Bloomington, In.: iUniverse, Inc, 2012.

Bell, Landon C., *Lunenburg County VA, Wills 1746–1825.* Berryville, Va.: Virginia Book Company, 1972.

——, *The Old Free State.* Richmond: The William Byrd Press, 1927.

Blomefield, Francis, *An Essay Towards A Topographical History of the County of Norfolk: Volume 5.* London: W. Miller, 1806. Transcription by British History Online, `http://www.british-history.ac.uk/topographical-hist-norfolk/vol5` : 2017.

Bond, Paul Stanley, et al., *The R.O.T.C. Training Manual: A Text Book for the Reserve Officers Training Corps, Volume 4.* Baltimore: The Johns Hopkins Press, 1921.

Brien, Cora and Clarence R. Geier, "Third Time's the Charm: Historical Archaeology and the Sarah Spindle House on the

Battlefield of Spotsylvania Court House." *Fredericksburg History and Biography, Vol. IV.* Fredericksburg, Va.: Central Virginia Battlefields Trust, 2005.

Brock, R.A., *Virginia and Virginians: Eminent Virginians, Montgomery County.* Reprint. Signal Mountain, Tenn.: Mountain Press.

—— *Virginia and Virginians: Eminent Virginians, Vol. I.* Richmond: H.H. Hardesty, 1888.

Burtchaell, G.D., compiler, *The Knights of England, vol. II.* London: Sherrat and Hughes, 1906.

Carthew, G.A., *The Hundred of Launditch and Deanery of Brisley, Volume III.* Norwich, England: Miller and Leavins, 1879.

Civil War, Compiled Service Records. Carded Records, Volunteer Organizations. Record Group 94: Records of the Adjutant General's Office, 1780s–1917. National Archives, Washington, D.C.

Crozier, William Armstrong, editor, *Virginia Court Records: Spotsylvania County, 1721–1800.* New York: Fox, Duffield & Company, 1965.

Cunningham, S.A., editor, *Confederate Veteran, Volume X,* compendium of magazines (Nashville, 1902).

Custalow, Linwood "Little Bear" and Angela L. Daniel "Silver Star," *The True Story of Pocahontas: The Other Side of History.* Golden, Co.: Fulcrum Publishing, 2007.

Daughters of the American Revolution, *Historical Collections of the Joseph Habersham Chapter, Daughters American Revolution, Volume II.* Atlanta: Blosser Printing Co., 1902.

——, *Lineage Book, volume LXIV.* Washington: National Society of the Daughters of the American Revolution, 1907.

——, *Lineage Book, volume LXV.* Washington: National Society of the Daughters of the American Revolution, 1907.

Evans, Anselm Evans, editor, *Confederate Military History: A Library of Confederate States History, Vol. 3.* Atlanta: Confederate Publishing Company, 1899. Stroud, U.K.: The History Press, 2015

Fisk, Proctor M., *History of the Three Hundred Fiftieth Regiment of U. S. Infantry, Eighty-Eighth Division, American Expeditionary Forces.* Cedar Rapids, Iowa: The Laurance Press Company, 1919.

Fitch, Tad and Michael Poirier, *Into the Danger Zone: Sea Crossings of the First World War.*

Fox, Joseph M. III and David E., "Y-DNA Testing of a Paper Trail: The Fox Surname Project," *Journal of Genetic Genealogy*, Volume 8, Number 1.

Hodges, Frances Beale Smith, *The Genealogy of the Beale Family, 1399–1956.* Ann Arbor, Mich.: Edwards Brothers, 1956.

Hollister, C. Warren, *Henry I.* New Haven, Conn.: Yale University Press, 2008.

Kelso, William M., *Kingsmill Plantations, 1619–1800.* New York: Academic Press, 1984.

Killen, Linda, *The Whartons' Town: New River Depot, 1870–1940.* Radford, Va.: Radford University, 1993.

King, George H.S., "Memorial to Henry Fox, Gentleman, of 'Huntington', King William County, Virginia." *Genealogies of Virginia Families: From Tyler's Quarterly Historical and Genealogical Magazine.* Baltimore: Genealogical Publishing Co., 1981.

Lord, Erin M., Mallary J. Orrison, Katharine A. Goins, E Thomas Ewing, *Edgar A. Long, Principal of Christiansburg Institute: A Life Devoted to Education.* Blacksburg, Va.: Virginia Tech, 2011.

McIlwaine, H.R., editor, *Minutes of the Council and General court of colonial Virginia, 1622-1632, 1670-1676.* Richmond: Virginia State Library, 1924.

d'Orleans, Louis-Philippe-Albert, *The Battle of Gettysburg: From The History of the Civil War in America.* Philadelphia: Porter & Coates, 1886.

Pettus, William Walker IV, *Thomas Petyous of Norwich, Eng-*

land and His Pettus Descendants in England and Virginia, Volume I. Baltimore: Otter Bay Books, 2011.

———, Thomas Petyous of Norwich, England and His Pettus Descendants in England and Virginia, Volume II. Baltimore: Otter Bay Books, 2013.

Rhea, Gordon C., The Battles for Spotsylvania Courthouse and the Road to Yellow Tavern. Baton Rouge: Louisiana State University Press, 1997.

Roberts, Emily Griffith, Ancestral Study of Four Families. Terrell, Tx.: self-published, 1939.

Robertson, James I. Jr., 4th Virginia Infantry. Lynchburg, Va.: H.E. Howard, 1982.

———, The Stonewall Brigade. Baton Rouge: Louisiana State University Press, 1977.

Sayers, Jane E., "The English Royal Chancery: Structure and Productions." Diplomatique royale du Moyen Age XIIIe-XIVe siècles, online publication, http://elec.enc.sorbonne.fr/cid/cid1991/art_03 : 2017.

Sherwood, George, editor, The Pedigree Register, Volume III. London: self-published, 1916.

Simpson, Homer E., Over There and Back: The Diary of Homer E. Simpson as Kept During the Great War, https://www.google.com/culturalinstitute/beta/u/0/exhibit/QRAX8hg8 : 2017.

Stacy, Pocahontas Hutchinson and Alice Bömer Rudd, The Pettus Family. Washington: self-published, 1957.

Steadman, Joseph E. and compiler Shirley Faucette, Ancestry of the Fox family of Richland and Lexington Counties, South Carolina. Batesburg, SC: self-published, 1972.

Tagg, Larry, The Generals of Gettysburg. Baton Rouge: Da Capo Press, 2003.

de Walden, Howard, Some Feudal Lords and Their Seals. London: De Walden Library, 1904.

Wharam, F. Douglas Jr., "Only a Matter of Time: Christiansburg Institute and Desegregation in Southwestern Virginia: 1959–1960," thesis. *Television News of the Civil Rights Era 1950–1970*, University of Virginia (http://www2.vcdh.virginia.edu/civilrightstv/ : accessed 17 Mar 2017).

Williams, Charles E., *Along the Allegheny River: The Southern Watershed*. Charleston: Arcadia Publishing, 2006.

Collections

"Alabama, Texas and Virginia, Confederate Pensions, 1884-1958," database with images, *Ancestry.com*, http://search.ancestry.com/search/db.aspx?dbid=1677 : 2017.

"City and Town Population Totals Datasets: 2010-2015," database with images, United States Census Bureau, https://www.census.gov/data/datasets/2015/demo/popest/total-cities-and-towns.html : 2017.

"Cohabitation Registers," database with images, Library of Virginia, http://digitool1.lva.lib.va.us:8881/R/5A6II5KTK8UQ8ETJY99BTDPLTPJCHRLQT4EJDG2JLPH2Y8NUF5-02420?func=collections-result&collection_id=1522 : 2017.

"Confederate Disability Applications and Receipts," database with images, Library of Virginia, http://lva1.hosted.exlibrisgroup.com/F/?func=file&file_name=find-b-clas11&local_base=CLAS11 : 2017.

"England, Select Births and Christenings, 1538-1975," database, *Ancestry.com*, http://search.ancestry.com/search/db.aspx?dbid=9841 : 2016.

"England, Select Deaths and Burials, 1538-1991," database, *Ancestry.com*, http://search.ancestry.com/search/db.aspx?dbid=9840 : 2016.

"England, Select Marriages, 1538-1973," database, *Ancestry.com*, http://search.ancestry.com/search/db.aspx?dbid=9852 : 2016.

"Family Data Collection - Births," database, *Ancestry.com*, http://search.ancestry.com/search/db.aspx?dbid=5769 : 2016.

Find A Grave. Database with images. `http://www.findagrave.com` : 2017.

"Find A Home," database with images, *Redfin,* `https://www.redfin.com` : 2017.

"Historic Registers, Montgomery County (Western Region)," database with images, *Virginia Department of Historic Resources,* `http://dhr.virginia.gov/registers/Counties/register_Montgomery.htm` : 2017.

"Jefferson Papers," database, *Founders Online,* National Historical Publications and Records Commission, `http://founders.archives.gov` : 2016.

"Lancaster, Pennsylvania, Mennonite Vital Records, 1750-2014," database with images, *Ancestry.com,* `http://search.ancestry.com/search/db.aspx?dbid=60592` : 2016.

"Lunenburg County, Virginia, Marriage Bonds Index, 1763-1839," database, *Ancestry.com,* `http://search.ancestry.com/search/db.aspx?dbid=5685` : 2016.

"Marriages of Lunenburg County, Virginia, 1746-1853," database with images, *Ancestry.com,* `http://search.ancestry.com/search/db.aspx?dbid=49051` : 2017.

National Geologic Map Database, United States Department of the Interior, `https://ngmdb.usgs.gov/ngmdb/ngmdb_home.html` : 2017.

"North Carolina, Marriage Records, 1741-2011," database with images, *Ancestry.com,* `http://search.ancestry.com/search/db.aspx?dbid=60548` : 2016.

"Online Collections Database," database with images, American Civil War Museum, `http://moconfederacy.pastperfectonline.com/` : 2017.

"Papers of the Continental Congress, compiled 1774–1789," database with images, *Fold3,* `https://www.fold3.com/browse/1/hrRUXqv6R` : 2016.

"Pennsylvania, Veteran Compensation Application Files, WWII, 1950-1966," database with images, *Ancestry.com,* http://search.ancestry.com/search/db.aspx?dbid=3147 : 2016.

"Record of Pay and Service of Officers and Men of Virginia, New York, and Georgia. 1775-1856," *Fold3*, https://www.fold3.com/browse/1/hEW9YnTE8t1XIqIyh1UboQ8qw9JjPJ-CE : 2016.

"Revolutionary War Pensions," database with images, *Fold3*, https://www.fold3.com/title_467/revolutionary_war_pensions : 2017.

"Revolutionary War Rolls," database with images, *Fold3*, https://www.fold3.com/title_469/revolutionary_war_rolls : 2016.

"U.S. and Canada, Passenger and Immigration Lists Index, 1500s-1900s," database, *Ancestry.com*, http://search.ancestry.com/search/db.aspx?dbid=7486 : 2017.

"U.S. and International Marriage Records, 1560-1900," database, *Ancestry.com*, http://search.ancestry.com/search/db.aspx?dbid=7836 : 2016.

"U.S., Appointments of U. S. Postmasters, 1832-1971," database with images, *Ancestry.com*, http://search.ancestry.com/search/db.aspx?dbid=1932 : 2017.

"U.S., World War I Draft Registration Cards, 1917-1918," database with images, *Ancestry.com*, http://search.ancestry.com/search/db.aspx?dbid=6482 : 2016.

"U.S., World War II Draft Registration Cards, 1942," database with images, *Ancestry.com*, http://search.ancestry.com/search/db.aspx?dbid=1002 : 2016.

"U.S., Social Security Death Index, 1935-2014" database with images, *Ancestry.com*, http://search.ancestry.com/search/db.aspx?dbid=3693 : 2016.

"U.S., Social Security Applications and Claims Index, 1936-2007," database, *Ancestry.com*, http://search.ancestry.com/search/db.aspx?dbid=60901 : 2016.

"U.S., Social Security Death Index, 1935-2014," database, *Ancestry.com*, http://search.ancestry.com/search/db.aspx?dbid=3693 : 2016.

"Virginia Chancery Records Index," database with images, *Virginia Memory*, the Library of Virginia, `LibraryofVirginia` : 2017.

"Virginia, Compiled Marriages, 1740-1850," database, *Ancestry.com*, `http://search.ancestry.com/search/db.aspx?dbid=3723` : 2016.

"Virginia, Select Marriages, 1785-1940," database, *Ancestry.com*, `http://search.ancestry.com/search/db.aspx?dbid=60214` : 2017.

"Virginia, Deaths and Burials Index, 1853-1917," database, *Ancestry.com*, `http://search.ancestry.com/search/db.aspx?dbid=2558` : 2017.

"Virginia, Death Records, 1912-2014," database, *Ancestry.com*, `http://search.ancestry.com/search/db.aspx?dbid=9278` : 2017.

"Virginia, Freedmen's Bureau Field Office Records, 1865-1872," database with images, *FamilySearch.org*, `https://familysearch.org/search/collection/1596147` : 2017.

"Wisconsin, Deaths, 1820–1907," database, *Ancestry.com*, `http://search.ancestry.com/search/db.aspx?dbid=4984` : 2017.

"WWI Officer Experience Reports - AEF," database with images, *Fold3*, `https://www.fold3.com/browse/250/hpOrbDPgT` : 2017.

Newspapers

Bluefield Daily Telegraph, Bluefield, Va., clipping via Ancestry.com, 2016.

Clinch Valley News, Tazewell, Va., `https://www.newspapers.com/title_3331/clinch_valley_news/` : 2017.

Daily State Journal, Alexandria, Va., `https://www.newspapers.com/title_1800/the_daily_state_journal/` : 2016.

The Free Lance-Star, Fredricksburg, Va., clipping via Ancestry.com, 2016.

Melita New Era, Melita, Manitoba, Canada, `http://www.melitanewera.ca/community/local-community/melita-museum-did-you-know-1.2033781` : 2017.

New York Times, New York, NY, https://www.nytimes.com :
2016.

Palm Coast Observer, Palm Coast, Fl., http://www.
palmcoastobserver.com/ : 2017.

Patawomeck Tides, Fredericksburg, Va.

Pittsburgh Gazette Times, Pittsburgh, Pa., https://www.
newspapers.com/title_3518/pittsburgh_postgazette/ :
2017.

Richmond Dispatch, Richmond, Va., https://www.newspapers.
com/title_1721/richmond_dispatch/ : 2017.

Richmond Times-Dispatch, Richmond, Va., http://www.
richmond.com/archive/ : 2016.

Rind's Virginia Gazette, Williamsburg, Va., https://www.
newspapers.com/title_1263/rinds_virginia_gazette/ :
2017.

Roanoke Times, Roanoke, Va., https://www.newspapers.com/
title_1742/the_roanoke_times/ : 2016.

The Times, Richmond, Va., https://www.newspapers.com/
title_1735/the_times/ : 2017.

Virginia Gazette, Williamsburg, Va., https://www.newspapers.
com/title_1262/the_virginia_gazette/ : 2017.

Washington Post, Washington, DC, clipping via Ancestry.com,
2016.

U.S. census records

All via Ancestry.com*; databases with images, accessed 2016–
2017, as cited in the text.*

Virginia. Lunenburg County. 1830.
Virginia. Spotsylvania County. 1830.
Virginia. Lunenburg County. 1840.
Virginia. Charlotte County. 1850, population schedule.
Virginia. Lunenburg County. 1850, population schedule.
Virginia. Spotsylvania County. 1850, population schedule.
Virginia. Stafford County. 1850, population schedule.
Virginia. Mecklenburg County. 1860, population schedule.

Virginia. Montgomery County. 1860, population schedule.
Virginia. Montgomery County. 1860, slave schedule.
Virginia. Montgomery County. 1860, agricultural schedule.
Virginia. Spotsylvania County. 1860, mortality schedule.
Virginia. Spotsylvania County. 1860, population schedule.
Virginia. Spotsylvania County. 1860, slave schedule.
Virginia. Montgomery County. 1870, population schedule.
Virginia. Faquier County. 1880, population schedule.
Virginia. Montgomery County. 1880, population schedule.
Virginia. Pulaski County. 1880, population schedule.
Nebraska. Douglas County. 1900, population schedule.
Virginia. Auburn County [sic]. 1900, population schedule.
Virginia. Montgomery County. 1900, population schedule.
Virginia. Montgomery County. 1910, population schedule.
Pennsylvania. Westmoreland County. 1910, population schedule.
Pennsylvania. Centre County. 1920, population schedule.
California. Los Angeles County. 1930, population schedule.
Pennsylvania. Cambria County. 1930, population schedule.
Virginia. Montgomery County. 1930, population schedule.
Virginia. Tazewell County. 1930, population schedule.
Virginia. Montgomery County. 1940, population schedule.

Index

Symbols

—

Anne
  wife of George Alsop
    the elder   77
  wife of George Alsop
    the younger   78
Christian   57
Delphia   78
Emma   258
Esther   72
Gertrude   257–258
Mary   51, 61, 87, 88
Winifred   85

A

Abdill
  Anne Louise   13
  Claire Victoria   7, 14
  Kathy Jeanne   13
  Katie Rebecca   7, 14
  Peter Henry   13, 303
  Richard John
    b. 1928   12–13

    b. 1960   13
    b. 1989   7, 14
Alexander, Charles Lyde 35
Alsop
  Ann G.   83
  Anne
    daughter of George
      and Anne   78
  Benjamin   260–261
    b. 1758   79–85
    d. 1777   78
  Elizabeth
    b. abt 1760   79
    b. abt 1730   78
  Elizabeth C. 69–70, 83
  George
    b. 1735   78
    the elder   77
    the younger   78
  Ignatious   79
  Isiah   78
  Jane   79
  John
    b. abt 1768   79

THE ANCESTORS OF HENRY STONE

"I sit beside the fire and think
Of people long ago
And people that will see a world
That I shall never know

But all the while I sit and think
Of times there were before
I listen for returning feet
And voices at the door..."

—J.R.R. Tolkien,
The Fellowship of the Ring

www.ingramcontent.com/pod-product-compliance
Lightning Source LLC
Chambersburg PA
CBHW021613270326
41931CB00008B/672

* 9 7 8 0 6 9 2 8 4 0 4 7 4 *